Pater in the 1990s

The 1880–1920 British Authors Series

Pater in the 1990s

Edited by

Laurel Brake & Ian Small

Number Six
in the
1880–1920 British Authors Series

ELT PRESS

of

English Literature in Transition, 1880–1920

University of North Carolina

Greensboro, NC 27412

Number Six

in the

1880–1920 British Authors Series

Distributed in Europe

by

Colin Smythe, Ltd.

Gerrards Cross

Buckinghamshire

England SL9 8XA

ISBN 0-944318-05-3

Library of Congress Cataloging in Publication Data

90-086290

Contents

Walter Pater
(After a photograph by Elliott & Fry, c. 1889)

Foreword

LINDA DOWLING

THE PRESENT VOLUME of essays, collected from the second international Pater conference held at Queen's College, Oxford in 1988, registers a decisive turn in Pater studies that has been gathering considerable force in recent years, a turn toward the "New Historicism" and its project of re-embedding the literary work in history, with "history" understood as an already-symbolic field of significations, "the literary work" as an open and heterogeneous discursive web rather than a unified and self-enclosed artifact. Nonetheless, as the reader will discover, roughly half of the fifteen essays of *Pater in the 1990s* remain within the older tradition of interpretive formalism that in a real sense originated with Pater himself, whose notion of the "House Beautiful" as enclosing a simultaneous and timeless order of artworks is the very image of that autonomous art—unified, self-enclosed, possessing its own laws and center of gravity—that was to constitute the focus, first, of Anglo-American New Criticism and later, by way of a critique in kind, of Euro-American deconstruction.

This Aestheticist tradition of formalist or immanent interpretation has provided the basis for some of the most noteworthy earlier efforts in Pater interpretation—the numerous studies of Gerald Monsman come readily to mind, or, more recently, the minutely detailed readings of Carolyn Williams's *Transfigured World*. This tradition has by no means exhausted itself, as Jonathan Loesberg's even more recent *Aestheticism and Deconstruction* so persuasively demonstrates, and as is demonstrated in these pages by such essays as Maureen Moran's intriguing account of the way in which Pater's language of myth ultimately exposes the very myth of interpretation upon which Pater's own work depends. At the same time, there is a palpable sense in the present volume that the scope and energies of formalist criticism are diminishing, that the outlines of one sort of picture at least have largely been filled in.

Against this background of approaching completion or saturation within the formalist project of Pater studies it is, paradoxically, an older mode of biographical and historical criticism that today seems most compellingly to suggest the outlines of a newer approach, not least because that mode so indispensably provides, in its patient investigation of primary materials, the basis of any New Historicist focus on power or ideology or systems of representation. For what the researches of the older historicism continue to demonstrate is that the specific or local details of history and biography are always in Foucault's sense archival, belonging not to any actual archive but to a vast network of silent relations, the relations of power and knowledge as these stretch invisibly away on every side of any actual surviving document and supply the ultimate conditions of its intelligibility.

No essay in the present collection better demonstrates the continuing value of such traditional research, perhaps, than that in which B. A. Inman, building upon the work of David Newsome, Richard Ellmann, Alon Kadish and Laurel Brake, brings to light hitherto unknown materials relating to the crisis Pater suffered during the period 1873-1877 when he was attacked by Oxford officials as a demoralizing moralizer, was denied a routine promotion to the valuable post of university proctor, and was exposed to humiliating satire in W. H. Mallock's *The New Republic*. Earlier Pater scholarship had been compelled to assume that these defeats flowed chiefly from his contemporaries' persistent hostility to the irreligious and hedonistic message of *Studies in the History of the Renaissance*. Now in an important discovery Inman reveals that Benjamin Jowett, the Master of Balliol College, moved to block Pater's promotion because he knew him to be involved in a homoerotic relationship with a Balliol undergraduate, William Money Hardinge. Among the Balliol undergraduates through whose assistance Jowett obtained his information about the affair, and some letters signed "yours lovingly" that had passed between Hardinge and Pater, may have been W. H. Mallock.

Mallock's role may in any event be taken to illustrate the New Historicist claim that such episodes as this must always be viewed against a background of symbolic struggle within Victorian society, an inevitable concentration of antagonistic forces around issues concerning gender or class or sexual identity. For Mallock's portraits of Pater as Mr. Rose, Hardinge as Robert Leslie and Jowett as Dr. Jenkinson (i.e. the "son" of Richard Jenkyns, an earlier Master of Balliol) were instantly decoded by Victorian readers, and the portrait of Pater was decried as ungentlemanly for its invidious and invasively personal character. The immediate effect of *The New Republic* was to drive Pater from the field of candidates competing for the Oxford Professorship of Poetry in March of 1877. Mallock's invidious portrait then continued to overshadow Pater's career, as when André Raffalovich would much later contrive a real-life meeting between "Mr. Rose" and "Robert Leslie," recording with an almost salacious glee that Pater, always so "affectionate to young men *as they were*," had found the willowy undergraduate Hardinge of 1874 grotesquely transformed by the mid-1880s into a portly roué more than anything else resembling, says Raffalovich, the Duke of Cambridge.

The picture Inman's essay provides of a sexually predatory Pater— the "ingratiatory vampire" and "Minotaur" of Raffalovich's reminiscence—thus illustrates in particularly dramatic terms the sense in which the Victorians themselves would always view Oxford as a symbolic site, a veritable battleground on which undergraduate minds, bodies, and souls were daily being contested for in deadly earnest. By the same token, the story as it involves Pater, Hardinge, and Jowett illustrates in an equally exemplary way the point of the New Historicism in insisting that "Oxford" in any such account is the name less of a single institutional entity than, in Foucault's terms once again, a conjuncture of discrete and competing discourses, an abstract convergence of power relations which, constantly shifting and entering into new strategic combinations, underlie all local groupings in any struggle for cultural legitimacy. This is the context in which, for instance, the one bit of condemnatory evidence in the Hardinge affair—the fact that Pater, at a time when he was teaching as a Fellow at Brasenose, had signed his letters to an undergraduate "yours lovingly"—must be taken as nothing less than a locus in a war of antagonistic discourses.

To understand how so innocuous a phrase could carry so momentous a significance in the Hardinge episode, moreover, is to have seen that the invisible battleground involved is really the Oxford tutorial system, that unique mode of instruction that had put generations of undergraduates in an always potentially intimate relationship with a Fellow of their college. For it is an earlier revolution in the tutorial system that had made the phrase "yours lovingly" a wholly conventional bit of undergraduate slang, the insistence of Newman and others in the Oxford Movement that the tutorial, having been originally and most importantly a pastoral relationship, could not be meaningfully conducted on any other grounds. As adopted by subsequent generations of Oxford undergraduates—by, for instance, William Morris as a closing in letters written to his Oxford friends—"yours lovingly" will thus testify merely to a culture of spiritual intimacy that had survived the Tractarian collapse of 1845, the attempt of undergraduates like Morris, arriving at an Oxford that seemed chillingly empty of idealism and noble aspiration, to recover something of the Tractarians' sense of fervent religious brotherhood.

By the time it became available to Pater and Hardinge in 1874 as the codeword for an unconventional physical relationship, then, "yours lovingly" had become, precisely in its seeming innocence, a phrase in which Jowett would instantly sense a threat to the entire tutorial system. For, freed by precisely Jowett's brand of university reform from having to declare for the Anglican priesthood in order to hold his fellowship at Brasenose and teach at Oxford, Pater had nonetheless inherited the quasi-pastoral powers and permission that had been developed for college tutors by the Tractarians and preserved for them by university reform as the most efficient means of producing a leadership class for imperial Britain. In that crucial transformation from disinterestedness to instrumentality, and in that shift from soul to mind, had opened the discursive space in which Pater could begin to make claims for the sensuous experience of the body, enacting his own larger interest in the polemical project that Richard Dellamora, both in *Masculine Desire: the Sexual Politics of Victorian Aestheticism* and in his essay in this volume, has described as intended "to revalorize desire, especially between males."

It is a tribute to Pater's genius, no doubt, that for more than a century now the notion of an anti-polemical, apolitical, transhistorical "Art," Pater's own most significant contribution to Victorian culture, has tended to obscure for us the otherwise unmistakable signs of personal and political struggle in his writing, the symptoms of an underlying warfare of values and assumptions that has not ceased today. Yet the ostensible autonomy of Pater's literary art from the tumultuously shifting matrices of Victorian culture is no longer, as Paul Tucker's essay on Pater's ethical Aestheticism in the present volume cogently demonstrates, the unexamined premise from which Pater studies may innocently begin. Within the wider perspective suggested by the New Historicism, it is itself the assumption that most demands scrutiny and analysis. As the reader will discover, one of the larger and more invigorating implications of *Pater in the 1990s* is that the already acknowledged richness of Pater's prose—"brooding over itself with delight"—is only further enriched when we understand it in the fuller complexity of its ideological negotiations, and more fully grasp it in the torsions of its shifting historical moment.

Walter Pater
(Rebecca Lasley 1991 ©)

Pater in the 1990s

1

LAUREL BRAKE & IAN SMALL

THE UNDISGUISED DISTASTE for the work of Walter Pater a generation ago—in, for example, René Wellek's disparaging dismissal in 1965
that "today Pater is under a cloud"—now seems very distant.[1] The
advent in the past decade of new ways of thinking about text and of the
relationship between "literature" and culture has led to insights into
the work of Pater which traditional critical practices did not permit. In
particular two general trends can be perceived. In the first place
readings of Pater's work have been enlivened by emphases on language
as a system, by attention to discourses other than simply the "literary,"
and by the tolerance of disruption, plurality, and self-consciousness
within texts; all of these have allowed the distinguishing characteristics
of Pater—his relativism and subjectivism—to be welcomed rather than
dismissed. The second trend is an interest in the production and reception of works which in its turn has led to a reassessment of the
importance of Pater's career as a teacher, and a renewed interest in his
transactions with publishers and late nineteenth-century publishing
institutions, particularly the periodical press. The general impetus of this
research has been to revalue what was hitherto considered marginal or
secondary in Pater's work, such as the early or uncollected essays. In the

1990s Pater the critic and Pater the novelist will be joined by other, less familiar Paters—the university teacher, the professional, the writer of philosophy and of mythography. All in all these lines of research have alerted critics to the diverse elements which make up the construction of "Pater"—elements which Pater himself was the first to select. The essays contained in this volume gather together the strands of this recent research. They include documentary, theoretical, and exploratory work on a broad range of Pater's criticism, fiction, philosophy, and art history. The volume appreciates the past yet looks to the future by engaging with current projects, such as editing the *Collected Works* and the biography. It offers to the critic of Pater, the postgraduate student, and the interested reader a summary of the current state of research, but it also isolates what will be the main areas of interest in Pater for literary critics and historians in the coming decade.

It has often been noted that Pater's work tests most of the rules of orthodox literary history. As Ian Fletcher remarked, Pater is a novelist, an essayist, and an historian of philosophy and art whose work exists at the margins of all of these genres. For these reasons describing and, more importantly, accounting for these "anomalous" generic features and for the accompanying unique textual qualities of his work has proved remarkably difficult. For many years the study of Pater was hampered by a relative paucity of essential material—no proper edition, no bibliography, no biography, and so forth. In the past two decades some significant work has begun to rectify this situation: it includes an edition of the letters, two biographies and a two-volume monograph on the life and work, two bibliographies, annotated scholarly editions of *The Renaissance* and of *Marius the Epicurean*, and a detailed analysis of Pater's reading sources. The two central developments in Pater studies in the 1990s will take place in the areas of editing and biography: a scholarly edition of his collected works is in train and a new biography is due in 1994. Both projects will provide basic materials for research. It is fitting, then, that the issues of editing and biography form the subject of the first group of essays in the present volume, presenting new discoveries about the life, and addressing some of the most intractable problems faced by the editors of the *Collected Works*.

The first—and perhaps most startling—essay is by Billie Andrew Inman who, in an exemplary piece of scholarly investigation, pieces together the events in Pater's private life in the fateful years between 1874 and 1876. Critics have known for some time that Pater's career at Oxford was marked by a scandal and the first specific details of it emerged in 1980. In her examination of the correspondence between Philip Gell and Alfred Milner, Inman has discovered confirmation of the homosexual relationship between the Balliol undergraduate, William Money Hardinge, and Pater. She suggests that the relationship with Hardinge and the trauma of its discovery had lasting consequences for Pater's work. Inman gives important new insights into the relationship between Pater, Jowett and W. H. Mallock, and in so doing corrects some errors of fact in Richard Ellmann's biography of Oscar Wilde (1987). Editorial issues relate to the biography in obvious ways: they are discussed in the essays which follow Inman's. The problems of editing Pater, practical and financial as well as intellectual, have taxed the group of scholars working on the *Collected Works* for some time. The conditions under which the texts of Pater's works have been transmitted to twentieth-century readers are well-known. Much of his work was written in the first place for various periodicals, and subsequently heavily revised for book publication. Most of the remaining material—the unfinished, or unpublished, or uncollected work—has come down to us via the filtering medium of his literary executor, Charles Shadwell. The resulting "Pater" is very like Robert Ross's "Wilde" in the sense that it is partly a product of editorial rather than authorial decisions. The problems produced by the textual history of Pater's works are addressed by Gerald Monsman, Ian Small and Laurel Brake. Monsman discusses the issues raised in editing the unpublished manuscript chapters of *Gaston de Latour*, and he examines the ways that work has been, might be, and will be produced. Small discusses how some of the larger issues involved in theories of textual editing and annotation are manifested in particular works by Pater, and he examines their implications for any future editions of the works. The forthcoming edition of the *Collected Works* is (for the most part) printing Pater's texts in their earliest published (that is, largely periodical) form. Writers as varied as Pater, Oscar Wilde and George Gissing well knew that the conditions for professional authors in the late nineteenth century determined to a large extent how their work was received. The complex relationship between the conditions and circumstances of periodical and book publication, and the ways in which Pater has been (and is) read is a topic discussed in this volume by Laurel Brake.

The second group of essays links the biographical with the textual by way of addressing the intertextual elements of Pater's work. One strand of recent research on Pater has taken his reading of other writers as its subject. Pater's commerce with other authors was once dismissed as dishonest, unoriginal or inaccurate, most famously perhaps in Christopher Ricks's comparison of Pater's use of quotation with that of Matthew Arnold. One of the happy consequences of the apparatuses of the scholarly editions published in the 1980s was a demonstration of how complex Pater's intertextual strategies are. The emphasis of much contemporary research is upon the special nature of Pater's engagement with other writers, seeing in his use of their work a highly radical instance of intertextuality. In the present volume three contributors discuss some intertextual elements in Pater's work. J. P. Ward assesses the significance of the influence of Wordsworth on Pater. Lesley Higgins throws fresh light on the relationship between Pater and one of his best known students, Gerard Manley Hopkins, showing that although Hopkins's undergraduate essays for Pater are saturated with the latter's thought, they at the same time reveal a critical engagement with it. F. C. McGrath discusses—and in a useful appendix prints— Joyce's parodies of Pater in *Ulysses* and the general implications about Joyce's notion of style which may be drawn from them.

The next group of essays discusses from radically different starting-points a more familiar concern—the concepts of the aesthetic and the ethical in Pater's work. Taken together, these essays aim to controvert traditional, almost orthodox, ways of viewing the relationship between

Pater's aesthetic or "impressionist" criticism and contemporary ethical or cultural concerns. Paul Tucker retains an interest in the notion of intertextuality for, by reexamining the German influences on Pater's thought, he is able to reassess the nature of the ethical and aesthetic in Pater's work, arguing that they are concepts which have been inadequately discriminated in the past. The next essay, by Richard Dellamora, retains an interest in biography. A recent development in cultural theory—the foregrounding of gender by women's and gay studies—has radically affected perceptions of Pater. Here the guiding proposition is that all writing is gendered, and that Pater's is no exception. Dellamora analyzes Pater's work in the context of late-nineteenth-century constructions of masculinity, and argues that such an analysis exposes the blindness of some modern critical accounts of Pater, particularly that of Harold Bloom.

The final and largest category of essays in this volume takes as its subject the context of Pater's work. That context, particularly Pater's commerce with European culture, has become an important topic in recent scholarship. Critics as varied as John Conlon, Patricia Clements and Linda Dowling have documented both the extent and the significance of European culture for late nineteenth-century British writers, Pater included. Some papers here suggest ways in which such research might proceed in the future. Indeed the essays in this group employ some of the new approaches suggested by recent theoretical developments in literary studies. They reveal that the "Pater" favoured by anthologists from W. B. Yeats onwards—the author, that is, of *The Renaissance, Marius the Epicurean* and some of the essays in *Appreciations*—is a very partial one. Works hitherto considered as "secondary" or "not literature"—*Gaston de Latour, Greek Studies* and *Plato and Platonism*, for instance—now attract critical attention. Hayden Ward examines "Pascal," Pater's last essay, setting it against recurrent concerns in the *oeuvre*, but also emphasizing its uniqueness. Indeed, the essays by Hayden Ward and Gerald Monsman (and, later, by Jane Spirit), add considerably to our knowledge of the "unfinished" Pater and of his preoccupations and achievements during the last four years of his life. J. B. Bullen examines a further context to Pater's early work, illuminating his view of the Renaissance by comparing it with the main currents of mid-nineteenth-century Renaissance historiography and some modern theories of history. Bullen perceives a shift in some of the essays of *The Renaissance* from the metaphoric to the metonymic, and in his view such a shift corresponds to Roland Barthes's distinction between the writing of history as "analysis" and the writing of history as "enactment." In a paper which complements Bullen's, M. F. Moran discusses Pater's mythic fiction, seeing in it Pater's view of mythology as "the expression of the experience of a culture," and an interrogation of the processes of interpretation and ascribing meaning. Here, as elsewhere, a new and quite different Pater comes into view. A context of a different sort is adduced by Bernard Richards, who continues the themes of the "undervalued" Pater of the preceding essays. He takes his subject from some of the less well-known later essays, and addresses a hitherto neglected topic—Pater's accounts of architecture. Anne Varty returns to another neglected piece, "Diaphaneitè," one of Pater's earliest writings, but one published only posthumously. The context which she uses to explain the concerns of the essay is—as with Paul Tucker—Pater's exposure to contemporary German thought. Hayden Ward argues that Pater's last essay, "Pascal," contains elements of his earlier work; Anne Varty explains how the early "Diaphaneitè" is reappropriated and recapitulated in fragments in the later work. Finally Jane Spirit continues the theme of rehabilitating the "unknown" and late Pater by discussing a philosophical context—the nineteenth-century European reputations of two thinkers who influenced him, Michel Montaigne and Giordano Bruno. In so doing she provides both a new way of regarding *Gaston de Latour* and a companion study to Monsman's earlier account of the manuscript of it.

The essays contained in this volume are important, then, in several distinct ways. In the first place they reflect upon the scholarly and critical achievements of the past, often, as with Richard Dellamora's engagement with the hidden biases of Harold Bloom's views of Pater, through a revaluation of them. The volume also engages with current concerns, particularly in its discussions of projects such as the biography or scholarly editions. Most importantly, though, the essays contained here point to the future for Pater studies. By exemplifying the relevance of new thinking about how texts and works are to be understood in the study of discourses such as historiography or myth or masculinity, or of compositional strategies such as intertextuality, *Pater in the 1990s* indicates where new research on Pater will be most fruitful.

Pater at Oxford, 1872
(Simeon Solomon)

Estrangement and Connection:
Walter Pater
Benjamin Jowett
and William M. Hardinge

_____ **▬** _____ 2

BILLIE ANDREW INMAN

EVER SINCE THOMAS WRIGHT stated in his biography of Pater in 1907 that Benjamin Jowett, Master of Balliol, applied a "salutary whip" to Pater in somehow snatching from him in 1874 a virtually promised University Proctorship, students of Pater have wondered whether the story were true and, if so, what Pater could have done to make Jowett think he should take such uncharacteristic action against a Fellow of Brasenose. Wright implied that although Jowett was not happy about Pater's philosophic stance in *The Renaissance*, it was loose talk of Pater's that really motivated Jowett,[1] but he gave no details. At the first international conference on Pater, at Brasenose College in 1980, Laurel Brake galvanized her audience by bringing forth the first real evidence pertaining to the, by that time, famous mystery regarding Pater, Jowett, and the Proctorship. She reported that Jowett's action was prompted by letters written by Pater that were carried to him by W. H. Mallock, known to Pater scholars primarily as the creator of Mr. Rose in *The*

1

New Republic. She had found in the *Diary* of A. C. Benson evidence of this transaction that had been suppressed by Benson in his life of Pater in the English Men of Letters series (1906). As Brake reported, Benson in his *Diary* gives no facts about the content of the letters, but implies a good deal through his comment upon them—"What a donkey P[ater]. must have been to *write* them"—and his statement that they prompted a "dreadful interview" between Jowett and Pater, which left Pater "old, crushed, despairing."[2] Benson's source of information about the letters and the interview was Edmund Gosse. Laurel Brake assumed in her paper, printed in 1981 as "Judas and the Widow," that this incident occurred before Pater was passed over for a University Proctorship in February 1874.

In "Oscar at Oxford," an essay published in 1984 in the *New York Review*, Richard Ellmann approached the Pater-Jowett estrangement from a different direction, placing its onset in 1876 rather than 1874. He reported that "[a]n undergraduate of Balliol named William Money Hardinge, whom Wilde knew as one of Ruskin's roadbuilders, was disclosed to have received letters from Walter Pater signed, 'Yours lovingly'."[3] He adds: "Hardinge had also written and circulated some homosexual poems. The affair was brought to the attention of the authorities by Balliol students who feared that the 'Balliol Bugger', as Hardinge was called, was giving the college a bad name. Early in 1876 the master of Balliol, Benjamin Jowett, was apprised of the Pater letters and the sonnets. He now broke with Pater—a famous rupture—and summoned Hardinge on the official charge of 'keeping and reciting immoral poetry'."[4] In his biography of Wilde, Ellmann repeated the story about Hardinge and Pater[5] and reported, additionally, that it was Leonard Montefiore, a Balliol student, who complained to the authorities, while Alfred Milner and Arnold Toynbee, also Balliol students, tried to help Hardinge.[6] Ellmann still placed the incident in 1876.

Since it stretches the imagination too far to suppose that two similar incidents leading to an estrangement between Pater and Jowett occurred, one in 1874 and the other in 1876, Brake and Ellmann must have been writing about the same incident. But how can the discrepancies in dates and the names of their informer be accounted for? Further, what was the source of Ellmann's account? And what sort of person was William Money Hardinge? My intention is to answer some questions pertaining to this matter, but I cannot help raising new questions as I proceed.

Ellmann based his account of the Hardinge incident upon information given him by Dr. Alon Kadish, a member of the Faculty of Humanities at the Hebrew University, Jerusalem, who had found it in the Gell Correspondence at Hopton Hall near Wirksworth, Derbyshire, when doing research for his *Apostle Arnold: The Life and Death of Arnold Toynbee*.[7] In the summer of 1988, I read the pertinent letters in the County Record Office at Matlock, Derbyshire, with the permission of Major Anthony Gell, the grandson of Henry Wellington Gell, the brother of Philip Lyttelton Gell, who was the preserver of the letters crucial to this inquiry as well as hundreds of other letters. The problem regarding the dating of the Hardinge incident quickly dissolved when I observed that the letters describing it were written in February and March 1874—not 1876. How could Alon Kadish, and therefore Richard Ellmann, have been mistaken about the year? Perhaps for four reasons: the Hardinge affair was not Kadish's primary concern, nor Ellmann's; some of the pertinent letters are dated only with month and day; a commemorative essay on Jowett written by Hardinge refers to his leaving Balliol College for good in 1876; and Philip Gell, to whom the letters were written, went down from Balliol because of illness in both February 1874 and February 1876. What Kadish did not realize is that Hardinge went down twice: in February 1874, under a cloud of disapproval, to stay until November, and in June 1876, after becoming seriously ill. At the time of his second departure, his father, who had played a very important role in the events of 1874, was dead.[8] The error in dating leads Ellmann to say that Oscar Wilde knew Hardinge at the time of the incident "as one of Ruskin's roadbuilders."[9] However, when Hardinge was sent home in February 1874, Ruskin's road-building project had not begun[10] and Wilde had not matriculated at Magdalen College, and would not do so until October. Both Hardinge and Wilde later joined in Ruskin's road-building. The error also leads Ellmann to infer that "[u]nder pressure, he [Hardinge] gracefully acknowledged himself to be too ill to . . . [read his Newdigate Prize poem in the Sheldonian], and Bodley [John Edward Courtenay], like others, pretended to accept the reason as true."[11] Actually when his poem "Troy" won the prize in 1876, Hardinge *was* too ill to read. The poem was read on 21 June 1876, by Philip Gell.

Ellmann's account of the Hardinge crisis in *Oscar Wilde* is correct, however, in regard to the persons involved and the main charges. Still, since the crisis was so important to Pater's reputation at Oxford, it deserves a detailed treatment from one who is interested primarily in the nature of Pater's participation. I shall begin by introducing the correspondents and the central figure, mainly from facts in the *Balliol College Register, 1832-1914*, the *Alumni Oxonienses 1715-1886*, and *Who Was Who*, and then give as detailed an account of the incidents as can be derived from the Gell papers.

Philip Lyttelton Gell, who in time would become Benjamin Jowett's literary executor and later Director and President of the British South Africa Company; Alfred Milner, who would become the first Viscount Milner and Governor of the Transvaal and Orange River Colony; Arnold Toynbee, who would blossom early as an influential social philosopher and economist, but die in his thirty-first year; and William Money Hardinge, who would become a novelist—all were friends at Oxford at the beginning of 1874. Gell, Milner, and Toynbee had been together at King's College, London, before Gell and Milner matriculated at Balliol in January 1872 and February 1873 respectively, and Toynbee at Pembroke, in January 1873. As 1874 opened, Toynbee, who had been so dissatisfied at Pembroke that he had withdrawn, was reading in Oxford; he would enter Balliol in 1875. Hardinge states in "Some Personal Recollections of the Master of Balliol" that he "had known Toynbee years before at a tutor's."[12] *Who Was Who* names the Reverend J. M. Brackenburg, Wimbledon, as Toynbee's tutor. Hardinge had matriculated at Balliol on 3 February 1873 with Milner. In a letter to Gell written in December 1873, Toynbee concludes by saying,

"Remember me to Milner, Rendel and Hardinge."[13] James Meadows Rendel, who had also entered Balliol in 1873, will be present during the period to be described, but will not play an active role. Leonard Abraham Montefiore, who had matriculated in February 1873, with Milner and Hardinge, was a good friend of Rendel's and Milner's, but not of Gell's. It is clear in one of Milner's letters that he and Gell judged Montefiore differently.[14]

By the middle of February 1874, Philip Gell had gone down from Balliol because of illness, and was therefore not present when the news broke within the group that Montefiore had provided information to Richard Lewis Nettleship, a Balliol don, about Hardinge's "unnatural" behavior, which had prompted Jowett to ask Hardinge's father to call him home and keep him there until November. It was necessary for Milner and Toynbee to write letters to Gell to explain how matters stood with Hardinge and, on Milner's part, to defend Montefiore's action. Thus were written the letters of interest to Pater scholars, only a few in a personal correspondence between Gell and Toynbee extending nearly to Toynbee's death in 1883 and a personal and professional correspondence between Gell and Milner extending to Milner's death in 1925.

The letters that mention Pater by name are Toynbee's to Gell written 25 February 1874 and Milner's to Gell written 1 March 1874. These two letters are dated with only month and day, but another letter of Toynbee's linked in content to the letter of 25 February, is plainly dated "March 11, 1874." All other evidence points to 1874 as the year of the incident.

The pertinent paragraph in Arnold Toynbee's letter of 25 February 1874 is as follows:

—Hardinge has gone down till November, and as Jowett now [?] knows all about Pater—at any rate quite enough—and his parents eyes before strangely closed are now wide open to the inferences that are & may be drawn from his manner & conversation, and as Hardinge himself for the first time seems distinctly to realize the peril in which his conduct has placed him, there is some hope of his working sufficient change in character & circumstances to prevent the catastrophe which otherwise must only have been a question of time.[15]

Milner's letter of 1 March 1874 is twenty-six pages long, and is
written from a defensive stance, although he blames himself (rather
than Gell) for what he thinks to be Gell's misinterpretation, because he
had not written a full explanation earlier. Hardinge had apparently
written Gell a letter containing what Milner calls "an unprincipled
pack of lies," and Gell, incensed, because he believed Hardinge to be
telling the truth, had written a letter to Montefiore, which had caused
Milner "pain" when he had read it. Milner begins his long, corrective
explanation:

On Saturday night (Feb. 21st) Hardinge, who had been down to London for
a day, came into my room, telling me he was in the greatest mess he had ever
been in / during his life. Jowett had been down to London & requested his
father to withdraw him on the general ground, that he was living up here in a
way wh. might ultimately harm himself & was already throwing discredit on the
College. His conversation & writing were indecent, his acquaintance bad, his
work = 0^2. Why should he remain at Oxford?/

I don't doubt Jowett said to Harding's [sic] <u>père</u> at that time what he said
in his own words to me on Sunday "I can't allow this sort of thing to go on,
& yet I don't want to ruin the man for life." With what I cannot help
regarding as a sound mixture of wisdom & kindness he suggested Hardinge's
withdrawal by his father without any fuss or public inquiry.

Well, Hardinge went home & denied everything. He came back to Oxford
& told me, that he had been to/ see Jowett and had denied everything &
proceeded to ask me, if Jowett should send for me, to assert that I had never
heard from his mouth any indecent poetry or words, wh. could be construed
into an allusion to <u>unnatural</u> profligacy. You know, how utterly impossible it
would have been for me to deny such charges, but you do not know, that only
one or two nights before Hardinge had repeated in my rooms a sonnet / yet
more filthy & yet more unnatural than anything I had heard from his lips
before. I pointed out to Hardinge, that he was asking me to commit myself to
wholesale falsehood, wh. I could not do, but promised at the same time to give
the most favourable colouring to the matter. Shall I confess it? At that moment
I really felt sorry for Hardinge. He looked all this pretence—the devil's own
pretence, of contrition, affected me. Besides I thought, as I told him, / that his
going down would do him more harm than good—an opinion, of wh. at this
moment I do not retain a single shred.

Next day much to my surprise Jowett did send for me. I made the very
best of Hardinge's case. The sonnets, about wh. he asked, were in my
representation mere literary exercises, the indecent language merely intended to
<disgust> startle men. In confirmation of this theory, wh. I still believe / to be
partially true, I cited the fact, that he often used blasphemous expressions,

which seemed to me the mere echoes of sharp things he had heard from other men. These words of mine are, as far as I can discover, the whole sum & substance of the material, wh. under Hardinge's plastic hand has grown into a deliberate charge of blasphemy & impiety directed against him by Montefiore. [Milner's underlining] Before I left Jowett told me, that he had at least two witnesses, who were prepared / to affirm his first charge against Hardinge, wh. Hardinge had denied the day before. "His levity," said Jowett, "was perfectly disgusting. He has no sense of truth & nothing makes any impression on him." [Milner's vertical line]

That afternoon Jowett saw Hardinge & placed before him an alternative, wh. I think you will on calm consideration decide to have been substantially fair. "You are discrediting the College. I do not wish to discredit you. Go down quietly, or, if you adhere to your denial of yesterday / wh. I believe to have been absolutely false, we will have an inquiry." That inquiry Hardinge shrank from. He came here on Monday morning & told me, that he was going to accept the first alternative. "You know yourself Milner," these were his words—I can swear to them, "I could never stand an investigation. My character is too bad." I agreed with him & told him, we would all do our best—we are all doing it, to hush up matters. . . . Now for Montefiore's conduct in the matter.

And in the first place let me say, that I have not the least wish to influence your judgment of Montefiore otherwise than by putting before you the plain facts./ We have never quite agreed about Montefiore & I don't expect us to agree now. We have both <agreed> decided about his injudiciousness. . . . Montefiore made no charge against Hardinge. He only spoke about him to Nettleship [Richard Lewis Nettleship, 1846-1892, B.A., Balliol 1869; elected Fellow at Balliol, 1870], not as a don, but as a / personal friend, a step wh. Rawnsley [Hardwicke Drummond Rawnsley, 1851-1920, matriculated at Balliol 24 October 1870; B.A. 1875; vicar of Crosthwaite, Cumberland, 1883] had taken on several previous occasions. [Milner's underlining] There can be no doubt that Nettleship, (as he has told both Rendel & Toynbee), was fairly well aware & exceedingly anxious to get rid of Hardinge. The only effect Montefiore's speaking had was the attempt on the part of the Dons to get his father to withdraw Hardinge quietly, on the whole the kindest thing they could have / done. For my own part, I do not see, that Montefiore was to blame even in the time of the step. <You> The very fact, that Hardinge had not yet irretrievably committed himself with Pater was all the more reason why the evil should be prevented. It seems more strongly absurd to say, that one should not interfere till the mischief was done. And it is vain to pretend that there was not evidence of the strongest character/ against Hardinge. When a man confesses to lying in another man's arms kissing him & having been found doing it, as there is the strongest evidence to prove <in Hardinge's case>, or when letters pass between them in wh. they address one another as "darling" & sign

themselves "yours lovingly," & such a letter I̲ have seen, when verses are
written from one man to another too vile to blot this paper, what hope can you
have, that a criminal act, if not committed already, <will> may not be
committed any day? / Why, if it does not occur, it is pure "good luck," & not
"good management." For my own part I am thankful that Montefiore did take
this step. It was no longer to be reconciled with one's conscience, that such a
life as Hardinge's and such notoriety as Hardinge's—you can have no idea how
he was spoken of all over the Varsity—should go on getting worse & worse, till
some day we were startled by the news of the worst and [met] with the/
unanswerable question "How could you suffer these things to proceed under
your eyes"? If as I believe, Hardinge's character is the result of "Nature's
spite," no amendment could be hoped for & the longer the blow was delayed,
the more fatal must it be not only to himself but to his reputation.

Milner goes on to say that Montefiore's motive might be attributed by
some to personal spite, since he and Hardinge had quarreled, and that
Hardinge had seized upon this interpretation, to assume the role of
victim. And he adds, "It is all very / well to say he should have spoken
to Hardinge first, but you know what the result would have been.
Hardinge would have giggled blasphemed stared [?] & said 'Go then'."
Milner begins the penultimate paragraph:

> In conclusion, it's a [?] mercy, that neither Jowett nor Nettleship know the
> worst, that Toynbee made Hardinge destroy his most culpable letters, I mean
> such as could be adduced against him in a court of law, & that for the future
> we all mean to keep absolute silence to the outside world & speak as little as
> possible among ourselves upon a subject, wh. has become [word after *become*
> blotted out by liquid] painful to most of us.[16]

Two days later, 3 March, Milner tried to explain a passage in this letter:
"When I said Montefiore spoke to Nettleship as a friend, I did not
mean to assert that he had blurted the matter out. But there / is a
difference between bringing a deliberate charge before the constituted
authorities & speaking seriously to a friend, who happens to be more
or less an authority, about the conduct of a third person, who is
distinctly going wrong & whom you both want to prevent from coming
to worse harm." And he continues: "I still differ as to Hardinge's
supposed innocuousness (to coin a word). His reputation as the 'Balliol

B. . . r' is injuring the College as a whole, though I think with you, that it did not harm individuals."[17] Gell was apparently still more sympathetic towards Hardinge than Milner was, and Gell had been conveying some information from Milner and others to Hardinge. Where Milner was concerned, Gell probably just sent on to Hardinge a letter enclosed by Milner in his letter of 3 March, in which Milner showed himself willing to express opinions "to Hardinge's face," as he said, as well as "behind his back," and in regard to which he told Gell to use his discretion whether to send it to Hardinge or return it to him. But that Gell had been in communication with someone besides Milner and Toynbee is shown in the following new detail, one especially interesting to Pater scholars. It is included in the second paragraph of Milner's letter to Gell written 13 March:

> Hardinge with his usual delicacy has written an abusive letter to Rawnsley, in wh. he says, / that he has just heard from you, telling him that the three chief agents in his removal were Miss Pater, Montefiore & Rawnsley, who as it appears, had had a great row with Mac-Ewen [Alexander Robertson] in Hardinge's rooms, the night before the latter went down, in wh. he denied having been in any way instrumental in H[ardinge]'s dismissal, was very indignant at the receipt of this letter, both with Hardinge for disbelieving his word & with you for prompting him.[18]

It is easy to infer from the passage following the one just quoted, that Milner had thought Rawnsley was Jowett's second witness. When Rawnsley assured Milner that he had not spoken to Nettleship for two terms, Milner apologized to him. After reporting this fact to Gell, he adds: "For my own part the question is more of a mystery to me than ever. Jowett distinctly told me, that he had / two witnesses against Hardinge in the matter of the indecent sonnets. The one of course was Montefiore, but who was the other?" Who, indeed? Perhaps another acquaintance of Hardinge's at Balliol could have been called in by Jowett as Milner was, to be questioned about Hardinge's sonnets and unacceptable behavior. Hardinge's circle included Walter Sydney Sichel (1855-1933),[19] who was a student at Balliol from 1872 to 1877, and Thomas Herbert Warren (1853-1930), a student at Balliol from 1872 to 1876. Warren had been educated at Clifton, where, upon Jowett's recommendation, Hardinge studied before entering Balliol.[20] When Hardinge returned to Oxford in 1893 to attend a Balliol dinner, he visited Warren at Magdalen,[21] and Warren was one of Benson's sources for his life of Pater. Also, Hardinge probably knew John Edward Courtenay Bodley in 1874 as in 1875 (when Bodley entered in his diary for 15 April that he had visited Hardinge's rooms and found him playing Weber),[22] since he and Bodley matriculated at Balliol at the same time. Or perhaps the second witness to the sonnets and unacceptable behavior was an alarmed Miss Pater,[23] who went to the Master of Balliol and asked him to avert danger by sending Hardinge home.

Who suggested the name of Miss Pater to Philip Gell? There is no record of W. H. Mallock's ever having written a letter to Philip Gell, and it is unlikely that he would have. Milner's only two references to Mallock in the letters of the 1870s and, likely, in his entire correspondence with Gell, are the following in a letter dated from Balliol on 6 February 1876: "The Union [Oxford Union, of which Milner was the President] is peculiarly lively & peculiarly troublesome. Mutual friends are in *status quo* except that Sloman has gone down, Mallock too as it seems, he being however hardly a mutual friend. . . . Toynbee is at last working for Greats. . . . Montefiore is going down next term[24] & Glazebrook will take rooms in the same house with Rendel & me in the Broad. . . . Mallock allowed himself to be drawn out to a considerable extent about his books.[25] He is the greatest *autologist* I know - a nice new word that, don't you think so?"[26]

Benjamin Jowett himself was one of Gell's correspondents. The Gell collection contains forty-three letters from Jowett, written from 5 August 1873, to near the end of his life (the late letters are undated). Most of these letters are brief and rather formal, like many of Pater's letters, but Jowett did not hesitate to give Gell personal advice, for example, about positions he should not accept, or boys he should be pleased to see him tutor. There are no letters from 1874, but as Jowett's literary executor Gell knew that Jowett had burned all of his personal correspondence that was at his command, and Gell might have removed letters from his own collection that he knew Jowett would have wanted to be destroyed. This is pure speculation, but if Jowett did not introduce the name of Miss Pater, I cannot imagine who did.

How Philip Gell came to say that Miss Pater wanted Hardinge out of town is just one of several questions we are left with. Another is, "Were letters handed to Jowett?" From Toynbee we learn that Jowett and Nettleship were not told everything the friends of Hardinge knew, much less given letters, and that Toynbee supervised Hardinge's burning of letters that could be used against him in a court of law, letters like the one Milner saw. Jowett was genuinely disturbed about the sonnets that at least two witnesses had thought to be indecent and unnatural, as well as by Hardinge's flippant attitude. Milner does not report that Jowett mentioned letters. When talking to Benson, Gosse might have been imaginatively filling in blanks in a story he knew imperfectly. Perhaps W. H. Mallock did not take letters to Jowett. The possibility that no letters were delivered is strengthened by the statement of Thomas Wright, who appears to have known more than he told, that a "common friend" of Pater and Jowett informed Jowett of Pater's loose talk by making a "casual observation."[27]

But let us assume that Gosse was remembering and reporting correctly to Benson. What could Mallock's motive have been in taking letters to Jowett? Did the motive have anything to do with Pater at all? It is clear that to Milner, Gell, and Toynbee, Pater was simply a given in Hardinge's situation. They do not express surprise, sympathy, regret, or condemnation regarding his relationship with Hardinge. Montefiore had no motive relating to Pater. Perhaps Mallock, too, was concerned only about Hardinge's welfare and the reputation of Balliol College.

Certainly, Mallock would not have delivered letters to Jowett simply to strengthen his hand against Pater, as some Paterians tended to assume when Laurel Brake first presented the apparent evidence of his involvement. Mallock, even as a youth, when Jowett came to his house to "inspect him" and decide on his suitability for Balliol College, felt a temperamental antipathy to him.[28] He continued to be "repelled" by Jowett.[29] From his second term at Balliol, he thought Jowett's unorthodox support of Christianity was vague and intellectually absurd, but he knew his adverse feeling was not based altogether on intellectual grounds.[30] The sharpest satire in *The New Republic*, which Mallock began writing in his second year at Balliol,[31] 1871, is directed at Dr. Jenkinson, the stand-in for Jowett.[32] Mallock's treatment of Pater shows no personal animus. He does not accuse Mr. Rose of "doubleness" as he does Dr. Jenkinson. It is interesting, too, that his Mr. Rose is oblivious of Dr. Jenkinson's antipathy to him as of the implication that he has had a pernicious influence upon the education of the eighteen-year-old boy who has written "Three visions in the watches of one night," a sonnet which he reads.[33] In general, Mr. Rose is a happy Hedonist who does not realize what effect his words have on other people. He seems also very naive in asking openly for a book that describes the rites of Priapus, which the more discreet Laurence has kept locked up.[34]

But whatever his motive for taking letters to Jowett, if indeed he did, how could Mallock have gained possession of letters written from Pater to Hardinge or Hardinge to Pater? Certainly only Hardinge, Pater, or someone very close to one of them could have placed such letters in his hands. Did Mallock know Hardinge? Neither Hardinge nor Mallock mentions the other as far as I know, and, apparently, the only suggestion of a link is Geoffrey Faber's statement in a footnote in *Jowett: A Portrait with a Background* that Robert Leslie in *The New Republic* "was said to be a 'Mr. Hardinge'."[35] Faber adds: "But there were several Mr. Hardinges: None of them seem quite to fit. And who was 'Laurence'? Can he have been a wishful self-projection of Mallock himself? If so, Leslie might be a projection of W. M. Hardinge, novelist and poet, who was his younger contemporary at Balliol?"[36] Faber also calls attention to Leslie's early statement that " 'Dr. Jenkinson is the only one [of the distinguished people at Laurence's house-party] I know, and, naturally enough, he forgets me'."[37] But if Hardinge and Mallock knew each other well enough in 1874 for Hardinge to have given Mallock letters from Pater, it was likely before Montefiore's report and the burning of other letters, and certainly Hardinge did not intend that Jowett see them.

Philip Gell's mention of Miss Pater suggests another scenario, equally speculative but more plausible. Clara or Hester Pater happened to see in Walter's room letters written by Hardinge, and she feared that this young man would expose and disgrace her brother. She called upon Edmund Gosse, a friend of the family, for help, and he turned to a fellow Devonshireman who was a Balliol student with access to Jowett. Suppose that Gosse asked Mallock to show Jowett the letters so that he would send Hardinge down, for the welfare of Pater as well as Hardinge. If Gosse did not give Mallock letters, how would he have known that Mallock had them? Jowett would not have been inclined to reveal the identity of the informant to Pater, who might have told Gosse if he had. Mallock is not likely to have told Gosse or anyone else. He was the most circumspect of all circumspect men. In his *Memoirs*, he rarely if ever gives a date, and he names very few persons besides famous authors and influential aristocrats. About Pater he states only that in his *New Republic* he was represented by Mr. Rose, and he does not mention Hardinge. An Oxford outsider like Gosse would not have been likely to hear by chance from any man at Oxford what Milner, an insider, never learned, in spite of his curiosity on the subject of the second witness. However, it is possible as Lesley Higgins suggested at the Pater Conference, that R. L. Nettleship, who might have been privy to all the information Jowett had, might have told his older brother Henry Nettleship, who might have told Pater, who might have told Gosse.

In spite of all the unanswered questions, one can say that only seven months after Simeon Solomon was arrested for deviant behavior, Pater was involved in a homosexual romance with a nineteen-year-old student who had a tendency, before faced with consequences, to advertise his homosexuality. It was not a "platonic" relationship, but unless Hardinge mischaracterized it to Milner, Gell, and Toynbee, it was unconsummated. Since the very day Hardinge left Oxford, 25 September 1874, is the day Brasenose nominated John Wordsworth to be

University Proctor, it is likely that Jowett did tell the President of Brasenose that Pater was not the sort of man who should have a wider influence, although the Fellows of the College, almost all clerical, might have passed over Pater on the grounds of irreligion even without Jowett's advice.

But it was not in official Oxford's nature to "ruin a man's life" over manifestations of "unnatural" tendencies, but to remove temptation, keep publicly silent, and speak as little as possible about it among themselves. There was also much plain empathy with homosexuality (although Victorians did not use this word in the 1870s). When another young man, Charles Edward Hutchinson, who matriculated at Oxford in 1873, at Brasenose rather than Balliol, published a pamphlet entitled *Boy Worship* anonymously in 1880, he said that the worship of beautiful boys was by no means rare in Oxford or elsewhere:

> Men of all tastes become boy-worshippers. It is not only Sayge Greene who goes into ecstasies over a boy's face and figure, (he may, it is true, express himself more eloquently than some of his more robust brethren,) but the devotees of the cricket and football fields have ere now furnished many an ardent follower.
>
> The Upper River, as well as a certain College Chapel, has its little band of *habitués*. Here I would remark, that although sundry restrictions have, in some quarters, placed difficulties in the way of free intercourse, an ardent boy-worshipper will always find means of access to the shrine.[38]

When selecting a headnote for his pamphlet, Hutchinson borrowed the first two and a half lines from the sonnet which Mr. Rose reads in the *New Republic*, the one written, he says, by an eighteen-year-old boy.

> Three visions in the watches of one night
> Made sweet my sleep—almost too sweet to tell
> One was Narcissus.[39]

The use of these lines on the title-page and the first page of text in *Boy Worship* seems to link the subject of the work especially to Pater, but the main theme is that boy worship was not limited to aesthetes, much less to one aesthete, but was rather common at Oxford.

Yet all this is not enough to explain the estrangement between Jowett and Pater. Jowett tended to assume the role of kind fatherly adviser with "errant men." Geoffrey Faber quotes the following from a letter written by Josephine Butler to Lewis Campbell, Jowett's friend and early biographer, dating the incident "very much later" than 1869:

> At one time . . . there was an outbreak of abnormal immorality among a few of the young men in Oxford. To such he [Jowett] was (I know) the wisest, most prudent and gentlest of counsellors. He was extremely severe and tender at the same time. We [she and her husband] had the unhappiness of having to try to guide for a time one of these youths (now dead) and thus I got to know how implicitly such misguided or guilty creatures might confide in him, and seek and follow his advice.[40]

Jowett treated Hardinge in much the same way in 1874, and he accepted him back later that year, befriended him in 1876, was delighted, according to Hardinge, that he had won the Newdigate Prize for Poetry that year, visited him in London in later years, and invited him to the prestigious dinner at Balliol on 24 June 1893.[41] Neither Swinburne's blasphemies nor John Addington Symonds's homosexuality caused an estrangement from Jowett. But these men, like Hardinge, accepted Jowett's kindness and called him master. Pater's estrangement from Jowett probably had its incipience long before 1874, because of Pater's independence. No man was less inclined than he to cater to or cultivate friendships with his older contemporaries. He did not write adulatory letters across the Channel to Renan as Carlyle did to Goethe; he did not evoke Rydal Mount as if it were "holy ground," as Arnold did. Although he bought *The Ring and the Book*, and five of Browning's books published afterwards, he apparently did not try to meet Browning. The fact that Rossetti, upon meeting Pater, " 'disliked him extremely' "[42] is a good sign that he was not approached by Pater with the enthusiasm that young William Morris had exhibited in his approach. And there is no evidence that after he emerged from the student status he remained attentive to Jowett as many other younger men did.

If the interview which Gosse reported between Jowett and Pater was "dreadful" for Pater, it can be safely assumed that it was not satisfactory for Jowett either. Jowett confided to his diary in 1877: "I seem to have great power in thinking and in dealing privately with persons, but no power in public or society."[43] It is likely that with Pater, Jowett failed in the type of personal influence upon which he prided himself. What he probably found in Pater was not gratitude and a willingness to be counselled, but a resistant attitude based on a sense of superiority. Such an attitude, more than anything else, could have caused the estrangement between Jowett and Pater.

It is impossible to say now, how Pater felt about Hardinge in 1874 and afterwards. It is not difficult, however, to make an informed inference about the nature of Hardinge's feelings for Pater and to see the effects of the trauma of 1874 upon Pater's works.

Although Milner's letters describe Hardinge's untruthfulness, spitefulness, and cockiness, and Toynbee refers to his "doubleness," all these traits were probably defenses marshalled for protection in a crisis, not settled traits of character. There are no traces of them in "Some Personal Recollections of the Master of Balliol," written primarily to show how kind Jowett could be to an individual over a long period of time in spite of the multifarious demands upon his time and strength. Hardinge expresses pride in having introduced Toynbee to Jowett[44] and when describing Jowett's funeral procession states, casually: "I walked with Alfred Milner, who had been my very first Balliol associate."[45] In 1874, Hardinge was full of literary and linguistic promise. His Newdigate Prize poem, "Troy," is felicitously written, and it contains the interesting idea that if Helen had been a woman instead of a "soulless spirit" sent by the gods to torment men, she would (like Pater's Aphrodite) have grown weary of the havoc she caused. Hardinge later published in *Nineteenth Century* translations of a considerable body of ancient Greek poems and French poems, with commentary ("Chrysanthema Gathered from the Greek Anthology," 1878, and "French Verse in English," 1881), and contributed stories and reminiscences to *Temple Bar*, *Universal Review*, and *Magazine of Art* in the late 1880s and the 1890s. He published four novels: *Clifford Gray: a Romance of Modern Life* (1881); *Eugenia: an Episode* (1883); *The Willow-Garth* (1886); and *Out of the Fog* (1888). All of the novels are heterosexual love stories, but the first is perhaps personally revealing and is interesting for some parallels with Wilde's *The Picture of Dorian Gray*, written later. Clifford Gray is a prominent artist whose fate is strangely bound to one of his paintings, a portrait, although of a woman, which is exhibited at the Royal Academy after his death. There is "all hell and all heaven in the woman's face," and the portrait is absolutely true to life. Clifford Gray suffers the misfortune of being in love with this woman, Vera de Trekoff, although it is plain that the male narrator has a deeper appreciation of and a more tender love for Gray than she does, and is the only one who really mourns his death. Vera does, however, express a few Paterian sentiments. For example, she says, "Ask not what has become of passed sunlight and shadow, whither have vanished the glory-rays on tree and hill; look into your friend's face and find them there. . . ."[46] The novel is dedicated, not to a person, but to the years 1876-77, which Hardinge apparently spent in France; and it was completed in 1877. The prefatory sonnet to this novel probably resembles the sonnets Alfred Milner called "filthy" and "unnatural":

'Lean over me—lean over, dear, awhile,
One while ere yet mine eyelids swoon to death;
For one live moment give me of your breath
And one last shaft of sunlight in your smile!
Stoop down and kiss me once, and reconcile
My soul to hear the word this instant saith;
For the spent heart within me travaileth,
Sense being so faint and this world's worth so vile.

Speak not at all: but fold your hands in mine,
Dim not with tears my stars that are your eyes;
Lean low and listen . . . closer, closer bend!
It is not I that speak—a voice divine
Whispers through mine its heavenlier harmonies—
"Lo! I am with you always, to the end." '

Paris, 18--

"(from a MS.)"

The Willow-Garth is dedicated to the unnamed person addressed in
the poem below:

> To . . .
> Because outside this region of my life
> There lies for ever something known not yet,
> A world wherein you enter and find set
> Your crystal throne of rest from human strife,
>
> Because beyond these bounded eyes of mine
> There spreads the vision of a wider sphere,
> And there your daylight is as mine is here
> And there you know what I at most divine,
>
> Because my hoped-for future is yours now,
> Because you have all that I have not and I
> Having nothing that you have not,—by and by
> Might have, when reaching you, yet dream not how—
>
> Therefore this vase whereinto memory pours
> Wine that is stranger not to tears or blood,
> With whatsoever of hope be here or good,
> —This book of mine—is yours as I am yours.

August 1886

I do not maintain that this poem was written to Pater, in spite of the
"crystal throne." Twelve years had passed since 1874. But I think it
illustrates the attitude the aspiring writer of nineteen had toward the
celebrated writer of thirty-five, a self-effacing adulation for a superior
man, which Pater thought natural to women in love and to men with
"female souls," men like his Raoul in *Gaston de Latour* (unpublished
chapter 10) and his Emerald Uthwart. It is reasonable to assume that
in the relationship between Pater and Hardinge, Pater was the
"seigneurial species of soul," like Jasmin and James Stokes, and
Hardinge was the "servile species," a " 'servant of servants' to his
brother" (terms from *Gaston de Latour*, chapter 10).

That Pater became Socrates, with his circle, can be inferred from the
following commentary of Alexander Michaelson (Marc André Raffalovich):

There would have been something irresistible about Pater at the height of his power had he cared to exert his personal influence. Those unacquainted with his writings, or prejudiced by Mallock's *New Republic*, could describe him as "a black, white, ingratiatory vampire." Of course we who knew and loved him saw and understood the feelings of that delightful youth (now a distinguished novelist)[47] when first face to face with that Minotaur. And we were not less aware when we watched with malicious amusement the less delightful and vainer youths who expected to make an impression. What fun it must have been, what fun it was, for aspirants to praise of so rare a quality when they compared notes. Well! it was worth while to have performed in his presence, he would never think the worse of one for that. Few men, I suppose, have been kinder and more affectionate to young men *as they were*; it is so much easier to be kind and affectionate to the men we imagine.[48]

Like Socrates, Pater thought the love of refined men for one another the highest type of love. But he also thought the adoring, selfless love of a "noble" woman for a man to be a fine thing (thus his appreciation of Octave Feuillet's selfless heroines); and the patriarchal home, which depended upon "the discretion of wives," was to him the basis of "civilised order."[49]

One can infer that what Pater felt after the disclosure of his relationship with W. M. Hardinge in 1874 was not shame, but anger, pain, and recognition of the circumscribed boundaries within which he would be constrained to live if he were to remain acceptable to polite society. I have shown in detail in *Pater and His Reading* that the theme of victimization and the tendency to glorify suffering entered Pater's works after 1874 and that most of his works published over the next four years were written as veiled responses to criticism of his life and influence;[50] in short, the personal crisis of 1874 had distinct ramifications in his writings, as did the religious crisis of 1860. I will repeat here only one reference to Pater's new stance. His revision in 1877 to his characterization of Abelard in *The Renaissance* contains his most revealing protest against the type of persons who had judged him:

The opposition into which Abelard is thrown, which gives its colour to his career, which breaks his soul to pieces, is no less subtle opposition than that between the mere professional, official, hireling ministers of that system, with their ignorant worship of system for its own sake, and the true child of light, the humanist with reason and heart and senses quick, as theirs were almost dead, reaching out to and attaining modes of ideal living, beyond the prescribed limits of that system, though possibly contained in essential germ within it. As always happens, the adherents of the poorer and narrower culture had no sympathy with, because no understanding of a culture richer and more ample than their own; after the discovery of wheat they would still live upon acorns—*après l'invention du blé ils voulaient encore vivre du gland*; and would hear of no service to the higher needs of humanity with instruments not of their forging.[51]

The image of the soul (or the body) being torn to pieces becomes a recurring motif in Pater's works, with a poignant representation of it to be found in "A Study of Dionysus" (1876), where the *Zagreus* in *Dionysus Zagreus* means literally "torn to pieces."

Without the crisis of 1874 Pater might have given us *Marius the Epicurean*, most of the essays in *Appreciations*, and parts of *Plato and Platonism*, but not *Imaginary Portraits*, the major essays in *Greek Studies*, *Gaston de Latour*, "Lacedaemon," and "Emerald Uthwart."

Editing Pater's *Gaston de Latour*:
The Unfinished Work
as "A Fragment of Perfect Expression"

3

GERALD MONSMAN

WHAT MAKES THE TEXT of *Gaston de Latour* problematic is that Pater published the first five chapters in monthly installments in *Macmillan's Magazine* in 1888; then, unable to sustain the monthly pace, he abandoned serial publication but continued to work on the novel intermittently until his death in 1894. Several years after his death, his colleague at Oxford, Charles L. Shadwell, published the five *Macmillan's* chapters and two additional ones as *Gaston de Latour: An Unfinished Romance* (1896). Shadwell spoke of Pater's remaining half dozen unpublished holograph chapters as "for the most part unfinished: and they have certainly not received that revision which he would have been careful to give them before he allowed them to appear among his published writings." Hence Shadwell withheld the rest because he and Pater's sisters felt that "nothing more remains of his writings in a shape sufficiently finished for publication," and that it is "not their wish that any work of his should appear in a form less complete than he would himself have approved."[1] Fortunately, neither Shadwell nor Pater's sisters destroyed these—what they called—"fragments," suggesting that for them a certain amount of *déshabillé* among intimates was proper and accepted: Pater's family and most intimate colleagues could enjoy his unfinished thought, if not the world at large. Describing a number of Pater manuscripts at Harvard's Houghton Library, Elizabeth Falsey reported in the 1984 issue of *English Literature in Transition* that

> [s]ome are undated, scattered notes from Pater's reading, bits of translations, isolated sentences or phrases written on the slips of paper which we know Pater kept by him to be used (or not) in lectures and essays. Even in the longer pieces there are sentences with blank spaces in them, as though the right thought or the right word would be visible only from a different "perspective." To consult them is to be aware of some of Pater's preoccupations at work in the process of his own writing, the movement of his own thought. The tension between centrifugal and centripetal forces, for example, is present in our—and perhaps, his—provisional ordering and reordering of the sheets, bringing them into different relationships, one to the other. Pater's description of the "home-grown method of Socrates" in "The Doctrine of Plato" is useful in approaching his own papers: in them one sees the "philosophic temper," a long and complex dialogue of a mind with itself.[2]

The *Gaston de Latour* holographs at both Harvard and (eventually) at Brasenose reflect the same tensions of ordering and re-ordering, Pater's preoccupations at work in the process of writing, and the movement of his thought.

Heretofore, in *Gaston* as edited by Shadwell, little of that quality has emerged. Indeed, for Shadwell the unfinished and unpolished must be decorously hidden away—a certain amount of his editorial energy seems to have gone into constructing the equivalent of those fig leaves which so proliferated on nineteenth-century statuary. Not only did Shadwell withhold substantial passages of Pater's working drafts, but he disregarded many of Pater's emendations—presumably because he may have felt they were not finally decided upon. Quite simply, Shadwell's decision not to print the inchoate chapters of *Gaston* is largely a function of what may be called the concept of the single meaning. But language in general and literary language (or the visual arts) in particular is made of signs which function so that even the work of perfect expression is a fragment that resists "dogmatic interpretation"[3] and gives rise to multiple meanings. Like Shadwell, Charles Lamb in

"Oxford in the Vacation" cannot tolerate the different readings of manuscripts that have not arrived at a perfected and definitely settled meaning: "Those *variae lectiones*, so tempting to the more erudite palates, do but disturb and unsettle my faith." In a footnote he added:

> There is something to me repugnant at any time in the written hand. The text never seems determinate. Print settles it. I had thought of the Lycidas as of a full-grown beauty—as springing up with all its parts absolute—till, in an evil hour, I was shown the original copy of it, together with the other minor poems of its author, in the library of Trinity, kept like some treasure, to be proud of. I wish they had thrown them in the Cam, or sent them after the latter Cantos of Spenser, into the Irish Channel. How it staggered me to see the fine things in their ore! interlined, corrected! as if their words were mortal, alterable, displaceable at pleasure! as if they might have been otherwise, and just as good! as if inspirations were made up of parts, and those fluctuating, successive, indifferent! I will never go into the workshop of any great artist again, nor desire a sight of his picture till it is fairly off the easel; no, not if Raphael were to be alive again, and painting another Galatea.[4]

Shadwell and Pater's sisters would have agreed with Lamb—whom Pater admired also—although Pater himself, according to William Sharp, preferred reading the Greats in their own hands (certainly the poetry, perhaps the prose also, but most assuredly their letters). But now a century later I and my colleagues at work on the *Collected Works* of Pater have taken it upon ourselves to overrule Shadwell and the sisters and to publish these "fragments." What I am doing with the *Gaston* holograph would certainly seem strange, perverse even, to the nineteenth century—Pater caught, as it were , without clothes. In effect, I propose to go into Pater's "workshop" (if not his dressing-room) because I think we in the twentieth century have a different way of regarding art. Indeed, deliberately flying in the face of the previous assumption that the latest text is the best, the Pater edition takes as its copy-text not the last version Pater revised for publication but its first published appearance. I would like to explain why, contrasting present editorial principles and assumptions with those of Shadwell; and I believe Pater's own imagery characterizing the handwriting of authors in some measure may be transferable to a scholarly edition including

verbal variants and, possibly, a "formulaic" descriptive transcription of
the unpublished holographic chapters: "Imagine the pleasure of reading
the intimate letters of Michael Angelo, of Giorgione, of Leonardo, of
Dante, of Spenser, of Shakespeare, of Goethe, in the originals! It would
be like looking on a landscape in clear sunlight or moonlight, after
having viewed it only through mist or haze."[5]

Some of Pater's unpublished material is indeed hurried and
fragmentary, but other chapters are, as Samuel Wright described them,
"good, clear and incisive." Of course, Wright is suggesting there a
value judgment—some material is "good," whereas other is markedly
less valuable. Yet what is hurried and fragmentary—even though not
regular, ordered, and complete—may nevertheless be informative,
fertile, and afford a glimpse of excellence, *comely*, to use a Paterian
word. Indeed, the fragmentary, looked at from the perspective of
Romantic poetry or music, is perhaps one of the most significant genres
of the nineteenth century. Lamb may pretend not to like literature in
process, but his own essays are themselves celebrations of spontaneity,
haphazardness, and non-closure (trailing off in rambling afterthoughts).
In short, in the nearly one hundred years since Shadwell's first and only
editing of *Gaston* (I am excluding mere reprints, here) critical and
aesthetic standards have taken a major turn. If it is no longer important
that biography serve to idealize its subject—Wordsworth can have an
illegitimate French daughter and still be an important poet; Swinburne
is now universally seen as justified in making use as an artist of his
pathologic condition—then, if this is so, perhaps also the more spontaneous, less polished writings of any author should be judged not in terms
of some ideal of finished Platonic form, but as process. To paraphrase
remarks of some years ago by G. Thomas Tanselle, one might say that
apart from canceled passages, it is often not possible to know what a
writer or his publisher finally may have done with insertions, substitu-
tions, blanks or false starts; but these idiosyncrasies are an essential part
of the writer's compositional habits and personal make-up. For Tanselle,
to preserve the inadvertencies, to make no more than a provisional
decision between or among superscripts or alternative words and

phrases, is to recognize that all art is process, and any closure provided by the editor is a mere superficial ornament.

A work of art is not like an engineer's blueprint—a configuration that attains within certain tolerances the single archetypal ideal, and the closer the engine comes to this single, final shape the nearer its approach to perfection. In contrast, the artist theoretically could revise his work in mutually exclusive directions: the *King Lear* Quarto of 1609 and its 1623 Folio version, for example, do not belong to a single Ur-text but present essentially different yet equally valid versions of well-known passages. Or take, for example, Thomas DeQuincey's *Confessions of an English Opium-Eater*: it first appeared in 1823 anonymously in the *London Magazine*; many years later DeQuincey revised it carefully, but its expanded, polished 1853 form lacks the spontaneous, candid immediacy of the earlier version. Which is the real *Confessions?* At times the final form or meaning of art is necessarily provisional: consider the Homeric epics and folk-tales altered generation by generation—who is to say which of the versions hundreds of years apart is better or worse, which is the perfected version? At other times the indefiniteness of closure is highly self-conscious, as in the double ending of John Fowles's *French Lieutenant's Woman*; but no less here the reader must live with ambivalence as his permanent legacy.

Were one to make an argument for the principles behind Shadwell's editorial practice, one could do worse than cite Hans Walter Gabler's 1984 edition of James Joyce's *Ulysses*. Joyce's novel underwent constant compositional revisions and expansions, so much so that Gabler rejected the first edition of 1922 as too corrupt to serve as a copy-text:

> The deeper faults of the text as published originated throughout the pre-publication transmission from drafts to fair copies to typescripts to print. The rich array of surviving documents that record the work's development made it possible to catch the text before these corruptions occurred and to rebuild *Ulysses* as Joyce wrote it. . . A new original text established from the acts of writing as recorded in the documents through which the novel developed, this reading text for *Ulysses* is thus, as nearly as editorial skill and critical understanding have been able to render it, a non-corrupted counterpart to the first edition of 1922.[6]

Gabler explicitly promises "an ideal text freed of the errors with which *Ulysses* was first published"; however, his edited version is based on a copy-text that "is not assembled in a unified holograph manuscript at a state of development corresponding to the first edition text" but is, rather, what he calls "a continuous manuscript text . . . extending over a sequence of actual documents." The key to such an editorial undertaking, of course, is the "rich array of surviving documents" enabling Gabler to make emendations and reconstructions based on principles that are rooted in objective editorial criteria derived from very precisely established relationships between versions.[7] Yet to speak of rebuilding *Ulysses* "as Joyce wrote it" is, for all Gabler's data and precision, still a conjectural process—Joyce never wrote it that way, never on any day held it in his hand completed in that form. And so one cannot say with certainty that on that hypothetical day Joyce would not have rejected or incorporated textual bits according to personal urgencies about which Gabler's objective principles knew nothing. For classroom purposes one might like to have a Gabler-like reading text of *Gaston*; however, scholars would have to admit that it would *not* quite be Pater's text. Moreover, although Shadwell might have been able to assemble a Gabler-like collection of drafts and proofs, he clearly belonged to an age which lacked both the inclination and the technical command to undertake that sort of editing; and at this present temporal distance the necessary data are no longer available.

I would like to consider, however, one small example of the text of *Gaston* from Chapter II, "Our Lady's Church." Monseigneur Charles Guillard, here described as the Bishop of Chartres, is a Paterian version of Robert Browning's Bishop who orders his tomb. No Tertullian whose "Credo quia absurdum est" ratifies belief in a spiritual reality, the worldly Guillard nevertheless is judged by Gaston as Browning invites readers to judge the Bishop of Saint Praxed's church: "equitably; the religious sense too, had its various species." What I am about to recreate for this passage is the simplest possible stemma, perhaps conflating stages in Pater's often tortuous progress from draft to finished literary work; however, this hypothetical set of relationships will serve to illuminate Shadwell's editorial principles. Bearing in mind that numerous permutations complicating the stemma are certainly possible, the reader nevertheless may be able to envision something of the textual transmission of the whole novel, from manuscript through magazine to the book edition of Shadwell.

Plate number 1 is Pater's holograph in the Berg Collection of the New York Public Library:

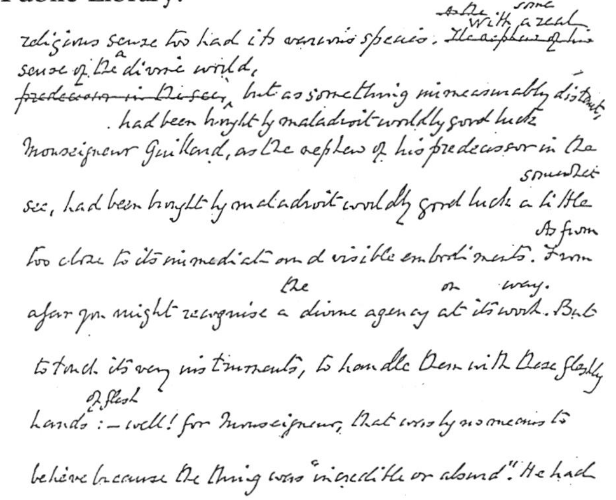

Plate 1

Though one generally assumes a holograph precedes first publication, the passage on pages 396-97 of the *Macmillan's* version of "Peach Blossom and Wine," later moved to *Plato and Platonism*, is not in the holograph, raising the interesting possibility that Pater here copied anew already published material, as he did just before his death with "Hippolytus Veiled" (although for "The Child in the House," he instead revised the offprint).[8] In numerous places the Berg holograph contains emendations of published passages, suggesting that Pater may have copied and then revised—or even revised *as* he copied—the *Macmillan's* text. Edmund Gosse recalled that Pater characteristically made *several* handwritten copies of his manuscripts.[9] This raises another possibility: that because choices in wording are left open in the Berg holograph (as Pater's "Rossetti" and "Sir Thomas Browne" prepared for the printer did not do) the Berg may be a penultimate draft prior to *Macmillan's* publication. Pater possibly may have saved his selections for a final fair copy, no longer extant, in which he included the passage later moved to *Plato*.

Whether prior to or subsequent to *Macmillan's*, the revision toward which Pater was working in the Berg holograph is given in Plate 2. Superscripts are omitted unless a clear choice is indicated by a caret or by cancellation of the original wording. Thus, in the penultimate line of the holograph example, the superscript, "hands of flesh," would be the rejected variant; but the superscript beginning the passage *is* chosen because Pater canceled the original:

> With a real sense of the divine world, but as something immeasurably
> distant, Monseigneur Guillard, as the nephew of his predecessor in
> the see, had been brought by maladroit worldly good luck a little
> too close to its immediate and visible embodiments. From afar you
> might recognise a divine agency at its work. But to touch its
> very instruments, to handle them with these fleshly hands:—well!
> for Monseigneur, that was by no means to believe because the thing
> was "incredible or absurd."

Plate 2

The holograph version clearly is quite distinct from the magazine version given in Plate 3:

> The nephew of his predecessor in the
> the see, with a real sense of the divine
> world, but as something immeasurably
> distant, he had been brought by a
> maladroit worldly good fortune a little
> too close to its immediate and visible
> embodiments. Afar, you might trace
> the divine agency on its way. But to
> touch, to handle it, with these fleshly
> hands—well! with Monseigneur it was
> not to believe because the thing was
> "incredible or absurd." He had smiled,

Plate 3

How does Shadwell deal with these different passages? Is his 1896 *Gaston* a product of sound editorial practice or possible malpractice? Plate 4 shows the changes in the *Macmillan's* text needed to produce Shadwell's 1896 edition, given in Plate 5. Certainly the least problematic correction would be the silent elimination of the redundant article—"predecessor in *the the* see":

The nephew of his predecessor in the the see, with a real sense of the divine world but as something immeasurably distant, he had been brought by a maladroit worldly good-fortune a little too close to its immediate and visible embodiments. Afar, you might trace the divine agency on its way. But to touch, to handle it, with these fleshly hands,—well! with Monseigneur it was not to believe because the thing was "incredible or absurd." He had smiled,

Monseigneur Guillard

From / *l.c.*

by no means

Plate 4

sense too, had its various species. The nephew of his predecessor in the see, with a real sense of the divine world but as something immeasurably distant, Monseigneur Guillard had been brought by maladroit worldly good-fortune a little too close to its immediate and visible embodiments. From afar, you might trace the divine agency on its way. But to touch, to handle it, with these fleshly hands:—well! for Monseigneur, that was by no means to believe because the thing was "incredible, or absurd". He had smiled, not

Plate 5

Shadwell's text of 1896 follows the *Macmillan's Magazine* large-scale variants. For example, Shadwell's text gives the *Macmillan's* wording for the opening sentence: "The nephew of his predecessor. . . ." But Shadwell omits many of the smaller-scale variants: the short middle sentence that in the Berg reads "From afar," reads in the magazine "Afar"; but Shadwell follows the manuscript wording: "From afar." If Shadwell instead had taken the Berg as his copy text, he then would have rejected many of its readings, including several that seem settled; he would have accepted fully just a single eight-word emendation— "well! for Monseigneur, that was by no means"—and, though incorporating in his opening sentence the Bishop's name, would have utilized only this smallest part of the most extensive variation.

Why does Shadwell fail to follow a single Edition text, critically constructed? Just possibly his choice of readings for his 1896 edition may reflect reliance upon a lost fair copy (more like the Berg than like *Macmillan's*). The penultimate sentence in Chapter V of Shadwell's 1896 text is found nowhere else and clearly was meant to bridge from the chapter on Montaigne to the following one on the St. Bartholomew's Day Massacre. Since Pater discontinued publication in *Macmillan's* with Chapter V (all the previous chapters had been marked "To be continued," but not this chapter), one might assume that Pater did write such a sentence but canceled it and that Shadwell restored it for his edition. Moreover, such a transition sentence is more characteristic of a later than an earlier draft; and if the Berg holograph is the most complete and corrected text, that sentence ought to have been found in it. Still, this is tenuous evidence for a fair copy. Yet if there was no fair copy, Shadwell can be accused of substantial editorial tampering, regardless of where in the order of compositional development the Berg holograph belongs.

Assuming that Shadwell created a hybrid text in 1896, the most likely explanation of why he combined the holograph with *Macmillan's Magazine* for his edition is that by his own standards Shadwell wished to guard against corruptions—to be absolutely certain that the words we read are the words not only that Pater wrote but that they were the choices he would have made had he lived long enough to complete his novel. In a letter of 25 January 1895 to Gosse, Clara speaks of Shadwell liking "to make his own emendations from the original MS rather than from the printed article."[10] But Shadwell employs guidelines that destroy any meaningful concept of a critically constructed Edition text—he is intuitive, graceful, reluctant to concede authority to either holograph or magazine versions unless they agree. In the case of divergence, he prefers the holograph, but by no means all of the time. Shadwell does not really have a single text; he blends the manuscript and the magazine texts together to produce the ideal archetypal version, Pater's Platonically perfect full-grown beauty. Shadwell would have thought of this as his posthumous tribute, justifying it in scholarly terms as more correct than the hurried product of periodical publication or incomplete revision. But, of course, this ideal text is the creation of final choices not Pater's, howsoever he may have generated the options among which these choices are made. Shadwell even made small changes in punctuation on his own authority—he hyphenated "good-fortune"; he deleted one comma, added another.

Unlike Shadwell, I will choose the *Macmillan's Magazine* version as my Edition text. To forego Shadwell's apparently subjective, hybrid version and select a single text is to select a flawed, less than perfected version. This is not to say that the double "the" in lines 1 and 2 of the *Macmillan's* sample would not be edited out; nor does it mean that other objective emendations are precluded; rather, it is to accept failures of euphony, to risk word choices that may have been contributed by the compositor, to tolerate ambiguous antecedents, to forego more felicitous phrasing—in short, it is to recognize the limitations of any single text. This is very much analogous to the decision to publish the unpolished drafts which Shadwell had suppressed. But it is also to privilege the author's compositional process in a manner that Shadwell, seeking some text finally free of process, never did. Seeking Pater's ideal perfected expression, Shadwell obscured the actual Pater. However much Pater himself may have loved a heavy layer of varnish on his oils, the "varnish" Shadwell applied to *Gaston* is about to be stripped away.

Editing and Annotating Pater

4

IAN SMALL

IN BRITAIN, theorizing about texts on the one hand, and the editing of texts on the other, have long been taken to be completely opposed intellectual enterprises. Traditionally theorists have been concerned with the "large" issues: the notion of literature, practices of reading, the constructions of meanings, the ideology of literature, the relationships of discourses, and so forth. And by contrast textual editors have often been held to be the poor relations in literature departments. The collation of texts, the establishing of stemmata, the privileging of one textual variant over another—in general these have been taken to be crudely mechanical and naively historicist tasks, which, when set against the more ambitious projects of theorists, seem to be unproblematic. Of late, however, some editors have challenged the implicit separation of literary theory and text-editing and have pointed out ways in which the interests of editors and theorists overlap. So recently G. Thomas Tanselle, for example, has indicated that some of the concerns which editors and deconstructionists have with texts are not, and should not be, mutually exclusive.[1] Indeed, he goes so far as to suggest that some of the concerns of editors have a direct bearing upon the practices of deconstructionists. The argument that I wish to propose is broadly in

33

keeping with these views; in particular I want to suggest that some of the practical difficulties of text-editing do indeed have profound theoretical implications. An example is provided by the complexity of the editorial problems encountered in the production of the projected *Collected Works* of Walter Pater.

The most immediately pressing question facing any editor, and the editors of Pater's *Collected Works* are no exception, is the choice of copy-text. Ideally every textual editor would like the complete stemma, from first manuscript draft to the last printed edition, for the work in question. But for Pater, there is no possibility of such a reconstruction. Although we know from the evidence that we have, inconclusive and anecdotal as it tends to be, that Pater oversaw the production of his texts from first draft to printed book with a scrupulous enthusiasm, much of the material necessary to construct a stemma of any one of his works has simply not survived. We are best served in this respect by the unpublished elements in the *oeuvre*, as various essays in this volume make clear. But, as I shall suggest, the real problems with the choice of copy-text in Pater present themselves in much more stark terms. In the absence of virtually all manuscript witnesses to the text, of proofs and corrected proofs, Pater's editors have to choose between the various published texts of the same work. Which text does an editor choose, and on what grounds?

In the case of some texts, the issues are clear-cut. The textual history of *Marius the Epicurean* presents a good example. There are no known surviving manuscripts or proof-copies of the novel. The first edition, published in 1885, is the first text of the work to which an editor has access. Pater revised that edition for a second edition later in the same year. He revised it again, and on a massive scale, for the third edition in 1892. There was a fourth edition of the novel published in 1898, of dubious authority[2] which does not include all of the revisions made for the 1892 edition. Finally there is the 1910 Library edition of the novel which reprints the 1898 text. Further editions have, almost universally, followed the Library edition.[3] The choice facing the editor is thus quite straightforward. A tradition of textual scholars would, in general terms, determine such choices on the basis of the known intentions of the author with regard to the text in question. They allow an editor to choose a text for a variety of critical or historical reasons, but, in Tanselle's words, the task of the editor is "the historical reconstruction" of a text "which reflects the intention of its creator(s) at a particular time."[4] Under such a rubric, and given that the 1892 text is the last evidence which we have for Pater's intentions towards *Marius*, the choices facing the editor are not complicated, despite the fact that, as the brief history of the texts of *Marius* given above indicates, the editions which most readers have encountered are, by this definition, corrupt.

The argument against proposals such as these is on philosophical grounds: they privilege the author's intentions, and generally last known intentions, towards a text; and they assume a theory of art which is dependent upon a concept of expressivity. These two issues are too complex to be adequately discussed at any length here, but the following qualifications have a bearing for editors of Pater. The concept of intention needs to be characterized very carefully; it has to take account of such different forms of intention as generic intention as well as an author's intended meaning. Such a procedure is still, of course, problematic, because "intention" has become a highly contested concept among literary theorists. On the one hand, a group of critics—most famously W. K. Wimsatt and Monroe Beardsley—while not denying the concept of intentionality and authorship, have thrown into question the possibility of access to the intention (or intentions) behind a text; and on the other, more recent theorists, seeing the text produced as much by a common *langue* as an individual *parole*, and questioning the whole concept of authorship, have rendered the relationship of intention to textual understanding a problematic one. These latter qualifications have a great deal in common with the reservations about the concept of expressivity made by some philosophers of art. Both sets of reservations concern the social nature of works of literary art, and when applied to textual editing, concern the *social existence* of a text. So, for example, we now know that the texts of *The*

Importance of Being Earnest or *King Lear* which have commonly been held to be authoritative are in fact plays which Wilde and Shakespeare respectively never wrote; they are editorial constructs, made from collating early and late versions of the play in the case of Wilde, or folio and quarto texts in the case of Shakespeare. But the point at issue is, of course, that these "corrupt" texts have some authority—in this case, that given by an interpretative community. What may be called the social history of a work, this line of argument holds, is a key consideration in textual scholarship. Jerome McGann, for example, has suggested that the search for the "originary moment" of a text's production should be modified by attention to what he later calls "secondary" elements in text-production—to the consideration of the fact that a text may have an existence in and through history.[5] Such an argument has a considerable relevance for the choice of copy-text for some of Pater's works, in particular *Marius the Epicurean* and *Gaston de Latour*.

It is worth noting at this point that editors of important recent editions of some modern writers have experienced difficulties in the choice of copy-text which may have some lessons for the editors of Pater. Both H. W. Gabler and Michael Black have written about the inappropriateness of the single, simple, and stable text for writers such as Joyce and Lawrence. With these two writers there are of course both constitutional and institutional reasons why the search for a stable and uniquely authorized text will fail. In the case of Lawrence, Black points to the well-known publishing restrictions which Lawrence had to contend with, and he suggests that in the case of what he calls the "constantly-revising author"[6] we should be much more concerned with presenting a text (or texts) which reveals the work in evolution. A principal task for the editor then becomes, as H. W. Gabler has argued *à propos* of *Ulysses*, one of finding an apparatus suitable for the presentation of such an edition.[7] As I have indicated, these observations, if not directly applicable to Pater's entire *oeuvre*, nonetheless have some large implications for some of his works.

Marius, for example, underwent virtually constant revision in the years between 1885 and 1892, and so each text *may* have a claim, stronger or weaker, on the editor, as may the 1910 text (although on quite different grounds). But the position is made immensely more complicated with those works in which Pater collected, and substantially revised, material already published in periodical form. In fact, collections of previously published essays or stories represent about half of the works which Pater published in his lifetime, and well over half of the material collected together for the Library edition. The prospective editor has a further claim upon his attention for choice of copy-text in the case of these collections: he or she can go to the original periodical publication. So it is quite possible to argue that the periodical texts of the essays which make up *Appreciations*, or of the stories which make up *Imaginary Portraits*, should be reproduced as part of a collected edition in the manner of R. H. Super's edition of Matthew Arnold. But the resultant text would not be *Appreciations* nor *Imaginary Portraits*; it would be an editorial rather than an authorial construct. The broad justification for editors using procedures such as those proposed by Super exists in the view (and whether or not it is explicitly articulated is irrelevant) that they are engaged in editing documents rather than literary works. Such a proposition immediately runs into, and threatens to fall foul of, a debate about the nature of value, particularly of literary value.[8] So while it might be possible to justify editing, say, Pater's essay on Wordsworth as a document in a debate about that poet, it is difficult to see what the documentary nature of a work such as "Duke Carl of Rosenmold" might be. In the second place, and much more importantly, such an editorial procedure would involve ignoring a whole set of distinctions, all too familiar to textual critics, between texts and works.

The Renaissance presents perhaps the best example in the Pater canon of a situation where editorial problems are not accessible to simple prescriptive solutions. The successive editions which the book went through involved two sets of changes. In the first place, there are the major revisions to the contents of individual essays; and secondly there are the changes which Pater made to the contents of the book as a whole. In these senses it is perhaps not really accurate to talk simply of "editions": the various published versions of the book (in 1873, 1877, 1888 and 1893) have different contents. At what point these different "editions" can be said to be different works is not easy to determine; moreover, it is possible to make a case for each of those separate editions to be taken as copy-text. But in addition, the textual history of each of the essays in the book is complex: in general, the first appearances of the essays were in very different forms, in a very different context (in, that is, periodical publications) and intended for very different markets and readerships. So an argument for publishing the first edition of *The Renaissance* (the book edition, that is) would involve accepting the authority of Pater's changes from the first (that is, periodical) publication of some of the essays, but not accepting the authority of any subsequent revisions to its subsequent editions. Of course, it might well be possible to argue such a case, but the arguments could not be those suggested by Super for Arnold's essays. The social impact of the book—that is, of *Studies in the History of the Renaissance* (1873)—was much greater than that of its constituent essays. Thus, for example, if we are to believe Pater, it was the "Conclusion" to *The Renaissance*, and *not* the review of William Morris, which threatened to "mislead" the young men who read it. In this case, Super's argument would have to be reversed. The argument for documentary editing would have to reject the claims of the periodical text: the choice of it as copy-text would have now to depend solely upon critical grounds. Such an argument would remove the potential dispute between critics and textual scholars: it gives them a text to agree upon, but for very different reasons.

However, the logic of this argument, when it is applied to other elements of the Pater canon, becomes a handicap. A large proportion of that canon is an editorial construct: the arguments for a documentary edition of the *Collected Works* make no case for reprinting *Miscellaneous Studies, Essays from the 'Guardian', Gaston de Latour* or *Greek Studies*. The organization of these texts is of course principally the work of Charles Shadwell. The logic of a decision to take as copy-text the first book-edition produces a Paterian canon of the following works alone: *The Renaissance*, *Marius the Epicurean*, *Imaginary Portraits*, *Appreciations*, and *Plato and Platonism*. These are the only books for which an authorial sanction exists. Such a definition of copy-text problematizes the books published posthumously, not of course because the individual essays in those volumes do not possess authority (they manifestly do so), but because the *organization* of them by Shadwell into their various forms does not. It would be quite possible to consider other principles of organization. A chronological ordering of the texts has at least as much claim upon an editor as a thematic one does; and so does a principle which arranges essays in terms of the periodicals for which they were first intended, a principle used later in *Essays from 'The Guardian'*. However, the problem with such counter-proposals is that they fly in the face of social or cultural history. Many thousands of readers have encountered books entitled *Greek Studies* or *Miscellaneous Studies* despite the absence of any authorial sanction for their existence. Any complete edition can reproduce them; but the grounds for such a decision cannot be authorial—Pater sanctioned no such books; but neither can they be based upon some principle of documentary editing, as Super's *Arnold* is. The rationale for their reproduction would have to resort to the arguments (such as those indicated by McGann) about the existence of a text through history and the social construction of texts. The major problem produced thereby is that such an edition would be drawing upon two quite contradictory editorial principles: for the proposals to reproduce the first book editions of Pater's canon, particularly *Marius the Epicurean*, for which no periodical texts exist, explicitly discount the social history of the works in question. However, the arguments for the reproduction of posthumous material of necessity depend upon these considerations.

Now exactly the same sorts of dilemmas seem to exist in the area of annotation. *Marius the Epicurean* is a very difficult text in this respect. I have suggested elsewhere that there might have been several quite distinct and quite different intended audiences for that novel, each with quite different areas of knowledge and of ignorance.[9] If this is true, it

makes the practical decisions of an editor or editorial team hazardous
in the extreme. Most contemporary editions of the works of major
writers have proposed for their contributing authors a set of prescriptions about annotation which are—not to mince words—intellectually
disreputable. So it is not unusual to see general editors requiring from
their contributors annotations of allusions which a moderately well-
educated non-native speaker of English would not understand. Under
such a prescription the phrase "James Stokes, the prefect, his immediate
superior" in "Emerald Uthwart"[10] would have to be glossed for three
kinds of audience. For a non-European reader the term might simply
be meaningless. For a European reader it might have contradictory
implications: thus for French readers the term "prefect" is alarmingly
similar to current French usage for the head of a police force. And for
readers educated in some Catholic institutions the term designates a
senior master (a teacher) in a Jesuit school. So for all of these cases
some modern general editors would require the elucidation of a term
still in fairly wide usage in Britain, particularly among those educated
in private or grammar schools. What such editors have done is to
assume a degree of ignorance based in the first instance upon assumptions about a limited knowledge of British culture.

Other, more thoughtful prescriptions for annotation have made
demands at a rather more abstract level. Martin C. Battestin has written
what is perhaps the best-known attempt to determine a rationale for
annotation.[11] He suggests that any annotator has to be aware of the
character of his (modern) audience, of his own (subjective) interests,
and of the precise nature of the text to be annotated. While he
concedes that there can be no "single rationale for literary annotation,"
and that an editor should distinguish between what he calls "notes of
recovery" and "explanatory" notes, he also finally suggests that a work
may be perfectly understood:

> The purpose of literary annotation, whether of "explanatory notes" or "notes
> of recovery," is to recover for the reader, as briefly and objectively as possible
> all essential information (and *only* essential information) necessary to render the
> author's meaning wholly intelligible, the "author's meaning" being understood

as not only the primary denotative significance of a passage but also, when appropriate, its full range of implicit associations, whether biographical, historical, or literary.[12]

As I hope I have indicated, the definitions of many items are begged here; so the difficulties of ascertaining what constitutes the real import of terms such as "essential information," "the author's meaning," "intelligibility," the "full range of implicit associations," are never adequately addressed, let alone explained. More importantly, Battestin's prescriptive programme gives too many hostages to fortune. In particular it lays the annotator open to the charge that he is required to take on the role of an *ideal, perfectly knowledgeable and perfectly competent reader*, a reader for whom all textual allusions and all possible reactions are available. Of course, no such beast exists.

Other programmes for annotation have been more modest; they have simply required the modern editor and annotator to make explicit the cultural and literary knowledge which was implicit for contemporary readers or to make explicit the cultural knowledge which a writer believed was implicit in the cultural assumptions of his contemporary readers:[13] to define, that is, in the language of Hans-Robert Jauss and German reception-theorists, the "horizon of expectations" of a work.[14] Now definitions of a readership in terms such as these are, of course, quite different, and in their turn beg further questions which are equally difficult to answer. What, for example, are "contemporary" or "original" readers? Do they form an homogenous group? Are their "horizon of expectations" thus capable of a simple characterization (granted, of course, that such information could both be practically and theoretically retrieved by an editor). Under general prescriptions such as these—and they are the best-theorized accounts of annotation yet available—all that the conscientious editor can do is to be aware that he or she is producing an edition for a modern audience, and make informed guesses about both that audience and about a writer's original audience. And any editor must be aware too that one can make only informed guesses about *any* audience's cultural knowledge and cultural assumptions.

However all these decisions about contemporary and modern audiences are seriously jeopardized by the possible choices of copy-texts which I have outlined above. The readership of periodicals in the 1860s and 1870s were, as Laurel Brake indicates in the essay that follows, quite different: each established a readership with different tastes, political and artistic affiliations, and so forth. But these readerships, taken together, were vastly different again from the readership of a book such as the 1873 edition of *Studies in the History of the Renaissance*. The first difference is one of size, with the periodical readership being many tens of times larger than the readership of most books, particularly for a work such as *The Renaissance*. The second difference would be one of geography and class, with the periodical readership being much less homogenous, much less metropolitan. And the third difference would be one of education, for readers of mid-century periodicals would certainly have been less academic than the readers of Pater's books. If the rationale for annotation depends upon the expectations of an original readership, and if the original readership of each of Pater's works was quite distinct, then a consequence would be an edition with very uneven annotation, even if the annotation for each volume were based on precisely the same editorial principles.

But perhaps these qualifications are not the deterrent which they at first sight appear to be. It is quite possible that each text within an *oeuvre* produces a set of problems which are unique and have therefore to be treated in an *ad hoc* manner. In other words, perhaps the search for uniformity of treatment in both the rationale for copy-text and for the provision of annotation is little more than an administrative convenience. It may well be that there is no simple theory of text-editing which can encompass the generic diversity of early modernist texts, and no theory of annotation which will allow an editor to accommodate the heterogeneity of contemporary or modern audiences. If this indeed turns out to be the case, then editors of Pater may have to take account of the fact that both their editorial practices and their principles for annotation will inevitably have—at least in part—to be unsystematic.

The Discourses of Journalism:
"Arnold and Pater" Again—and Wilde

_____ ▬▬▬ _____   **5**

LAUREL BRAKE

T. S. ELIOT'S ESSAY ON PATER, first published in 1930, stresses the continuities between Arnold and Pater rather than the disruptions.[1] Eliot undervalues Arnold's deep attachment to Christianity (and perhaps Pater's) and suppresses Pater's many challenges to Arnold's ideas. I would like to suggest that Pater attacked two of Arnold's key positions in the 1870s and 1880s, that of the inferiority of romanticism and the superiority of poetry. To these notions, rooted in Arnold's construct of a classical tradition, Pater counters positions that derive from identifications with modern literary forms and writing: he defends Romanticism, and assesses it from a position consciously and unapologetically within it; prose, he proclaims, is "the special art of the modern world."[2] The relationship between Pater and Arnold was largely one of disagreement and rivalry, voiced in public dialogue in print, in the press and in books, as well as in private conversation. In 1876 and 1888, in "Romanticism" and in "Style," the essays that begin and end *Appreciations*, the volume of collected essays published in 1889, Pater is, among other things, continuing the public dialogue.

As for Arnold, the second series of *Essays in Criticism* appeared in November 1888, a month before "Style" and a year before *Apprecia-*

tions. In his *Essays*, Arnold foregrounds his introduction to Humphry Ward's 1880 anthology of English poetry as the first essay, now newly entitled "The Study of Poetry": Arnold's 1880 essay does constitute a genuine referent of Pater's claims for prose in his essay on "Style" that appears less than a month later. Insofar as Pater had himself contributed to the Ward anthology which Arnold's then untitled essay served to introduce, Pater was familiar with Arnold's position and was addressing it. Pater's "Style" is placed analogously as the flagship of *his* collection a year later.

Enter Wilde. According to Frank Harris, editor of the *Fortnightly Review* in which "Style" appeared in December 1888, Pater, Arnold, and Wilde *discussed* style in 1886 at a London dinner party where Harris commissioned the essay from Pater.[3] Pater's defence of prose and Arnold's of poetry in the 1880s are related counter-statements that, with Oscar Wilde's interventions, inscribe a contest in the late nineteenth century between adherence to models from classical literature (which privileges poetry, nobility and the grand styles) and a challenging recommendation of contemporary literary forms (prose and its new popular form, the novel).[4] The apparent meanings of the ideological alliance between Pater and Wilde, and their differences with Arnold on this question, are disrupted, however, by an eloquent if unnoted harmony between Pater and Arnold in their common publisher (Macmillan) and periodical (*Macmillan's Magazine*). These parallel publications can be contrasted with the provenance of Wilde's work published by the small house of McIlvaine and originally in the free space of the *Nineteenth Century* and the *Fortnightly Review*. These aspects of production yield ideological meanings. Moreover, it may be that Eliot's choice as well as construction of Arnold and Pater as subjects is in part due to their implication in the problematic of culture and religion in the nineteenth century. Eliot's predisposition to matters of faith in the 1930s leads him to exclude Wilde and to minimize the ideological contest in the 1880s and early 1890s, just as Frank Harris's bohemianism ensures Wilde's prominence and exposure of the discontinuities.

Both Arnold's *Essays in Criticism* and Pater's *Appreciations* were published by Macmillan, and both included a large number of essays originally in *Macmillan's Magazine* or in books published by Macmillan. If these essays and books seem to have common origins and to be parts of the same discourse, that cannot be said for essays which were included in the *Nineteenth Century* in 1889 and 1890, signed Oscar Wilde, and published in book form by Osgood McIlvaine in 1891 as part of *Intentions*. The first, "The Decay of Lying," published in January 1889, prominently quotes notions of Arnold's and Pater's, either to reject them outright or to extend them beyond recognition. The second, "The True Function and Value of Criticism," in two parts or acts printed in July and September 1890, openly confronts Arnold's earlier pronouncements in 1864-65 in "Function of Criticism at the Present Time" and the first series of *Essays in Criticism*.[5] The wit, pace, and form of Wilde's essays distinguish them markedly from the contemporary work of Pater and Arnold; they combine argument and aphorisms with an unembarrassed and even exploitative topicality; and the Platonic dialogue, W. S. Landor's *Conversations*,[6] Frederick Harrison's 1867 "Culture: a Dialogue" (an analogous and influential critique of Arnold),[7] and Wilde's persistence from 1880 with writing drama contribute to his essay's distinctive and unexpected dialogue form which offers an alternative metaphor for the site of criticism: Wilde displaces Arnold's pulpit and Pater's academy with the Aesthetic drawing-room, and the setting of the public occasion and audience favoured by Arnold and Pater with the private. These qualities together make Arnold's and Pater's contemporary work appear rarefied and even constrained compared with Wilde's, and suggest Wilde's work is part of a different periodicals discourse.

If the definition of the "text" is extended beyond content and style to include the discourse and its readers, then the differences between Wilde's text and those of Arnold and Pater emerge more clearly. The flamboyance of Wilde's writing is indicative of the degree of freedom afforded by the periodical in which it appeared; indeed, through Wilde's exploitation, or, more neutrally, utilization, of that freedom, its capaciousness is revealed. Although neither Arnold nor Pater tested its limits as strenuously as Wilde did, they also availed themselves of the freedom of James Knowles's *Nineteenth Century*, which prided itself on tolerant, untramelled eclecticism, and fostered oppositional expression through the format of the symposium. The definition of the "text" includes the periodical of which Wilde's writing forms a part.

While signature, the signature of *individual* authors, that is, figured importantly in James Knowles's programme for his journal, the other signature, clear to the editor and the periodical reader of the day, is the "signature" of the journal itself; its significance, if not its identity, is now obscured to us. Moreover the production process whereby writing is translated from the ephemeral of the periodical essay into the permanence of the book engineers the obscuring of the ephemeral characteristics and, most important, origins, even to the original readers of the book. The corporate institutional authorship of a work is obfuscated, and authorship is shifted to a context which foregrounds the individual; the discourse of the book is now that of art, the collected work, with its emphasis on individual performance, genius, memorability—here the tarnished image of the artist-as-critic.

I write "collected" work because that is how the production process is perceived by the consumer. But for the author it is selected work, and what is deselected, left to the limbo of ephemera, is for our purposes as important. In this process of selection and omission the "text" by the *critic* is constructed by the writer. Another process of this construction is characteristic of this system of production: it is the systematic revision of the ephemeral writing to provide it with a "finish" allegedly not required by periodical publication. Disallowed as a characteristic of a form of publication associated with constraints of time and with the undignified labours of Grub Street authors whose livelihood depends upon meeting deadlines, "finish" comes to be exclusively associated with another form of production, leisured and gentlemanly, which may result in art which by implication is defined as "not journalism." Finish often involved the careful suppressions of topical allusions in order to enhance the illusion of timelessness of the new "art" text. This was often Arnold's purpose in the relatively few revisions of his periodical texts for book publication. In the course of restoring the periodical texts of Arnold's work to readers in his edition of the *Collected Prose Works*, R. H. Super stresses:

> I hope it has been apparent how much of Arnold's writing—which was almost all journalism on its first appearance—is embedded in the ephemera of his day . . . Arnold's relation, not with the monuments of Victorian literature, but with the multitude of forgotten and fallen leaves—seeing him read his daily newspaper and comment upon it, then seeing that newspaper take up his comment, until as with the *Saturday Review* and the *Daily Telegraph*, a tradition of mutual banter is set up.[8]

Wilde, like Pater and Arnold, selected essays to reprint in book form. *Intentions* (1891) consisted of four pieces, "The Decay of Lying" and "The True Function and Value of Criticism" from the *Nineteenth Century*, one other from the same periodical, equally uncompromising, now entitled "The Truth of Masks,"[9] and "Pen, Pencil, and Poison," from the *Fortnightly Review*.[10] A liberal and erudite periodical from its inception in 1865 when it was modelled on the *Revue des Deux Mondes*, the *Fortnightly* was edited in 1889 by the young Frank Harris, and open to publication of Wilde's libertine, provocative, and light-hearted defence of the aesthetic perfection of a life of a murderer and a forger. *Intentions* is a text to keep in view beside Arnold's *Essays* and Pater's *Appreciations*, with Wilde's selections from his critical essays characterized by inclusion of work from the two journals at the apex of the high culture which offered the widest moral parameters in the British press of the day. Wilde excluded, and never reprinted in his lifetime, for example, numerous reviews and articles from the daily *Pall Mall Gazette*, and his contributions to *Woman's World*, the *Court and Society Review*, *Queen*, and the *Speaker*. He constructs himself in *Intentions* as the irreverent and youthful upstart who takes on and displaces the ageing gurus. Arnold's death in April 1888 may have freed Pater and Wilde from critical constraint (would Wilde mock and attack Arnold at sixty-six so directly had Arnold been alive?), but Arnold *hors de combat* may also have consolidated his influence among critics and readers more generally.

By contrast a great part of the selections by Arnold and Pater from their respective books in 1888 and 1889 stemmed from a relatively staid periodical aimed at a family audience.[11] *Macmillan's* habitually carried fiction and this signalled its lighter magazine format and its intention to include women prominently among its readers. Unlike the *Nineteenth Century* or the *Fortnightly Review, Macmillan's Magazine* was implicated in its publisher's book publications; originally conceived as a vehicle of trailers for forthcoming books for the firm, the *Magazine* addressed the moral tolerance not only of its own immediate audience but that of the large circulating libraries such as Mudie's and retailers such as W. H. Smith; these possessed considerable economic and moral authority through their power to purchase books in bulk from publishers or not. An anonymous review of *Macmillan's* cumulative catalogue which appeared in the *Bookman* in 1891 makes plain this moral dimension of Macmillan's list in its diction, with value accorded to Macmillan's "honourable career," its "steadfast" adherence to "principles," and its efforts to "raise" the publication of books, while the alternatives of "bad books," "startling successes," and "big sales" are rejected. The association of the publication of aesthetically fine books with this high moral posture endorses the "worth" of the publications:

> This volume has been executed in a manner which is worthy of the honourable career it records. Some publishers may have achieved more startling successes than any even of Messr. Macmillan, but big sales of bad books the latter have never aimed at. None have done more to raise the whole manner of the publication of books. They have been steadfast to two great principles: first, never to publish a book which they did not think worth reading; next, always to give all books fair opportunity so far as printing and binding were concerned. Looking over this catalogue, it is with growing surprise one notices how very few of the titles are unfamiliar. . . . Everyone knows that it is almost always a pleasure to handle a Macmillan book—the binding is invariably tasteful, and some of the new sizes introduced by the firm peculiarly neat.[12]

The ideological link between Macmillan's and Smith's, renowned for its refusal to circulate "immoral" books, is revealed by the case of Wilde's novel *Dorian Gray*, which Macmillan refused to publish, and Smith to distribute.

Arnold's second series of *Essays in Criticism*, comprising ten essays, includes only two from non-Macmillan origins. Both are on controversial topics, and they appeared in the same two journals which harboured Wilde's work. *Essays* reprints one item from the *Nineteenth Century*; predictably, it is the most morally vulnerable in the opinion of Lord Coleridge, who appends a "Prefatory Note" to this selection of essays Arnold made before his death.[13] "C" (Coleridge) suggests that Arnold's review of Edward Dowden's biography of Shelley (it is the most recent essay in the volume, having appeared in January 1888)[14] is only part of what Arnold would have wished to say—while he would not have retracted what he does say, he would have said more about Shelley.

The other non-Macmillan essay, on Tolstoy, is from the *Fortnightly Review*, published only a month before the piece on Shelley, in December 1887.[15] We know that Tolstoy too was a morally delicate subject at the time, probably unfit for inclusion in *Macmillan's Magazine*, as an irate reviewer of *The Picture of Dorian Gray* in the Tory *St James Gazette* of 24 June 1890 indicates. Tolstoy's *Kreutzer Sonata* serves the reviewer as an example of Puritan prurience, which is one form taken by authors like Wilde who derive pleasure from treating a subject merely because it is disgusting.[16] These essays which originate outside of *Macmillan's* pages inscribe its familial audience and the limits of respectable morality as well as identify their subjects and the sites of their publication as marginalized and suitable for male readers, in a different discourse.

Pater's selection from his published work for *Appreciations* is far more eclectic in a variety of ways than either Wilde's or Arnold's. The essays are drawn from three decades, two from the 1860s, four from the 1870s, and five from the 1880s; partly in consequence the essays cohere less. Where Arnold's book overwhelmingly addresses poetry and Wilde's criticism and theory, Pater's volume includes essays on each of three

genres—four on prose, four on poetry, and three on drama; and two on
critical terms—"style," and "romanticism" and "classicism." These two
are carefully positioned at the beginning and end of the volume, and
the title of the last essay is even changed by Pater from "Romanticism"
to "Postscript" to enhance the illusion of unity and discernible
structure. Similarly, the sources of the essays show a greater range: four
from the *Fortnightly Review*, three from *Macmillan's Magazine*, two
from the *Westminster Review*, one from *Scribner's Magazine*, and one
from T. H. Ward's anthology, *The English Poets*. The faceted eclecticism
of *Appreciations* in part results from Pater's decision to give fiction his
serious attention in the 1880s; he is forced to dig more deeply into the
past than Arnold or Wilde to provide criticism suitable for translation
from ephemera to art.

Both Pater and Arnold include essays in their books which first
appeared in T. H. Ward's anthology of English poets (in 1880 and
1883), but the roles these essays play are contrasting: they reveal the
centrality of poetry to Arnold's literary production in the period, and
Pater's parallel preocccupation with imaginative and critical prose.
Arnold's three contributions to Ward (his niece's husband) were the
introduction (later titled "The Study of Poetry"), and pieces on Keats
and Gray. These were all written specially for the selections of poems
which they preface in Ward. Two other essays on Romantic poets in
Arnold's volume treat Wordsworth and Byron; these served as introduc-
tions to editions of their poems edited by Arnold and published by
Macmillan in 1879 and 1881 respectively. With his review of Dowden's
life of Shelley in 1888 Arnold could be said to have completed a
personal project, that of reconsidering his earlier views on the Romantic
poets stated in 1864 and 1865. Just as "The Study of Poetry"
genuinely states the programme of the 1888 volume, "The Function of
Criticism at the Present Time" itself served as the keynote to the first
series of *Essays in Criticism* in 1865. The essays Arnold did for Ward
were part of a larger, previously conceived, reconsideration of Romantic
poetry, a project which Arnold continued to pursue after Ward's
anthology appeared.

The coincidence of Arnold's interests with Ward's volume is not accidental. Darrel Mansell[17] strives to distinguish between the conception of Ward's project—with its twin emphases on the teaching of English poetry and the dispersal of authority implicit in the plurality of critics—and Arnold's well-known predilections for classical and European literature, and for authority. However true these differences, it is also true that Ward's project is itself significantly Arnoldian. As early as 1865 Arnold recommends "that a practice common in England during the last century, and still followed in France, of printing . . . a notice by a competent critic, to serve as an introduction to an eminent author's works, might be revived among us with advantage,"[18] and in 1877 he responds positively to his publisher's suggestion that he undertake a selection of Wordsworth and provide a preface. This appeared in September 1879, the same month in which Arnold probably began to prepare his introduction for Ward: Arnold's parallel selection of Byron's poems in 1881 immediately followed the publication of Ward's volumes 3 and 4 in December 1880, in which Arnold's Keats and Gray essays appear. All three, Arnold's selection from Wordsworth and Byron, and Ward's anthology, were published by Macmillan. The close interrelatedness of the projects is indicated by the common publisher; the family link between Arnold and Ward; and the Oxford associations of Arnold (graduate and former professor of poetry) and Ward (graduate and recent fellow of Brasenose), and most of the critics whom Ward employed in his anthology. These selections of Arnold's and Ward's anthology are productions of the same formation.

Comparison of Humphry Ward's proposal to Macmillan with Arnold's suggestion in 1865 shows that both took their idea from French models, probably the same model, as Sainte-Beuve had already attracted Arnold's attention in 1864 in "The Literary Influence of the Academies":

> The idea, which I wish to carry out is one which I think will mark off such a book from all similar collections in English, namely, that each poet or group of poets should be undertaken by a separate writer, who would select from his work, and write a short *critical* introduction, varying from a single page to ten

or twelve. This idea has been mooted in a most admirable collection of French poetry, called "Les poetes français," published in 1861 by Gide & now (I believe) issued under Hachette's name. That collection occupies four volumes. I should propose that the present book should be in three. . . .

I have already enlisted a good many friends to help in the work . . . I should say that Mr. Matthew Arnold has expressed himself strongly in favour of the scheme, & has promised to help if he can possibly find time. If I can induce him to write the general introduction, as Sainte-Beuve did for the French Collection, I think we would not fear for the success of the book.[19]

Ward's anthology slots easily into Arnold's endeavours at the time, allowing Arnold to lend his name and authority to Ward by agreeing to write the introduction. The flattery of the parallel with Sainte-Beuve and the authority it implied may also have induced Arnold to agree. Ward's project, a version of which Arnold is simultaneously engaged upon, is a variant of one proposed by Arnold fifteen years earlier, and now nurtured by a publisher common to both. Prompted to publish *because* Arnold endorsed it, Macmillan recognized its compatibility with aspects of its current list, while Arnold endorsed it out of recognition of its origins and those (familial and academic) of its youthful proposer.

Pater is also a Macmillan's author, publishing with the press in the 1880s a combination of fiction and criticism, *Marius the Epicurean* in 1885, *Imaginary Portraits* in 1887, the third edition of *The Renaissance* in 1888, and numerous articles, including chapters from *Gaston de Latour* in the *Magazine*. Ward's original proposal to Macmillan of February 1879 shows Pater as volunteering to take eight out of the twenty-seven poets in Volume III: Coleridge, Robert Southey, Samuel Rogers, Keats, Milman, John Keble, W. S. Landor, and possibly E. B. Browning. In the event, he only takes on Coleridge, and in 1883, for the second edition, Rossetti, now dead and thus eligible for inclusion. Southey and Rogers are undertaken by Henry Taylor, Keats by Matthew Arnold, Keble by A. P. Stanley, Landor by Lord Houghton, and E. B. Browning by W. T. Arnold. It is interesting that in theory Pater was willing to concentrate on nineteenth-century poetry in early 1879, and that circumstances intervened to prevent him. Poetry does not appear to be prominent in *Appreciations*, insofar as two of the four essays in poetry date from 1868 and 1874; the other two are derived from Ward, and one of those, on Coleridge, which Pater dates in the volume "1865, 1888," is created in 1888 by combining the Ward essay and his 1866 *Westminster Review* article on Coleridge's prose. Three out of the four essays on poetry were written over a decade before *Appreciations* appeared. Moreover, the introductory and concluding essays of the volume—which are both theoretical—discuss modern European prose texts; in this respect they parallel "Amiel" and "Count Leo Tolstoi," the only two parts of Arnold's 1888 *Essays* which do not treat Romantic poetry. However, where Arnold's first essay, from Ward, foregrounds poetry and anticipates the majority of the essays which follow, Pater's "Style" is recent. It foregrounds prose, and it marginalizes the essays on poetry, including those from Ward, which follow. What the poetry essays in *Appreciations* show is Pater's willingness to discuss recent literature in English, such as that by Rossetti and Morris. The list of poets Pater volunteered for Ward's third volume, which included contemporaries and near-contemporaries such as Keble, Landor, and E. B. Browning, bears this out. In this respect Pater, and Wilde after him, differ from Arnold, who clearly confines his published literary criticism on English literature to work by the previous generation, as he does in 1888.

Besides pieces on poetry and prose, Pater selects three essays on different types of Shakespearean drama for inclusion in *Appreciations*. This choice of subject typifies the apparent moral and intellectual respectability of the essays in this volume. Pater's essays from the *Fortnightly* do not probe its perimeters of tolerance as Wilde's do, and on the whole the distinctions between the *Fortnightly* and *Macmillan's Magazine* do not emerge as clearly as they do in Arnold's selection. The *Appreciations* essay which is to attract controversy was one of Pater's earliest reviews, originally entitled "Poems by William Morris" which appeared anonymously in the *Westminster Review* in 1868, a period when Arnold was to call it "the wicked *Westminster*." The Morris essay attracted adverse criticism then and in 1873, when part of it appeared as the "Conclusion" to Pater's *Renaissance* essays. Although Pater removed it from the 1877 second edition, he republished it twice in 1888-89, in the third edition of *The Renaissance*, and in a different form as "Aesthetic Poetry" in *Appreciations* (1889), as a companion piece, perhaps, to the Ward introduction to Rossetti. But because it again provoked criticism, it was withdrawn a second time by Pater, this time from the 1890 edition of *Appreciations*. If Oscar Wilde at this time sought to be provocative, exploiting the spectrum of latitude in the press, and Arnold was also, even as an elder critic, willing to reprint the Shelley and Tolstoi reviews, Pater emerges in his criticism of the period as the most sensitive to the prevailing morality of the readers of his books, most anxious to construct a reputation of rectitude to survive him.

The significance of the critic constructed by Pater is not only illustrated positively by what *Appreciations* includes, but also by the critical journalism not reprinted. All the articles published between 1873 and 1888 and excluded reveal facets of Pater's critical practice and reserve. Certain topics are carefully avoided, such as classical Greek culture and French fiction. Thus, the succession of pieces from 1875 on "The Myth of Demeter and Persephone" (1875), "A Study of Dionysus" (1876), "The Bacchanals of Euripides" (1878), "The Beginnings of Greek Sculpture" (1880), "The Marbles of Aegina" (1880) are not only excluded from *Appreciations*, which in the event is confined to English literature; the Greek essays remain uncollected by Pater, who is aware of the common association among his peers of classical Greece with homosexuality, and aware too of his own vulnerability on this score. These Greek studies, with others, were only collected posthumously.[20]

Pater's suppression of this material takes on an increased significance, even poignancy, when one notes that in 1889 he republished his treatment of the *revival* of Dionysus in a *French* setting, in the apparently protective guise of fiction, as one of the four *Imaginary Portraits*. Indeed, the whole of that volume suggests that prose fiction for Pater was liberating, and incurred less risk of personal liability. However, the suppression of the classical Greek essays registers the strength of presence of the vociferous moral majority among readers and institutions such as the church, the academy, and the critics; particularly vulnerable, it would appear, are collected prose essays, availing themselves of the authority art offers the ephemera of journalism in the form of printed books. In the light of this, Matthew Arnold's definition of Hellenism, characterized by sweetness and light, may be read, even in its earliest forms, as carefully excluding the homosexual aspect of Greek life while leaving the hearty manliness to Hebraism. This is a delicate distinction, and his advocacy of disinterestedness, most commonly read as an allusion to the affray of journalism and political life, may well exclude covertly this form of engagement in and with Greek life.

Pater's decision to risk the inclusion of "Aesthetic Poetry" in 1889 is of interest in the light of what replaces it in the second edition of *Appreciations* in 1890. Pater chooses a review he published anonymously in *Macmillan's Magazine* in 1886 of a French novel, Feuillet's *La Morte*.[21] The Victorian press shows that readers were kept well-informed through reviews about noteworthy writing of all kinds in Europe and nineteenth-century writing in Britain shows marked familiarity with its European counterparts. However, it is equally true that French fiction, associated with sordidness, moral laxity, and realism had for some time been labelled as unsuitable reading for a major group of novel readers, respectable women. It would be reassuring to such readers that Pater's review had appeared in *Macmillan's* (had they known it), but significantly its author chooses to publish it anonymously in just such a family magazine. When Pater made his selection of work for *Appreciations*, he may have judged that having restored the "Conclusion" to *The Renaissance* (1888), it was safe in 1889 to reprint the entire essay from which it was drawn, but having incurred criticism again, he substitutes in 1890—perhaps wryly—this moderate and "approved for the family" review of a French novel.

Pater's fear of castigation was not the result of individual neurosis or simply personal experience. In theological circles and the closely related academic world, the indignation and litigation following the publication of *Essays and Reviews* in 1860 was swift, long-lived, and well-known. In the wider national sphere, while *La Traviata* was performed in London in 1857, the libretto was "unavailable" and the novel banned. Censorship, the tyranny of the majority, was a live issue in the mid-1880s, and fiction—associated with light literature and women readers—was predictably a prime site of conflict.

If the issue of censorship is implicit in Pater's selection and deselection process, novelists whose work was its victim, such as George Moore and Wilde, protested openly and vociferously. In "A New Censorship of Literature," an article in an evening daily newspaper, the *Pall Mall Gazette* in December 1884, and in a pamphlet *Literature at Nurse* (1885),[22] George Moore exposed the refusal of the circulating libraries to stock *A Modern Lover* and subsequently *A Mummer's Wife*; he claimed that the consequential failure of fiction in this position was disastrous for contemporary English literature as well as for the author and publisher of the work refused. In noting that the reaction of the press to the pamphlet was cool, Pierre Coustillas quotes a review in the *Academy*, a journal written by and for men in the universities, which disapprovingly links the realism of George Moore's novels with that of Emile Zola's;[23] in 1888 the septuagenarian Henry Vizetelly, the publisher of Moore's pamphlet, was imprisoned for three months for publication of Zola's *La Terre*. In February 1891 Wilde included a riposte to the critics of his novel, *The Picture of Dorian Gray*, in an article he published in the *Fortnightly*, "The Soul of Man Under Socialism"; while his claim there is stylistically emphasized by hyperbole and italics, his contention that "[t]here is not a single poet or prose-writer of this century, for instance, on whom the British public have not solemnly conferred diplomas of immorality,"[24] refers to a contemporary climate that all of his *Fortnightly* readers would recognize. When one considers poets and novelists of the nineteenth century, many did attract the charge of immorality: Wordsworth, Coleridge, Keats, Shelley, and Byron, but also Dickens, Thackeray, Charlotte and Emily Brontë, Elizabeth Gaskell, George Eliot, Moore, Meredith, Hardy, Gissing, William Morris, D. G. Rossetti, and Swinburne.

Pater's careful behind-the-scenes regulation of what should be published on diverse occasions in different discourses, and Moore's and Wilde's explicit interventions to alter public opinion and behaviour provide two models of responses to censorship. The explorer, editor, and translator Richard Burton provides a third. He withdraws the potential object of controversy from the public domain by publishing for private subscribers; and in order to protect himself and his associates from charges under the Obscene Publications Act of 1857, he invents a false Indian company under whose imprint he publishes his edition of *The Book of a Thousand Nights and a Night* in 1885.[25] His edition of the *Arabian Nights* is copiously annotated, and its long "Terminal Essay" is largely devoted to the subject of pederasty; undoubtedly learned, the project is bound up with exploration and the anthropology of the period, and detailed sexual erotica is presented in the notes under the guise of the interest of cultural relativism. The two thousand subscribers to the first edition undoubtedly included a majority interested in this material. In the introduction Burton roundly defends this medieval Islamic work from charges of immorality and, contrasting it favourably with modern hypocrisy, identifies a French novel as a genuine purveyor of vice! No doubt he is appealing to his readers' knowledge of another, more familiar literature labelled exotica by the same censorship. But he too is attesting in 1885 to the existence of censorship, and the pressure emanating from its formation, such as the law. He also shows that in 1885 French fiction was still commonly regarded as an object of censorship:

> The morale is sound and healthy; and at times we descry, through the voluptuous and libertine picture, vistas of a transcendental morality, the morality of Socrates in Plato. Subtle corruption and covert licentiousness are utterly absent; we find more real "vice" in many a short French roman, say La Dame aux Camélias, and in not a few English novels of our own day than in the thousands of pages of the Arab. Here we have nothing of that most immodest modern modesty which sees covert implication where nothing is implied, and "improper" allusion when propriety is not outraged; nor do we meet with the Nineteenth Century refinement: innocence of the word not the thought;

morality of the tongue not of the heart, and the sincere homage paid to virtue in guise of perfect hypocrisy.[26]

We should therefore not be surprised that besides work on Greek culture, Pater does not select any of the four reviews of French fiction for *Appreciations* in 1889. He also leaves out a number of anonymous reviews of the work of friends which appeared in periodicals such as the *Oxford Magazine*, and newspapers such as the *Pall Mall Gazette* and the *Guardian*, reviews which seem to derive primarily from their function of the anonymous puff, as their authority would undoubtedly diminish were their authorship to be acknowledged. But there is also the factor of where the reviews appeared: these periodicals and newspapers lack the status of periodicals from which the selected articles originate. In particular, the newspapers in the 1880s and 1890s are identified with the vulgar mass medium, the "new journalism" and the non-professional man of letters at leisure to write the amusing or learned paper within the domain of letters.

Unlike Arnold and Wilde, Pater does not resort habitually to the latitude offered by the *Nineteenth Century*, making only four contributions to it in his lifetime, two book reviews in the late 1880s and two papers on the great French churches in 1894. Both of the reviews were not only signed but understood to be entirely the reviewer's work, with the initiation of the review and the choice of book his. The first of Pater's reviews of Noticeable Books appeared in April 1889 and treated a French novel; the second, published in December, proved to be Pater's most explicit manifestation of his interest in politics. Pater sees the potential of the space James Knowles offers, but avoids being associated with such a libertine journal. Two other decisions by Pater support this. In the June following the signed Ferdinand Fabre review in April, he reviews another novel by Fabre, but in a different periodical,[27] one which is allied to the Anglican church and which permits anonymity; it offers Pater double protection: non-exposure to the reading public, and the respectability of the Church for the many colleagues and critics privy to the authorship of unsigned journalism.

That Pater chose an Anglican weekly like the *Guardian* to place a review of French fiction suggests an element of wit as well. Pater's wish in the latter part of his career to identify himself and be identified with religious rather than libertine formations is also indicated by his decision to place essays on Plato and classical Greece in the *Contemporary Review*, the journal whose religious constraints its editor, James Knowles, left to create the unconstrained *Nineteenth Century*. Pater's association with homosexuality and paganism in the 1860s and 1870s, and the popular association by the 1880s of homosexuality with Plato meant that publication of these essays was potentially damaging to Pater. The appearance of such work in the *Contemporary Review* might forestall adverse response. The only other essay Pater placed in the periodicals before the publication of *Plato and Platonism* in February 1893, "A Chapter on Plato," appeared in *Macmillan's Magazine*,[28] another journal calculated to attest to the respectability of the material.

The last category of significant omissions from *Appreciations* is politically topical material, in particular two essays which deal with the question of English literature and English in the university syllabus, which appeared in the *Guardian* and the *Pall Mall Gazette*.[29] These may be thought too slight for inclusion, but fused in the way Pater constructed the essay on Coleridge, a suitable piece might have resulted, but for a different book. These pieces have no place in a collection of appreciations which identifies itself in its title as an aesthetic project pertaining to high culture. The contemporary debate about English is ruled out.

Pater's publishing tactic to avoid unwelcome exposure is well illustrated by his intervention in the debate following the appearance of *The Picture of Dorian Gray* complete in one issue in *Lippincott's Monthly Magazine* in July 1890. Ward, Lock & Co. published an expanded version the following April, incorporating a preface of epigrams which Wilde published in March in the *Fortnightly*, no doubt as a trailer for the novel. He followed it up with *Intentions* in May. Yet the bulk of the reviews of *Dorian Gray*, and Wilde's public response to them—in letters to the press and in his essay "The Soul of Man under

Socialism" which appeared in the *Fortnightly* in February 1891—were reviews of the periodical version, so sensational was the novel. A friend and former teacher of Wilde, Pater had been sent the novel in manuscript by Wilde for comment. We might expect that Pater would have been one of the supportive reviewers. Certainly, Wilde himself might have such an expectation, as he had produced at Pater's delicate request[30] a highly appreciative review of *Appreciations* in the *Speaker* just ten weeks before *Dorian Gray* first appeared; its last paragraph concluded:

> But in Mr. Pater, as in Cardinal Newman, we find the union of personality with perfection. He has no rival in his own sphere, and he has escaped disciples. And this, not because he has not been imitated, but because in art so fine as his there is something that, in its essence, is inimitable.[31]

More praise for Pater was incorporated by Wilde in the novel itself as published in July 1890 and in *Intentions* which appeared in May 1891. The significance of this sequence is that, although requested by Frank Harris to write a review for the *Fortnightly*,[32] Pater did not review the novel when it first appeared, when his favourable view might have been of value to Wilde.[33] Nor did Pater review it promptly when it appeared in volume form in April, or after *Intentions* was published in May. Only in November, seventeen months late, did Pater publish a review.[34] However, few reviews of Wilde's novel *were* published, and Pater's reticence was unquestionably shared by other critics.

The debates of Pater, Arnold, and Wilde on the nature of the subject of literary discourse are implicated in the wider contemporary discussion of the institutional role of literature: whether the classical model was to continue to prevail with its constituent validated literary forms, or whether the subject was to be defined so as to have its roots in the vernacular and its indigenous form: "The future of poetry is immense," Arnold proclaims at the opening of "The Study of Poetry."[35] Wilde and Pater demur: "Imaginative prose," Pater declares in "Style," "being the special art of the modern world,"[36] and the *decay* of lying of more concern to Wilde than Arnold's search for truth. If the ideological alliances are clear, their material forms show that Arnold and Pater share a periodical discourse and a publisher which are repudiated by and repudiate Wilde. The positions of the three critics on the late Victorian spectrum of gender and discourse of gender figure significantly in the equation. Self-censorship as well as external censorship is evident. This examination of a cluster of critical writing in the late nineteenth century reveals the process of authorial management of publication and the construction by authors of themselves as critics. In the interplay of debate and cultural formations, details of the relationship between the history of periodical and book publication, and kinds of discourse emerge. Insofar as the construction of the twentieth-century canon has marginalized Wilde's interventions, it reproduces the effect of Victorian publishers, publications, and critics.

An Anxiety of No Influence:
Walter Pater on William Wordsworth

6

J. P. WARD

WORDSWORTH'S INFLUENCE on the nineteenth century was massive. Yet it had largely dispersed by the century's end and, as Linda Dowling has recently underlined, it was Walter Pater who initiated the change, for he was the first to make writing a truly composed artifice rather than directly trusting the language of the heart.[1] More personally, if for Wordsworth poetry was the "spontaneous overflow of natural feelings," then one can recall Thomas Hardy's description of Pater's manner, on meeting him, as "of one carrying weighty ideas without spilling them."[2] So one wonders why there is, as I think there is, a slight but real subtext of Wordsworth running invisibly through Pater's work. It surfaced notably of course in the article on Wordsworth of 1874, but also in the three explicit namings of Wordsworth that Pater places, in isolated prominence, right at the start of perhaps his three most important works, *Renaissance, Marius the Epicurean,* and the essay "Style." Pater's historical moment was to write, as it were, going away from Wordsworth until the *fin-de-siècle* left the poet out of sight; and this seems symbolized by the markers to Wordsworth at the beginnings of the three works.

To illustrate, here first is a passage from the essay on the poet: "[h]is words are themselves thought and feeling; not eloquent, or musical words merely, but that sort of creative language which carries the reality of what it depicts, directly, to the consciousness."[3] That first phrase, "his words are themselves thought and feeling," is, I suggest, remarkable. It is as though Pater is surprised by his own remark as he makes it. He should be, for the Paterian belief (ancestor—if I have this right—of the deconstructionist belief) is that words, not minds, are already the only encapsulations of civilization's several hoarded meanings, which the writer then chooses from and deploys with studied purpose. But with this remark Pater himself departs from that practice and enters Wordsworth's own mode of simple existential language. It uses no one-to-one, word-for-thing method of the kind which Pater will himself later recommend in the essay "Style"; it is an emptied-out definition. But furthermore in so putting it, Pater himself enters a line of Victorian critics who have made such one-phrase judgments of Wordsworth, all of which underline, and with approval, the simple and even poetically negative quality of Wordsworth's poetry. Matthew Arnold put it of Wordsworth that "he has no style." Much earlier Coleridge had called this style "matter-of-fact" and then in his own "conversation poems" followed it; and John Stuart Mill, acknowledging a great personal debt to Wordsworth's poetry, called him "the poet of unpoetical natures." Harriet Martineau put the paradox most fully. She wrote that "with all their truth and and all their charm, few of Wordsworth's pieces are poems," yet "he taught us to say what we had to say in a way not only the more rational but the more beautiful."[4] I think Pater's is the best of these remarks, emphasizing, as it does, not the negation but the indissolubility in Wordsworth of "words" and "thought and feeling" as one and the same thing.

Pater appears to have first read Wordsworth when he was himself trying to write poetry, at school and as an undergraduate at Oxford. His first critical comment on Wordsworth of any length followed when he was twenty-six and published the essay on Coleridge in 1865. The assessment is straightforward. Pater sees Wordsworth there as stable, completely attuned to nature, and possessing a philosophy of universe and man quite free from the "doubts and uncertainties" which bore down Coleridge himself. Wordsworth "already vibrates with that blithe impulse which carried him to final happiness and self-possession"; he had "a joyful and penetrative conviction of the existence of certain latent affinities between nature and the human mind," and had as well a "flawless temperament, his fine mountain atmosphere of mind, that calm, sabbatic, mystic wellbeing which De Quincey, a little cynically, connected with worldly (that is to say pecuniary) good fortune."[5] This seems hardly recognizable as the Wordsworth who, in his own words, had "his unruly times, / His times when he is neither sick nor well," said of poets that they come in the end to "despondency and madness," and of them that "[a]s high as we have mounted in delight / In our dejection do we sink as low." Pater is of course concentrating on Coleridge here, but one senses too that the Wordsworthian wise equilibrium has sufficiently impressed him that there is not yet anything to say about it.

In 1868 came Pater's review of William Morris's poetry in the *Westminster Review*, the substance of which became the essay "Aesthetic Poetry," in *Appreciations* in 1889. The essay names Wordsworth only once, but he seems to hover elsewhere. First, that the essay is touched in a couple of places with echoes of the 1798 *Preface to Lyrical Ballads* of Wordsworth. William Morris's poem "The Earthly Paradise" evinces "the great primary passions under broad daylight. . . . the simple elementary passions—anger, desire, regret, pity and fear," and so on. Pater will quietly return to Wordsworth's preface on several future occasions. More intriguing though is the brief passage referring to Wordsworth. Morris's poem has "a strange power in dealing with morning and the things of morning. . . . There are hints at a language common to birds and beasts and men . . . and this simplicity at first hand is a strange contrast to the sought-out simplicity of Wordsworth."[6] Noticeable here is the double occurrence of the word "strange," (it occurs only twice more elsewhere in the essay) and, although it refers to Morris, it comes just where Wordsworth is the point of comparison. The word is of course not uncommon in Pater, but it stands out from his other characteristic adjectives—scrupulous, exquisite, graceful, fugitive and precise. "Strange," unlike the others, is knowingly imprecise, suggesting rather an uncertainty as to what the adjective should be. It will figure strongly in the essay on Wordsworth itself, and seems to be a first marker here for a complexity and depth in Wordsworth that Pater sensed from an early age but really did not finally fathom.

The word appears again in that oddly irrelevant paragraph on Wordsworth right at the start of *Studies in the History of the Renaissance* in 1873. That luxuriating, even-paced, gentle book almost seems to say that the beautiful works Pater examines, and their creators, exist perhaps in a remote dream, a silent lunar museum of Pater's own making; and so, before proceeding, it is as though he turns and faces the robust mountain and lake writer briefly for a moment outside, before going back into his museum and shutting the door. And this first example of an early Wordsworth marker enables Pater to summarize his impressed puzzlement briefly but squarely and for the first time:

> Take, for instance, the writings of Wordsworth. . . . Scattered up and down [them], sometimes fusing and transforming entire compositions . . . sometimes, as if at random, depositing a fine crystal here or there, in a matter it does not wholly search through or transmute, we trace the action of his unique, incommunicable faculty, that strange, mystical sense of a life in natural things, and of man's life as a part of nature, drawing a strength and colour and character from local influences, from the hills and streams, and from natural sights and sounds. Well! that is the virtue, the active principle, in Wordsworth's poetry.[7]

From his own very different standpoint, of reaching always for the last finished touch (one of the book's returning concerns and words), Pater is finding space to acknowledge, generously but perhaps also under silent pressure, the existence of another poetry; one where it is not merely no failing, but of the essence, to treat matter which the poet "does not wholly search through and transmute." The faculty is strange and incommunicable, even to the subtly refining Paterian mind, and

Pater will next turn to an examination of it, in the essay on Wordsworth of the very next year, 1874.

In *The Renaissance* Wordsworth is used to illustrate Pater's own critical questions: what does the work mean for *me*? What are its peculiar qualities? In the Wordsworth essay these questions are repeated. But this time they are preceded by an attempt to grapple with the now pressing question of why one is drawn to the perplexing Wordsworth at all, and why that effect is present. The answer is curious. To "those who, coming across him in youth, can bear him at all" Wordsworth's poetry cultivates in his readers "a habit of reading between the lines," for Wordsworth "meets us with the promise that he has much, and something very peculiar, to give us, if we will follow a certain difficult way; and seems to have the secret of a special and privileged state of mind." This way is like "some initiation, a *disciplina arcana* by submitting to which [readers] become able constantly to distinguish in art, feeling, manners, that which is organic, animated, expressive, from that which is only conventional, derivative, inexpressive."[8]

It is curious that Pater should see the simple Wordsworth, of the "real language of men," as the leader of some esoteric cult, difficult to comprehend and get into, especially since Pater again seems to write with Wordsworth's 1798 *Preface* beside him: "It is for [their] direct expression of passion, that [Wordsworth] values [the lowly people's] humble words. . . . He constantly endeavours to bring his language near to the real language of men . . . and what he values most is the almost elementary expression of elementary feelings."[9] One can certainly applaud in passing the way the earlier paragraph was prophetic of many tendencies in Wordsworth criticism. F. W. Bateson also said of Wordsworth that "the poetry is *between* the words," Geoffrey Hartman took up the line of the *via negativa* and the American poet Louis Simpson is only one of many who said he could not read Wordsworth before middle age.[10] But what has to be called Pater's confusion, at one level, is borne out further in this essay by his still seeing a content, stable Wordsworth, one whose life fell into "broad, untroubled, perhaps somewhat monotonous spaces"—hardly true surely of the first thirty years, and at least some of the rest. And Pater goes on, unpromisingly, by characterizing his subject with adjectives more Paterian than Wordsworthian: "delicate," "precise" and "finely scrupulous" and even picking out "precious morsels" from the whole, much to Mrs. Oliphant's rage and ire. Pater improbably offers us too a Wordsworth more apt as a poet of the south-east than the Lake District: "[T]he English lake country has, of course, its grandeurs. But the peculiar function of Wordsworth's genius . . . would have found its true test had he become the poet of Surrey, say! and the prophet of its life."[11] Something similar had been said in the essay on Coleridge, yet one look at Dorothy Wordsworth's journals suggest where the poet got his detailed observations of leaves, "mouldering" or otherwise. Mrs. Mark Pattison was only the first of those who have noted Pater's propensity to see in the work of others, qualities already in his own talent and nature.

Of course, Pater does not leave it there. In the second half of the essay he writes, sensitively and early in Wordsworth criticism, about the relations between nature, humble life and (in Wordsworth's phrase) "the philosophic mind": he sees clearly how Wordsworth viewed nature as tranquilizing, how that itself dignifies humble life, how unity of man and nature can be taken literally on a scale of being, and how too this can emerge, without loss of dignity, in pity for lowly people and their sufferings, always a matter of real feeling for Pater himself. I don't share the view of Michael Levey, in his excellent biography, that Pater merely chose the "eminently safe" topic of Wordsworth in the aftermath of the fiasco of *The Renaissance*.[12] Yet although Pater intriguingly encourages the habit of "reading between the lines" (a view not inconsistent, as I will suggest, with "the words themselves being thought and feeling"), he does reach somewhere in this essay a definite, if quiet, stopping-point.

For in this section of the essay we can almost see Pater standing back from going into the heart of this poetry, which he otherwise had seemed almost compulsively to want to acknowledge. Pater's style, and way of thought in writing perhaps, is horizontal; the precarious,

lingering sentences so laid end to end that if they were all put together
it would stretch one might say from Rome to Canterbury and on
around London to Brasenose. He disposes and distributes his thoughts
and phrases as though to occupy a level surface. Wordsworth's cast is
vertical; up to the high mountains and the "huge peak" which "strode
after me"; down into the valley, the bottomless lake, the "mind's
abyss" and, clearly as the psychoanalytic approach later came to see, the
profoundly suppressed, and then disturbingly revealed, subconscious.
When Wordsworth says, "Oh mystery of man, from what a depth /
Proceed thy honours!",[13] if "honours" there corresponds to Pater's
"civilization," then Wordsworth imputes it to a noncivilized source.

This is best symbolized in Wordsworth by what Pater's essay never
touches on—in so many poems the sudden, unnatural death and the
sad survivor. In "We Are Seven" children have died and their little
sister plays by the grave. In "The Thorn" a tormented mother sits by
a small mound containing the body of her newborn child. In "The
Brothers" a rural clergyman tells of how a villager fell off a mountain
ledge to his death, not knowing that the person to whom he is telling
this very story is the deceased man's long absent brother. In Book XI
of *The Prelude* a young girl wanders by the gibbet of a hanged
murderer, and in Book V the retrieved body of a drowned man shoots
"bolt upright" out of the lake, "his ghastly face a spectre shape / —of
terror even." The grimly vertical quality of these last three deaths only
emphasizes the underground location of the buried—below ground,
like repressed guilts the survivor cannot acknowledge, later to thrust up
generally across the poetry in Wordsworth's frequent melancholic
moods and self-confessed depressive self-examination.

Only once in his essay does Pater come near to looking down into
this abyss. This is when he is describing at some length the pathos
Wordsworth sees in humble rural life:

> The girl who rung her father's knell; the unborn infant feeling about its
> mother's heart; the instinctive touches of children; the sorrows of the wild
> creatures, even—their homesickness, their strange yearnings; the tales of
> passionate regret that hang by a ruined farm-building, a heap of stones, a

deserted sheepfold . . . those whom men have wronged—their pathetic wanness; the sailor "who, in his heart, was half a shepherd on the stormy seas;" the wild woman teaching her child to pray for her betrayer; incidents like the making of the shepherd's staff, or that of the young boy laying the first stone of the sheepfold;—all the pathetic episodes of their humble existence, their longing, their wonder at fortune, their poor pathetic pleasures.[14]

That is a long list. And yet nowhere in it are there more than two actual deaths even hinted at, and neither is in any way outside death's natural course.

Pater of course had his own preoccupations with death. It is a Keatsian threat however to "beauty that must die" and, both more barbaric and sicklier than Wordsworth's, it must have citadels built against it. Wordsworth by contrast feels drawn to that death's violent nature for something inherent in it for himself. So what does Pater do about this difference? *He blanks it out*; once again that word "strange" is the clear marker, five or six times in the few pages immediately following the long passage just cited, where ostensibly he is trying to consider the nature of Wordsworthian speculation itself: "A sort of biblical depth and solemnity hangs over this strange, new, passionate, pastoral world, of which [Wordsworth] first raised the image." Wordsworth "comes, from point to point, into strange contact with thoughts which have visited . . . far more venturesome, perhaps errant, spirits." He enlarges "so strangely the bounds of [that region's] humble churchyards." And, with a perception which will finally appear extended into a general theory in the "Postscript" to *Appreciations* nearly fifteen years later, Pater writes that "those who take up these poems after an interval of months, or years perhaps, may be surprised at finding how well old favourites wear, how their strange, inventive turns of diction or thought still send through them the old feeling of surprise."[15]

In short, in missing how Wordsworth is disturbed into this writing from below and within, and hence never seems remotely comparable to Pater's own mode of elongated, silky prose, Pater stops short at a border he himself declares Wordsworth to have crossed: "Wordsworth . . . seems at times to have passed the borders of a world of strange speculations, inconsistent enough, had he cared to note such inconsistencies."[16] And this stopping-short, at seeing what is in fact the source of Wordsworth's massive nineteenth-century influence, and its Victorian melancholy, is associated with Pater's (and surely Newman's and Hopkins's) crossing of a different border, into one or other version of ecclesiasticism with its sumptuous use of the artifactual rather than the natural in expression of its beliefs. One recalls chapter XXII of *Marius*—"The Minor Peace Of The Church." Meanwhile Pater himself is left with the one thing he is interested in, namely, Wordsworth's style. The rest of the essay is concerned with that; Pater identifies words with thought and feeling in the poet, and he shows his own clear understanding, if not of Wordsworth's mind, then certainly of how Wordsworth's art and mind were related.

But although he does not cross the Wordsworthian border into strangeness, Pater it seems was sufficiently impressed to take over one project, the examination of his own childhood. This culminates in *Marius*, but begins most markedly in the group of *Imaginary Portraits* of 1878, written not so long after the Wordsworth essay. In all these there is a fully Wordsworthian attempt at a remembrance of things past. But Pater's purpose is not self-knowledge for its own sake, but now finally to find and cultivate his style. As he says in *Marius*, a "true understanding of oneself is ever the first condition of genuine style."[17] And this emphasis on style is Pater's true mark, his kind of literary health. But the difference between Pater's and Wordsworth's search has a notable feature. With Pater, as he moves backward in time, there is always a "blockage" at the artifact. Pater can't or won't get beyond or below the artifact to its origins, as Wordsworth always did. There is no "mind's abyss"; rather, in *Marius* he speaks of the "house of thought," a metaphor of structure.

The project develops accordingly. In "The Child in the House" (1878) the most treasured evokers of exquisite memory are the ready-made objects in the attic: "glass beads, empty scent bottles still sweet, thrum of coloured silks." Even non-objects are written as objects: "the angle at which the sun in the morning fell on the pillow." In "Emerald

Uthwart" the broader canvas of the (still artifactual) Canterbury Cathedral and school are preceded by that ubiquitously Paterian piece of nature already made, already artifact, the walled garden. Most interesting of all is the unfinished "imaginary portrait" called "The English Poet," not published in Pater's lifetime and appearing for the first time in the *Fortnightly Review* as late as 1931. A young child born in France of an English mother who however then dies, is sent to be reared by relatives in the Cumberland mountains in the north of England. The child finds the landscape wholly alien, and when on growing up he returns south to France, it is like a release: "The smooth winds from the sea, their balm and salt . . . the sand dunes grown richly about with wild marigold and yellow horned poppies." All this is firmly contrasted with "the too-clinging humours of our English climate, which is also, in part, a matter of inheritance." Yet Wordsworth and the 1798 *Preface* are still ambivalently hovering. In compensation for disliking the lake scenery the boy discovers reading and language, developing his bent "among people to whom a great English poet attributed a certain natural superiority in the use of words." A number of writers are mentioned in the work, but Wordsworth is the only one alluded to first without name this time, and then in terms of his beliefs rather than his achievement. Indeed the absence of name makes the story's title ambiguous, for the young boy grows up to be a poet himself. But there is an even more intriguing feature. For the story has begun with the young woman, the boy's mother, who has discovered a gold coin in the soil on the smallholding where she and her French husband live. The coin has on it the head of a handsome young man, and one day such a man happens to pass the farm and smile and talk to the young mother before he leaves. The coin here is the blockage, both to nature itself (the soil in which it is found) and perhaps also, although less certainly, to whatever deep psychoanalytical secret, sexual or otherwise, the story may contain. By placing that coin in the soil, Pater is able to deflect himself away from that soil to the very different terrain of the lake district which he then—complicating the picture further— quietly rejects too; but not its poet, the unnamed Wordsworth, who in the lake district had found no blockage, only the unboundedness of the immensity, the water, the "universe entire."

In *Marius the Epicurean* (1885) and the essay "Style" (1888), Pater is out on his own territory with confidence and on a large scale. We are now well into the last part of the century, and the strong Victorian-Arnoldian bond between language and true morality, literature and high culture, has given way. Yet both these works still have the small reference to Wordsworth as *The Renaissance* had in 1873. *Marius*, still discernibly autobiographical, moves gradually away from nature, through small domesticities and their household gods to the *beata urbs* and the Catholic church, and finally to grace, the last word in the book, and one whose liturgical opposition to "nature" can be read as an intentional emphasis. Yet at the start—on page two to be exact—again we find the echo of the 1798 *Preface*: "The old-fashioned, partly puritanical awe, the power of which Wordsworth noted and valued so highly in a northern peasantry, had its counterpart in the feeling of the Roman lad, as he passed the spot, 'touched of heaven,' where the lightning had struck dead an aged labourer in the field."[18]

In the essay "Style" it is again Wordsworth, and again right near the start, who is given an accolade of large implication not then, however, made the main force of the essay itself: "A century after Dryden, amid very different intellectual needs . . . the range of the poetic force in literature was effectively enlarged by Wordsworth."[19] But the essay's main drift of course is now on style's scrupulous making: "minute attention" to the "particles" in each word; each syllable's "precise value"; the "punctilious observance" of the medium itself, and the "words [one] would select in the making of a dictionary"; the pictorial and sculptural analogies for the process; and the scholar and scholarly conscience. Surely Wordsworth's heaving parabolic periods, his most unPaterian repetitions and his most indefinite vocabulary of immensity, eternity, something, thing, time and the rest, could never have been the result of the fastidious process Pater seems now to be requiring of writing. To put it briefly, one suspects Pater is being defensive in this rather convoluted essay, and his declared aims are a tacit answer to hovering charges of corrupting aestheticism or amorality. There is comparable defensiveness in *Marius*, of whom we recall that "though the manner of his work was changed formally from poetry to prose, he remained, and must always be, of the poetic temper." In "Style" the suggestion is that "imaginative prose, it may be thought, [is] the special art of the modern world." Hence the curious need to claim Wordsworth too as one who wrote "with the tact of a scholar"; hence too, yet again, the brief but clear echoes of Wordsworth's 1798 *Preface*.[20]

Broadly Pater recognized in Wordsworth his own singlemindedness, solitary situation and search for happiness's habitation. Possibly the mid-Victorians overpraised the essay on Wordsworth while missing its main import. Pater never really confronted the deep disturbance in Wordsworth's writing; rather he always stuck at the 1798 *Preface*'s concern with "real language of men" and, in one brilliant phrase of his own, captured its significance. And, by recognizing with a remarkable honesty the authenticity of Wordsworth's achievement, even if not its full nature, he was able to see that his own more Platonic project for self-knowledge could gain from a search back into his own childhood. Unlike Wordsworth he did not go more deeply into any "intimations"; he fixed on the gold coin in the soil, not the soil itself. And finally, I think revealingly, Pater only half-glimpsed one real resultant difference in their two ways of writing. While he himself worked so hard to choose every word for those long sentences (and "choice," as of select best specimens, is a favourite Pater adjective), Wordsworth could so often make poetry out of the very failure of such choosing:

> It was, in truth,
> An ordinary sight, but I should need
> Colours and words that are unknown to man
> To paint the visionary dreariness
> Which, while I looked all round for my lost guide,
> Did at that time invest the naked pool,
> The beacon on the lonely eminence,
> The woman, and her garments vexed and tossed
> By the strong wind.[21]

By writing of failure, Wordsworth succeeds. To Pater this was always, one feels, a "strange" way of doing things, but it seems he could never stop respecting it, even while continuing his own painstaking search for the very different success which was to redirect literature for the last third of the century.

Essaying "W. H. Pater Esq.":
New Perspectives
on the Tutor/Student Relationship
Between Pater and Hopkins

7

LESLEY HIGGINS

WALTER PATER'S PRESENCE in Gerard Manley Hopkins's life and work was much more than an undergraduate phenomenon. Three phases of personal and intertextual connection can be identified: the formative months of tutoring and friendship in Oxford from 1866 to 1868; their renewal of personal contact a decade later, when Hopkins returned to the city of Oxford as a Jesuit priest; and the impersonal but affective instances in the mid-1880s when a despondent and nostalgic Fr. Hopkins, now consigned to his "winter world"[1] in Dublin, would review and "overhaul" his old correspondence and papers.[2] Fundamentally, though, theirs was a relationship predicated upon the indelible influence of the University: the attitudes towards life and learning fostered in its colleges and common rooms; the philosophical and religious controversies it sustained but never resolved. Although there has been a great deal of conjecture, and some learned commentary,[3] as to the relationship which existed between the Brasenose don and the "star of Balliol," critics have not been able to ascertain the full extent of Pater's impact on Hopkins. The documents and manuscripts central to this enquiry remain unpublished—including five of the six essays which Hopkins wrote for Pater in 1866 and 1867. By focusing on the latter, analyzing them in conjunction with the Pater articles to which Hopkins was responding, I hope to provide a more searching and complete account of their intellectual and intertextual communion. The discussion will also suggest, in brief, how all of Hopkins's extant undergraduate work illuminates our rather sketchy knowledge of Pater's undergraduate career and curriculum. Hopkins's papers are especially helpful in clarifying Pater's intellectual ties with Benjamin Jowett, the Regius professor of Greek and Balliol Fellow who played crucial roles in the lives of both men.

Walter Pater was born five years before Hopkins (1844-1889), and he outlived him by five years. Only two academic terms separated Pater's final classes with Jowett in the spring of 1862 and Hopkins's initial tutorials in April 1863. Three years later, in Trinity term 1866, Hopkins began "coaching" with Pater, now established as a fellow of Brasenose.[4] The circumstances of these preparations for Hopkins's impending Greats examinations enter into our discussion in several crucial ways. The twelve months before Hopkins met Pater were pivotal in Hopkins's life; they were also emotionally searing. Each intensely-felt anxiety—about his academic performance, religious beliefs, or personal behaviour—fed into and exacerbated all the others. Jowett, for example, his tutor since matriculating in April 1863, represented both intellectual achievement and apostasy. Hopkins's defection from Jowett's sphere of influence and absenteeism from his tutorials during this year of inner turmoil were openly encouraged by the Rev. Henry Liddon,[5] the chief disciple of High Church Puseyism who became Hopkins's confessor in February 1864.[6] It was Jowett, I surmise, who dispatched Hopkins to Pater, a private coach from outside Balliol who was the antithesis of Puseyism. The Master of Balliol, Robert Scott, was unacquainted with Pater. Jowett, on the other hand, had been extremely impressed with Pater as an undergraduate[7] and could rest assured that his former pupil would actively counter-balance Hopkins's ritualistic tendencies.

In what frame of mind Hopkins first arrived at Pater's rooms is another matter. As Gerald Monsman has shown us, as early as February 1864 Hopkins had been strenuously warned about Pater's "infidel" beliefs by Samuel Brooke, the Corpus Christi undergraduate and member of the Old Mortality essay society who denounced Pater's Old Mortality presentations about "subjective immortality" and "self-culture" to his diary, his friends, and the Rev. Liddon.[8] When tutor and student met in April 1866, Hopkins was in the throes of a religious crisis—whether to "Romanise" or not—and Pater was at his most anti-Christian. "Neology" was the then-popular term for sceptical or latitudinarian attitudes; and just as Hopkins's friend Edmund Geldart identified Jowett as Oxford's principal Neologian,[9] so Hopkins characterized his new instructor: "Coaching with W. H. Pater this term. Walked with him on Monday evening last, April 30. Fine evening bitterly cold. 'Bleak-faced Neology in cap and gown': no cap and gown but very bleak."[10] A month after this initial walk, he noted, "[a] little rain and at evening and night hard rain.—Pater talking two hours against Xtianity."[11]

Despite these outstanding disparities, a rapport between the two was established, testimony to a shared belief that "in unimpeded talk with sincere persons of what quality soever—there, rather than in shadowy converse with even the best books—the flower, the fruit, of mind was still in life-giving contact with its roots."[12] For Hopkins, one can imagine that the vaguely *avant-garde* Brasenose don represented a welcome change from the hothouse atmosphere of Balliol. From all accounts, Pater's was a gently ironic demeanour, and therefore far removed from the overtly judgmental attitudes of such would-be Pygmalions as Jowett and Liddon. As for Pater's status as a neologian, Hopkins could always look beyond a "reputation" in order to see the man for himself.

Pater's positive response to Hopkins would have been similarly multifaceted. One reason, I would suggest, was that he welcomed the opportunity to work with a genuinely bright and inquisitive pupil. Pater was always content at Brasenose, but the initial adjustment must have been considerable. Quite frankly, the college was an intellectual backwater. Balliol had Jowett, Lincoln had Mark Pattison, Christ Church had Henry Liddell—and Brasenose had its own beer.[13] "Brasenose was a college for the average man," writes John Buchan at his most diplomatic.[14] Humphry Ward, another student of Pater and a contemporary of Hopkins, is more forthright: "It must be owned that the Brasenose undergraduates of my standing were for the most part not clever. . . . [T]hey toiled at games and played at books."[15] Small wonder that Pater would enjoy working with promising young men sent to him by Jowett and others.

Friendship with Hopkins was a fortuitous and mutually gratifying result of a diligent and enriching academic association. Hopkins's eagerness to absorb Paterian ideas, the alacrity with which he adopted some of his tutor's phraseology, is demonstrated in many ways. Within two months of meeting his new instructor, "as Pater says" had become a popular qualifying statement. Advising a friend about holiday plans in late June 1866, Hopkins remarks, "Folkstone is a sorry place. . . . The Sussex downs are seductive as Pater says, if there is a church."[16] A year and a half later, Hopkins begins his "Notes on Greek philosophy,"[17] with outlines for the lessons he is to teach at the Birmingham Oratory School, with the following generalization: "Great feature of the old Gk. philosophy, Pater said, its holding certain truths, chiefly logical, out of proportion to the rest of its knowledge."[18] His favourite Paterian verb and participle are "to colour" and "colouring"; the adjective most admired is "strange"; the most adaptable Pater term is "undercurrent," which was transformed into Hopkins's "underthought."

Among the Hopkins manuscripts at Campion Hall are fourteen notebooks from his undergraduate days: journals which include notes from lectures, quotations from various authors, and forty-five essays for such tutors as Jowett, Pater, and T. H. Green. No notebook is so formally identified as D.III, the inside front cover of which is inscribed "Essays/ for W. H. Pater Esq./ Gerard M. Hopkins."

As Hopkins must have quickly learned, Pater relished the "really large and adventurous possibilities" of the essay form. For him, as for

Plato, it represented "a voyage of discovery."[19] What we have in Hopkins's D.III notebook are six such voyages, navigated (with varying degrees of success) according to the following charts: "The origin of our moral ideas"; "Plato's view of the connection of art and education"; "The Pagan and Christian virtues"; "The relation of Plato's Dialectic to modern logic and metaphysics"; "Shew cases in wh[ich] acts of apprehension apparently simple are largely influenced by the imagination"; and "The history and mutual connection in ancient ethics of the following questions—Can virtue be taught? Are virtue and vice severally voluntary and involuntary?" A. C. Benson states that Pater would often ask for the essays in advance of the tutorial, at which time he would discuss "his careful verdicts as to the style and arrangement."[20] This information is based on the recollections of Humphry Ward, who also states that Pater " 'was severe on confusions of thought, and still more so on any kind of rhetoric. An emphatic word or epithet was sure to be underscored, and the absolutely right phrase suggested'."[21] Of the six essays in D.III, only the first has been subjected to Pater's pencil. The underscoring is quite extensive, however, as might be expected with a first assignment, when both pupil and teacher take pains to impress. Pater's discrete underlining implicitly queries both what is said ("the chain of morals fr[om] one age to another is de facto and a succession") and how it is said ("so to call it," "much exception").

Often, Pater would not set a subject for the essay, preferring instead that the student select a topic "in which he was interested."[22] Some of the titles quoted above cover traditional Greats material. The Plato papers follow the general course charted in Benjamin Jowett's lists for student essays, and as such suggest that the new Brasenose tutor was trying to emulate his own teachers.[23] Aesthetic questions reflect the preoccupations of both student and tutor. Overall, the papers hint at the range and orientation of lectures on the history of philosophy which Pater began presenting at "the end of 1866 or beginning of 1867."[24] They also anticipate, quite strikingly at times, the formalized lectures later published as *Plato and Platonism*, and therefore help to correct the view that Pater's interpretation of Plato was wildly idiosyncratic. For the purposes of my discussion, I would like to comment on the essays and their constant interplay with Paterian ideas and texts according to a very basic itinerary: the papers dealing with moral philosophy (D.III.1, 3, and 6) will be considered first, then the arguments about metaphysics (D.III.4), and finally, deliberations on aesthetic matters (D.III.2 and 5).

For the same reasons that they preferred their aesthetics to be grounded on moral criteria, most Victorians emphasized the moral dimensions and ramifications of philosophy. Throughout his undergraduate notebooks Hopkins rehearses the crucial debates of classical and contemporary philosophy; the essays for Pater are distinguished by the range of comparisons the student feels compelled to consider (Plato and John Stuart Mill, Heraclitus and Marcus Aurelius), and the attention paid, at all times, to "first principles," questions which, according to D.III.6, "go very much to the bottom of things."[25] "First principles" was both a favourite phrase and a *modus operandi* for Pater; he embraced the dialectic "in all its forms" because, to quote *Plato and Platonism*, it constituted "a dialogue, an endless dialogue, with one's self; a dialogue concerning those first principles, or 'universal definitions', or notions, those 'ideas', which, according to Plato, are the proper objects of all real knowledge."[26]

"The origin of our moral ideas" is both the longest essay for Pater, and the most diffuse. Classical sources are cited or alluded to several times, but Hopkins is primarily interested in refuting Utilitarian theory, "which makes morality lie in what attains or tends towards attaining the greatest happiness for the greatest number."[27] Not only does Hopkins question the objectivist stance of the utilitarians, he also faults them for failing to realize that "the things which we consider most absolutely excellent in point of morality . . . are not the earliest but the latest in point of apprehension. . . . [C]ivilisation is always trying to realise to itself morality in .more and more disinterested, that is absolute, manifestations."[28] The latter sentences take on heightened significance when compared with Pater's essay on "Coleridge's Writings," in which praise for Coleridge's poetry is juxtaposed with a frank, disapproving critique of his theological and philosophical speculations, his "passion for the absolute." The article begins with deceptively general comments about the changing "currents" of "intellectual and spiritual culture," then proceeds to a direct statement of very un-Coleridgean dicta: "Modern thought is distinguished from ancient by its cultivation of the 'relative' spirit in place of the 'absolute.' Ancient philosophy sought to arrest every object in an eternal outline, to fix thought in a necessary formula, and types of life in a classification of 'kinds' or genera. To the modern spirit nothing is or can be rightly known except relatively under conditions."[29] Coleridge was therefore anachronistic in his frequent "attempts to reduce a phase of thought subtle and exquisite to conditions too rough for it . . . to fix [scientific truth] in absolute formulas."[30] He was also too limited in his theological views, according to Pater, because "Coleridge thinks that if we reject the supernatural, the spiritual element in life will evaporate also, that we shall have to accept a life with narrow horizons, without disinterestedness, harshly cut off from the springs of life in the past."[31] Hopkins is clearly trying to challenge Pater's argument on its own terms. When he considers "the questions into wh. the discussion of the spring of moral ideas will throw itself," he can only conclude that "the utilitarian formula requires much exception."[32]

Of all of Coleridge's so-called "arguments," the one which Pater was most reluctant to refute concerned unity. Simply by reading the quotations which he cites in the article one rediscovers a crucial source for the emerging aesthetic of Pater and Hopkins. This is especially true of the fragment from *Aids to Reflection* which states, "[i]n the world, we see everywhere evidences of a unity, which the component parts are so far from explaining, that they necessarily presuppose it as the cause and condition of their existing as those parts, or even of their existing at all."[33] In late 1865 and 1866, Pater was still wrangling with the implications of this notion. Although his mature art criticism is grounded on the belief that "the unity of the thing with itself"[34] is paramount, his early philosophical essays reveal a hesitancy towards the "constraining" forces of unity. Hopkins, on the other hand, accepted wholeheartedly the arguments for unity. His first essay for Pater concludes with this ringing endorsement: "All thought is of course in a sense an effort a[t] unity. This may be pursued analytically as in science or synthetically as in art or morality. In art it is essential to recognise and to strive to realise on a more or less wide basis this unity in some shape or other. It seems also that the desire for unity, for the ideal, is the only definition wh. will satisfy the historical phenomena of morality."[35] On this point at least the pupil's thinking was more settled and harmonious than the teacher's.

Thanks largely to Kant and Coleridge, the subject-object antinomy had become a staple of the British intellectual diet by mid-century, a "distinction," to quote D.III.4, "understood widely and reappearing in all discussions."[36] Jowett, however, stressed its absence in the ethical teachings of Socrates and Plato.[37] When the phrase "objective and subjective" is first employed in D.III.1, Pater underlines it, perhaps to indicate that further explication is needed. Hopkins tries to explain all of his terminology in D.III.3, "The Pagan and Christian virtues":

> One is struck by the different values given by Xtianity and paganism to what wd. be called the subjective and objective sides of morality. We cannot but recognise the vast benefit gained fr. the distinctions of will and deed or conscience and law . . . which Xtianity has established when we turn to the ethics of the ancients and see the slow and incomplete unwinding of moral from mental excellences and the far greater prominence given to the fulfillment of the outward ideal of right conduct.[38]

By the time Hopkins composed this third essay for Pater, they had obviously grown comfortable enough in each other's company to confront their differences openly. Pater's strident attacks on the "Christian religion" in the 1860s are exemplified in "Coleridge's Writings." The article applauds those "who have passed out of Christianity"; it insists categorically that "[t]he Catholic church and humanity are two powers that divide the intellect and the spirit of man."[39] Nothing could be more antithetical to this position than the support for Christian morality in general and Catholicism in particular voiced in Hopkins's essay "On Pagan and Christian Values." Even the most enlightened pagans, Hopkins argues, defined their morality and their virtues in terms of the state, the public good, "not with the individual."[40] Hopkins contrasts this at some length with Christianity, in which "the all-important relation is to God."[41]

In D.III.1 and again in D.III.3 Hopkins refers to Plato's "remarkable" belief that "goodness was knowledge, vice ignorance"[42]—an issue that Jowett always stressed in his lectures.[43] Pater asked Hopkins for a detailed analysis of the proposition, no doubt mindful that such a topic was standard Greats material. Accordingly, Hopkins assembled his thoughts on: "The history and mutual connection in ancient ethics of the following questions—Can virtue be taught? Are virtue and vice severally voluntary and involuntary?"—questions posed in Plato's *Meno*, *Protagoras*, and the *Apology*. Hopkins's essay draws on primary sources, "Jowetry," and George Grote's seminal study, *Plato, and the Other Companions of Sokrates*; Pater's complementary analysis is found in the third chapter of *Plato and Platonism*.

Although the substance of Hopkins's argument is very traditional, the epistemological strategies he must entertain reflect once again the contemporary debate about the relative or non-relative nature of human knowledge. While pursuing these pivotal questions in Plato, Hopkins discovered not one but several contrary expressions of thought. He responded: "It is to be observed that contradiction of this sort matters little: the point is not whether Plato in some places surrenders an opinion . . . but whether an opinion is treated strongly enough to appear one of the currents which draw his thought. His irony and the suspension of judgment which after all he allows on great questions, as Goethe did too, make us not wish to press him to a conclusion."[44] (The comparison between Plato and Goethe which springs to mind is a very Paterian gesture.) Hopkins's remarks are typical of what one could call the Oxford approach to Plato, a sage man who, to quote Pater, "in spite of the demand he makes for certainty and exactness and what is absolute, in all real knowledge," believes that knowledge remains somewhat "elusive, provisional, contingent, a matter of various approximations."[45] Pater too cites the master's irony and humour as touchstones of "Plato's actual method of learning and teaching," a method which embodies "what is still sometimes understood to be the 'academic spirit', surveying all sides, arraying evidence, ascertaining, measuring, balancing, tendencies, but ending in suspension of judgment."[46] Pater was very comfortable with such an approach—some would say, too comfortable. Hopkins on the other hand demonstrated from youth an obverse need to make and then act upon firm judgments. Accordingly, D.III.6 concludes with this statement: "But with or without irony it cd. not be avoided that Plato's ethical system shd. be criticised after his time and be forced to the conclusions which it suggests. This is done by Aristotle."[47]

Walter Pater was similar in many ways to the Giordano Bruno he recreated for *Gaston de Latour*, a man who "was careful to warn off the vulgar from applying the decisions of philosophy beyond its proper speculative limits."[48] What Pater always asked of his students was that they discover for themselves these philosophical boundaries. In Hopkins's case, the process was fully under way when he composed D.III.4, "The relations of Plato's Dialectic to modern logic and metaphysics." The essay builds upon the translation of the *Philebus* which Hopkins undertook for Jowett in Lent term 1866.[49] For Pater, however, Hopkins turns from the *Philebus* to the more difficult and intellectually challenging *Symposium*,[50] retracing the steps from the love of mortal beauty to the love and "knowledge of the beautiful itself"[51] first outlined for Socrates by the Mantinean Sibyl. In this "process of abstraction," Hopkins blithely insists, "the concrete [is] plainly being cast aside at each step of the ascent."[52] Pater would have vehemently challenged this point for two reasons: first, because he always privileged the concrete over the abstract; and secondly, because he believed that Socrates and Plato, masters of "visual expression"[53] and keen appreciators of the concrete world, achieved an understanding of the concrete within the Idea parallel to their concept of the Many within the One. The proof of Pater's persuasiveness is found in the argument which Hopkins puts forward in D.XII, the Birmingham commentary written some months after D.III.4. These notes begin by re-examining the concrete's relationship to the abstract:

> Great feature of the old Gk. philosophy, Pater said, its holding certain truths, chiefly logical, out of proportion to the rest of its knowledge, as Parmenides his dialectic abt. Being and Not-Being, Zeno the contradictions involved in Motion, the Meharians and Heracleitus the difficulties of identity. The explanation of this perhaps is that they argued on the Idea alone, on the thought at its first blush, unrealised. This is not the same thing as saying, what is obviously true, that they argued in abstractions without referring to the concrete, because that is just leaving the question open whether abstractions exist apart in any way fr. the concrete, of Nominalism and Realism in their merely logical bearing in fact. The Idea, it is to be remembered, is not the abstraction, indeed it is as much the concrete as the abstract and exists before the universal has been abstracted from the particulars and the particulars realised in the universal.[54]

He has definitely conceded Pater's argument, yet characteristically he draws the line between an appreciation of the material, concrete world and materialism itself. Hopkins goes on in D.XII.1 to distinguish between himself and those "grimed with the concrete," the Comtean positivists.[55]

This reference to Comte enables us to clarify our understanding of what Pater did *not* say about Positivism. Although he shared with Comte a belief in the relativity of knowledge, "there is no evidence," to quote Billie Inman, that Comte "ever had a strong influence on Pater."[56] When Pater does refer to Comte in the 1868 essay "Poems by William Morris," it is to warn his readers that "what we have to do is to be for ever curiously testing opinion and courting new impressions, never acquiescing in a facile orthodoxy of Comte or of Hegel or of our own."[57] If Hopkins's differentiation between Pater and Positivism is not made clear, then one of his best undergraduate essays, "The probable future of metaphysics,"[58] is likely to be misread. Written for T. H. Green in the term just preceding the Greats exam (spring 1867), when Pater was probably still coaching Hopkins, the paper defends metaphysics against a series of would-be usurpers, most especially psychology and Comtean sociology. Hopkins marshalls support from John Grote, Mill, and Hegel to counter the argument that "the end of all metaphysics is at hand."[59] He begins by refuting the Positivists, and saves until last the Paterian philosophy of flux.

"The probable future of metaphysics," I would suggest, constitutes Hopkins's response to some of the primary ideas expressed in Pater's essay on Winckelmann published in January 1867,[60] and to the theory of flux described in "Coleridge's Writings." From his first essay to his last, Pater eschewed metaphysics and "all dead metaphysical philosophies."[61] It is "easy to indulge the commonplace metaphysical instinct," he observes in "Winckelmann," "[b]ut a taste for metaphysics may be one of those things which we must renounce, if we mean to mould our lives to artistic perfection. Philosophy serves culture, not by the fancied gift of absolute or transcendental knowledge, but by suggesting questions which help one to detect the passion, and strangeness, and dramatic contrasts of life."[62] In these remarks Pater is seconding Benjamin Jowett, who "protested" with "vehemence," a student recalls, that "the chief use of metaphysics is to get rid of metaphysics altogether."[63]

Modern thought has abandoned the pursuit of the absolute, Pater insists in "Coleridge's Writings"; instead, the relative spirit, the spirit of the Heraclitean flux, is being cultivated. As further proof of his argument, Pater links the relative spirit with the wisdom of Hegel and Darwin to try to demonstrate that the "inexpressible refinements of change"[64] are common to moral philosophy, the sciences, and the arts. "Forms of intellectual and spiritual culture," he observes, "often exercise their subtlest and most artful charm when life is already passing from them. . . . Nature, which by one law of development evolves ideas, moralities, modes of inward life, and represses them in turn, has in this way provided that the earlier growth should propel its fibres into the later, and so transmit the whole of its forces in an unbroken continuity."[65] Pater's use of the term "continuity" may seem mystifying, because we no longer associate it with the concept of flux. Hopkins, however, was very familiar with the connection. In the latter half of "The probable future of metaphysics," he brings forward several points to "challenge the prevalent philosophy of continuity or flux."[66] The current philosophical "season" of "Hegel and the philosophy of development in time," he remarks, is characterized by "the ideas of Historical Development, of things both in thought and fact detaching and differencing and individualising and expressing themselves, of continuity and of time."[67] Taking up Pater's argument about Nature, Hopkins acknowledges that "[t]o the prevalent philosophy and science nature is a string[,] all the differences in which are really chromatic but certain places in it have become accidentally. . . fixed and the series of fixed points becomes an arbitrary scale."[68] However, he asserts, there are non-arbitrary, timeless forms in the realms of nature, art, and ideas which transcend the flux:

> [T]here are certain forms wh. have a great hold on the mind and are always reappearing and seem imperishable, such as the designs of Greek vases and lyres,. . .the fleur-de-lys, while every day we see designs both simple and elaborate wh. do not live and are at once forgotten; and some pictures we may long look at and never grasp or hold together, while the composition of others strikes the mind with a conception of unity wh. is never dislodged: and these things are inexplicable on the theory of pure chromatism or continuity—the forms have in some sense or other an absolute existence.[69]

One of the more remarkable features of this passage—a prototype for Hopkins's theory of "inscape"—is that Hopkins has used elements of Pater's own argument to contradict his tutor. It is in the same "Winckelmann" essay which sounds the death-knell of metaphysics that Pater celebrates the timeless beauty, repose, and "centrality" of Greek sculpture and praises any work of art in which we find "the clear ring of a central motive. We receive from it the impression of one imaginative tone, of a single creative act."[70] Pater was far more tolerant of inconsistencies in his thoughts and work than Hopkins was.

The primary point to be made concerning Hopkins's undergraduate essays on aesthetics is that the majority of the papers—and the best—were not written for Pater. This surprises us until we remember that Pater only gradually discovered his talents and tendencies in art criticism; his first public displays of combative erudition focused on philosophical subjects. Nonetheless, we are grateful for such Hopkins essays as "On the rise of Greek prose-writing,"[71] "On the signs of health and decay in the arts,"[72] and "On the true idea and excellence of sculpture"[73]—all composed before Hopkins met Pater—because they retrace the gestation of many aesthetic concepts with which both young men tried to wrestle. Principally, they direct us to the preoccupations and pedagogy of Jowett, for whom these essays were written. It was Jowett who lectured to both of them on the relevance of Lessing, Kant, and Hegel, and who always cast his arguments in terms of such antithetical pairs as Classical and Romantic, objective and subjective, centripetal and centrifugal. It was also Jowett who used sculptural metaphors to explain the unsurpassed artistry of Plato's prose style, his "perfect perception of the plastic power of words."[74] One Jowett lecture, entitled "On the style of Plato," stresses that the "manliness + simplicity," the "self restraint" of Classical art is also to be found in the best philosophical literature:

> You may look at a Greek statue and be struck with the flexure of the limbs, the majestic folds of the drapery, the simplicity, the strength; And yet scarcely any topics arise in the mind of the uncritical [viewer], only when the difference is pointed out to him between such work as the Venus Victrise and some muse of the Augustan age or later, with its flattened [paste *del.*] cardboard looking face and thin creased robe he sees a separation not of degree but of kind. The highest art is colourless like water, it has been said; it is a surface without prominences or irregularities over which the eye wanders impressed by the beauty of the whole with nothing to detain it at a particular point.
>
> The same image about style—colourless as water. Criticism cannot analyse but only imperfectly describe it. It is a smooth surface over which the hand may pass without interruption, but the curious work lies beneath the surface: the effect only is seen from without. The finer the workmanship the more completely is the art concealed.[75]

In this way Jowett alerted his auditors to the excellences of Greek sculpture and provided a peculiarly apt frame of reference for judging Plato's classical style—lessons that neither Pater nor Hopkins forgot.

Remarks in D.III.1 to the effect that "the clearest and most disinterested appreciation of beauty" comes from "education"[76] lead directly to essay D.III.2, "Plato's view of the connection of art and education." Pater may have been hoping that his pupil would challenge some of Plato's precepts, particularly the decision to banish poets from the commonwealth, but Hopkins refrains from doing so. Instead, he affirms previous arguments about the need for unity in art and morality, stressing that Plato depends upon music, drama, and poetry "to preserve unity in the distracting multiplicity of life."[77]

On the surface D.III.2 seems to contribute little to our further understanding of the intellectual exchange enjoyed by Pater and Hopkins. However, the education which Plato advocated consisted of two basic courses of instruction: *gymnasia* and *mousika*. The last, as George Grote explains, "includes all training by means of words or sounds: speech and song, recital and repetition, reading and writing. . . ."[78] Therefore, what we have in D.III.2 is an essay in which Hopkins reminds Pater that music, by virtue of *harmonia*, is the pattern of all the arts, and that the arts, like morals, contribute to and reflect the inner unity of humankind. Pater himself makes the latter point in *Marius the Epicurean*, when he observes that "the old Greek morality again, with all its imperfections, was certainly a comely thing—Yes! a harmony, a music, in man's ways, one might well hesitate to jar."[79] However, it is his recapitulation of the former point for which he is best remembered: "*All art constantly aspires towards the condition of music.*"[80] Various sources have been suggested for Pater's most pregnant and provocative axiom. Hopkins's essay reminds us that Plato was among the first to probe the metaphorical potential of music, as well as its formal properties. As Pater summarizes in *Plato and Platonism*, "accordingly, in education, all will begin and end in 'music', in the promotion of qualities to which no truer name can be given than symmetry, aesthetic fitness, tone. Philosophy itself, indeed, as he conceives it, is but the sympathetic appreciation of a kind of music in the very nature of things."[81]

Of all the essays in D.III, the only one that must have disappointed pupil and tutor alike was D.III.5, "Shew cases in wh. acts of apprehension apparently simple are largely influenced by the imagination." The initial paragraphs are quite promising: Hopkins attempts to distinguish between "Locke's sense of our consciousness"[82] and "Kantian" distinctions between imagination "in the logical sense, for conceiving" and imagination as "the faculty of art production."[83] But what eludes him is the point at which sensation becomes "influenced" by the intangible imagination. Consequently he soon becomes sidetracked by logical distinctions, and eventually abandons the assignment with the remark, "I now see this is not the subject of the essay."[84]

Hopkins was assigned this topic, I would suggest, to allow him to grapple with the same sensation-perception-imagination matrix which Pater himself tried to address in "Coleridge's Writings." Before evaluating the way in which Coleridge "weaves" into his own philosophy "Kant's finespun theory of the transformation of sense into perception," Pater pauses to expound his own views: "What every theory of perception has to explain is that associative power which gathers isolated sensible qualities into the objects of the world about us. Sense, without associative power, would be only a threadlike stream of colours, sounds, odours—each struck upon one for a moment and then withdrawn."[85] Coleridge's borrowed theory, he goes on to argue, fails to account for the fact that "this power of association, of concentrating many elements of sense in a object of perception, is refined and deepened into the creative acts of the imagination."[86]

To conclude my overview of Pater's intertextual presence in Hopkins's thinking and writing, I would like to pursue the Paterian "under-currents" informing Hopkins's theory of "inscape." Ruskin of course initially inspired both young men to identify and appreciate the beauty and science of form, the essential organic pattern (or "law") within the cloud, cathedral, or painting. Yet Hopkins was also privy to the ways in which Pater offset the lessons of *Modern Painters* with Platonic theory and Hegel's *Ästhetik*. Ruskin's immediate focus was landscape painting and the natural world; Pater's interests were both broader, in cultural terms, and different, because art for him was essentially artifice—a restructuring of sensation and emotions into a foreign medium made possible by the artist's recognition of the "hidden causes" of life and motion, the "truth of nature" underneath the "visible surface."[87] "The demand of the intellect is to feel itself alive," he wrote during the months he was coaching Hopkins: "[i]t must see into the laws, the operation, the intellectual reward of every divided form of culture; but only that it may measure the relation between itself and them. It struggles with these forms until its secret is won from each, and then lets each fall back into its place, in the supreme, artistic view of life."[88] What is Hopkins's search for inscapes in tress, bluebells, and sonnets but an engagement with their essential forms until the secrets of pattern and structure are won from each?

Soon after meeting Pater, Hopkins intensifies and refines his search for the law of aspects, and he does so with a new sensitivity to composition and form, sensation and impression. The terms "inscape" and "instress" may have sprung fully grown from his mind, but their final theoretical gestation is recorded in D.XII. As previously mentioned, these "Notes on Gk. Philosophy" begin with a review of Pater's thoughts on the subject, his essential lessons about the Idea and form. Then, on 9 February 1868, Hopkins combines the Ruskinian notion of "relation" with Pater's emphasis on expression, impression, prepossession,[89] and form to puzzle out the meaning of words and works of art. His conclusion: "The further in anything, as a work of art, the organisation is carried out, the deeper the form penetrates, the prepossession [of feeling] fuses the matter, the more effort will be required in apprehension, the more power of comparison, the more capacity for receiving that synthesis . . . [of] impression which gives us the unity with the prepossession conveyed by it."[90] These animadversions on "words" then give way to a series of notes on pre-Socratic philosophers, the second of which, "Parmenides," introduces and explains the terms "inscape" and "instress." Only when Hopkins understands for himself the relationship between impression, form, and inscape, does he truly comprehend the origins of beauty.

The essential paradigm of intertextuality outlined in this discussion is one of *answering*. Exposure to Pater's conversations and published works catalyzed Hopkins's thinking and writing—often in antithetical directions. The "underthoughts" which link Hopkins's canon to Pater's are verbal witnesses to a very rare phenomenon: a friendship, an understanding and rapport based upon personal and intellectual ties lessened by time but never severed. As *Marius the Epicurean* explains, "the saint, and the Cyrenaic lover of beauty, it may be thought, would at least understand each other better than either would understand the mere man of the world. Carry their respective positions a point further, shift the terms a little, and they might actually touch."[91]

Pater Speaking Bloom Speaking Joyce

8

F. C. MCGRATH

PATER'S THEORY OF STYLE was essentially Hegelian and expression-istic.[1] For Hegel all art was the sensuous manifestation of the absolute Idea. In adapting Hegel Pater typically ignored his emphasis on the absolute Idea and limited art to expressing the individual mind of the artist. Style for Pater was the external expression of an inner vision, an inner vision he characterized as the writer's "imaginative sense of fact."[2] Furthermore, he insisted on an absolute fidelity to that inner vision and on the precise accommodation of language to it.

Pater's expressive orientation, however, also anticipated contem-porary Heideggerian attitudes towards language as constitutive of expression.[3] Pater was fond of saying, "Style is the man." In his monograph on Pater, Ian Fletcher provides an effective gloss on this statement when he says that style for Pater was "a mode of perception, a total responsive gesture of the whole personality."[4] Without much effort or distortion, I think we can push Pater's notion of style even further towards its Heideggerian conclusion and give it a post-modern turn by looking at Pater's own style in the context of the stylistic experiments of Joyce in the second half of *Ulysses*, particularly Joyce's parody of Pater in the "Oxen of the Sun" episode.

Joyce was one of a number of Modernists who was profoundly influenced by Pater's views on style and language and who continued

95

to develop them. In *Ulysses* there appear to be two views of style contending with each other. One is a modernist view that is very close to Pater's expressive ideal. According to this view each character has a distinct style of expression and these various modes of expression provide multiple perspectives on the experiences portrayed in the novel. Joyce uses the metaphor of parallax throughout *Ulysses* to suggest this notion of multiple perspectives. Parallax refers to the apparent displacement of a heavenly body when viewed from two divergent points on the earth's surface.

Both Joyce and Pater realized that multiple perspectives did not amount to absolute or complete knowledge of anything. No work of art can exhaust all possible contexts or perspectives, for they are theoretically infinite. There is always another perspective, another way of looking at something, another style of seeing it. In *Plato and Platonism* Pater says that room "must be left to the last in any legitimate dialectical process for possible after-thoughts; for the introduction, so to speak, of yet another interlocutor in the dialogue." "Another turn in the endless road," Pater adds, "may change the whole character of the perspective."[5]

The second half of *Ulysses* is nothing but one turn in the road after another. Every episode shifts perspective dramatically and, except for Molly's concluding monologue, the characters' individual styles of expression become subsumed under a bewildering variety of discourse forms, what Bakhtin calls incorporated genres: in the "Cyclops" episode we see things through most of the printed sources available to the average middle-class Dubliner; in "Nausicaa" we see Bloom through the eyes of Gerty McDowell, or rather through her language, the language of sentimental romances; in "Circe" everything is altered by the hallucinatory effect of dream work; in "Eumaeus" we stumble through an old man's tired prose; in "Ithaca" we submit to a catechistical inquisition of scientific discourse.

In the "Oxen of the Sun" episode the stylistic pluralism of *Ulysses* achieves its most extensive form. Here a series of parodies proceeds through the history of English prose style from its Latin and medieval roots to modern slang. The point of the "Oxen" parodies has been construed in a number of ways: to suggest the evolution of English prose style;[6] to add to while enclosing all previous English prose (a very Hegelian notion);[7] to make words reproduce objects and processes;[8] to suggest the provisional nature of any one style;[9] to suggest the limits of English prose style;[10] to expose the inadequacy or futility of English prose style;[11] to chart the decay of English prose style;[12] to exhibit language as pure system;[13] to discredit the category of style as such.[14] Deconstructionists would say that the "Oxen" parodies suggest the ultimate displacement and indeterminateness of all discourse.

I would like to suggest another possibility that links the parodies of "Oxen" with the parodies and styles of all the other episodes in *Ulysses*, and that is to view style not merely as a way of perceiving but as a way of constituting what we see. In this sense style could be compared not so much to a mirror (as in classical mimetic theories) or to a lens that colors or distorts (as in Romantic expressionistic theories), but rather to a scientific instrument designed to detect or measure something we cannot observe directly, such as the wave-length of light or the behavior of atomic particles. As such an instrument of perception, style not only makes things appear but also determines how they appear. This post-modern view of style is adumbrated by Pater and brought to fruition in the second half of *Ulysses*.

Joyce critics have long noticed how repetitious the "Oxen" episode is. Many details and material that appear elsewhere in the novel, especially in episodes that come before "Oxen," appear in the different narrative styles of "Oxen" itself. In one sense, this repetition creates the possibility of multiple perspectives, or the parallax effect. The metaphor of parallax and the notion of multiple perspectives, however, do not adequately account for the stylistic effects of these incorporated genres.[15] These languages, these forms of discourse, are instruments of perception that give us access to what otherwise would remain unseen in *Ulysses*. In other words, they make things appear, and through the repetitions we observe not so much the same things from different perspectives as different things that bear varying degrees of resemblance to each other.

It might be useful to consider the analogy of two artists painting a person's portrait. Do they see the same person? Did Wyndham Lewis and Brancusi, for instance, see the same person in their drawings of Joyce?[16] Does each reader of *Ulysses* perceive the same text? It may be that in the end we have only our styles of seeing, which we often borrow from great writers like Pater.

At this point Joyce's parody of Pater can bring this insight into the open for us:

> The stranger [Leopold Bloom] still regarded on the face [of Stephen Dedalus] before him a slow recession of that false calm there, imposed, as it seemed, by habit or some studied trick, upon words so embittered as to accuse in their speaker an unhealthiness, a *flair*, for the cruder things of life. A scene [from eighteen years ago] disengages itself in the observer's memory, evoked, it would seem, by a word of so natural a homeliness as if those days were really present there (as some thought) with their immediate pleasures. A shaven space of lawn one soft May evening, the wellremembered grove of lilacs at Roundtown, purple and white, fragrant slender spectators of the game but with much real interest in the pellets as they run slowly forward over the sward or collide and stop, one by its fellow, with a brief alert shock. And yonder about that grey urn where the water moves at times in thoughtful irrigation you saw another as fragrant sisterhood, Floey, Atty, Tiny and their darker friend [Molly Bloom] with I know not what of arresting in her pose then, Our Lady of the Cherries, a comely brace of them pendent from an ear, bringing out the foreign warmth of the skin so daintily against the cool ardent fruit. A lad [Stephen] of four or five in linseywoolsey (blossomtime but there will be cheer in the kindly hearth when ere long the bowls are gathered and hutched) is standing on the urn secured by that circle of girlish fond hands. He frowns a little just as this young man does now with a perhaps too conscious enjoyment of the danger but must needs glance at whiles towards where his mother watches from the *piazzetta* giving upon the flowerclose with a faint shadow of remoteness or of reproach (*alles Vergängliche*) in her glad look.[17]

In this passage Joyce invokes his model in several ways: through the atmospheric effect achieved; through allusion to some of Pater's well-known texts; and by using some typical Paterian syntax, phrasing, and diction. For example, the prose is peppered with complex sentences marked by many qualifying or parenthetical phrases, such as "it would seem," "as it seemed," and "but must needs glance at whiles." Typical Paterian diction would include "wellremembered," "comely," his use of "there" in the phrase "really present there," and his sprinkling of foreign words. *Alles Vergängliche* also invokes a key Paterian idea—the fleeting nature of experience. Characteristic Paterian phrasing also would include "a perhaps too conscious enjoyment of the danger" and "the cool ardent fruit." "Fragrant sisterhood" and "linseywoolsey" are Joyce's exaggeration of Paterian diction.

But even more interesting is what Joyce does not do. He does not deploy any significant ideas of Pater beyond what is necessary to mark the passage as stereotypically Paterian. He also does not mimic some of the purple passages Pater was famous for, such as the "Conclusion" to *The Renaissance* or his description of the Mona Lisa, passages Joyce did imitate elsewhere, as in the bird-girl description in *Portrait*. Of course, Joyce had to make a few allusions to some of the more famous passages to ensure recognition of his model. He alludes, for example, to Pater's Mona Lisa, who becomes Molly Bloom characterized as "Our Lady of the Cherries." The phrase "that circle of fantastic rocks" from the Mona Lisa passage becomes "that circle of girlish fond hands." The phrase "a scene disengages itself in the observer's memory" and the reference to immediate pleasures and fleeting experience mimic ideas and phrases that can be found in essays like the "Preface" and "Conclusion" to *The Renaissance* and Pater's essay on Wordsworth. In general, however, Joyce's parody of Pater, which is typical of the other parodies in "Oxen," seems to be modelled on some of Pater's less notable descriptive passages from *Marius the Epicurean* and *Imaginary Portraits*, like those Joyce copied into his notebooks during 1919 and 1920 while he was working on the "Oxen" episode.[18] Compare, for example, Marius's first view of Marcus Aurelius with the description of Stephen in Joyce's parody: "The nostrils and mouth seemed capable almost of peevishness; and Marius noted in them, as in the hands, and in the spare body generally, what was new to his experience—something of asceticism, as we say, of a bodily gymnastic, by which, although it

told pleasantly in the clear blue humours of the eye, the flesh had
scarcely been an equal gainer with the spirit."[19] Or a description from
"Duke Carl of Rosenmold" with the parody's description of Mrs.
Dedalus: "From the comfortless portico, with all the grotesqueness of
the Middle Age, supported by brown, aged bishops, whose meditations
no incident could distract, Our Lady looked out no better than an
unpretending nun, with nothing to say the like of which one was used
to hear."[20] Or this description from "A Prince of Court Painters" with
the parody's description of the lawn scene: ". . . 'The evening will be
a wet one'. The storm is always brooding through the massy splendour
of the trees, above those sun-dried glades or lawns, where delicate
children may be trusted thinly clad; and the secular trees themselves will
hardly outlast another generation."[21]

Joyce's preference for Pater's quieter prose rather than his purple
passages had precedents in Lionel Johnson and George Saintsbury.
Johnson preferred the "passionate simplicity of tone" in *Marius* and the
"finely-wrought miniatures" of *Imaginary Portraits*, while Saintsbury
admired Pater's quiet rhythms more than the purple prose of the Mona
Lisa passage.[22] Joyce is known to have used Saintsbury's *A History of
English Prose Rhythm* while he was composing "Oxen of the Sun," and
the passage Saintsbury chooses from *Marius* is one of those Joyce
copied into his notebook.

By choosing less notable descriptive passages, Joyce could appropriate the signs or stylistic markers of Pater (the sentence structure,
characteristic phrases, allusions, and atmospheric effect), but emptied of
any significant content. Roland Barthes has noted how when myth
appropriates signs it "prefers to work with poor, incomplete images,
where the meaning is already relieved of its fat, and ready for a
signification, such as caricatures, pastiches, symbols, etc."[23] Signs,
however, as Barthes has demonstrated, are not transparent, and they can
never be completely emptied of their prior content. There is always a
residue. But by choosing other than famous passages, Joyce could
minimize the historical residue of the content and focus more on the
pure effects of style. Pater himself preferred landscape paintings where

the subject matter "counts for so little" and could be more readily shaped to the artist's inner mood and vision.[24] These overall effects of style, then, become the focus of the "Oxen" episode more so than the stylistic markers themselves.

One of the most typical effects of Pater's style, despite his reputation as a priest of sensory experience, is to rarify what he describes, to aestheticize it. Pater himself captures the spirit of his own prose in his characterization of William Morris's "aesthetic poetry" as "a finer ideal, extracted from what in relation to any actual world is already an ideal."[25] A passage from this early essay on Morris aptly illustrates the effect I am referring to. Calling Morris a "Hellenist of the middle age,"[26] Pater dwells upon the shading of religion "into sensuous love, and sensuous love into religion" that was evident in the tension between the "mystic passion" of medieval religion and the "rebellious flesh" of the great romantic lovers, such as Lancelot and Abelard.[27] According to Pater, this tension resulted in a "beautiful disease or disorder of the senses," which he captures in his description of typical lovers of the Middle Ages:

> Here, under this strange complex of conditions, as in some medicated air, exotic flowers of sentiment expand, among people of a remote and unaccustomed beauty, somnambulistic, frail, androgynous, the light almost shining through them, as the flame of a little taper shows through the Host. Such loves were too fragile and adventurous to last more than for a moment.[28]

This passage, fragile, precious, exotic, rarefied, and ritualistic itself, expresses a great deal of the Paterian temperament. This rarefied sensuousness, almost drained of its blood, diaphanous as it were, so that a taper's flame would shine through it, is an important quality of Pater's own sensibility.

Joyce captures this effect of Pater's style superbly, an effect that is readily apparent if we compare parts of the Pater parody to renditions of similar material elsewhere in *Ulysses*. For example, compare how Pater's style characterizes Stephen Dedalus's dissolute lifestyle with how the style of John Wyclif characterizes it earlier in the "Oxen" episode.

Thinking in Pater's style Bloom notes that Stephen used "words so embittered as to accuse in their speaker an unhealthiness, a *flair*, for the cruder things of life."[29] The style of Wyclif, on the other hand, is much more direct and specific. It says that Stephen "lived riotously with those wastrels and murdered his goods with whores."[30] Wyclif's characterization of Stephen comes at the end of a paragraph in which Bloom sadly ponders the loss of his son Rudy and grieves no less for another man's son (Stephen) who is squandering his health carousing with medical students. The passage Joyce imitates here is the parable of the prodigal son from Wyclif's translation of the Bible.[31] The phrase "murdered his goods with whores" is uttered in the parable by the jealous elder brother of the prodigal son who objects to his father's joyous celebration of the fallen son's return. Even in Joyce's context of Bloom grieving for his lost son, the phrase retains its tone of judgment and condemnation. Moreover, the phrase is quite specific if not graphic about the dissolute son's offences.

In the Pater parody Bloom again is contemplating Stephen, but the father's sorrow and the judgmental tone are gone. The unhealthiness becomes a decadent flair for the cruder things of life. What those cruder things are remains vague and undefined. In other words, Stephen is no longer the guilty black sheep returned to the fold. Moreover, Stephen no longer inhabits a moral universe. His misdeeds are not sins to be forgiven but rather a style to be flaunted; the prodigal son becomes an Oscar Wilde. The observer too undergoes a transformation. He is no longer the forgiving father who welcomes his prodigal child home, but a detached aesthetic observer trying to capture in an expressive phrase, *un mot juste*, the look and tone of the object observed. We have moved from a moral universe of sin and forgiveness to a decadent aesthetic universe where manners and morals are matters of style and precise phrasing. The atmosphere has changed and both the observer and the observed have become transformed. In a very real sense, the context and all the elements within it have been reconstituted.

To take another example, compare how Bloom describes a scene in his own voice with how he describes it in the style of Pater. Here is a passage from the "Hades" episode in Bloom's own voice. As in the Pater passage, Bloom is remembering a social gathering that took place about eighteen years previously at Mat Dillon's, where the men were bowling on the lawn:

> Mat Dillon's long ago. Jolly Mat. Convivial evenings. Cold fowl, cigars, the Tantalus glasses. Heart of gold really. Yes, Menton. Got his rag out that evening on the bowlinggreen because I sailed inside him. Pure fluke of mine: the bias. Why he took such a rooted dislike to me. Hate at first sight. Molly and Floey Dillon linked under the lilactree, laughing. Fellow always like that, mortified if women are by.[32]

Now compare this passage of Bloom speaking Bloom with Pater speaking Bloom from "Oxen":

> A scene disengages itself in the observer's memory, evoked, it would seem, by a word of so natural a homeliness as if those days were really present there (as some thought) with their immediate pleasures. A shaven space of lawn one soft May evening, the wellremembered grove of lilacs at Roundtown, purple and white, fragrant slender spectators of the game but with much real interest in the pellets as they run slowly forward over the sward or collide and stop, one by its fellow, with a brief alert shock.[33]

Notice the overall effect of these two contrasting descriptions. Notice the different choice of detail. In his own voice Bloom focuses on very specific, concrete detail—names, emotions, the english he put on the ball, and so forth. In the first version of the scene Bloom is trying to explain to himself why Menton dislikes him. Bloom speculates that it was because he embarrassed him before some women in a bowling match at Mat Dillon's. This speculation masks perhaps a more fundamental reason, Menton's anti-semitism, which Bloom prefers to ignore, as he does most anti-semitic slights he encounters throughout the day from other Dubliners.

When the scene is rendered in Pater's voice much of the specificity evaporates, especially the emotions: the bowling match almost disappears; it becomes a generic game; the balls become pellets; the participants disappear; the spectators become the lilacs; and the competitive emotions of the match are given to the lilacs and reduced to the abstract phrase "much real interest." In this instance Bloom remembers the scene in connection with Stephen rather than Menton. His relation to Stephen here, however, lacks the emotional content of the earlier recollection of Menton. As with the Paterian description of the dissolute adult Stephen, the Paterian memory of the younger Stephen is from the point of view of a detached aesthetic observer, not of someone involved in the scene. At the end of the Pater passage the child Stephen is described with the same precious quality as the description of the adult Stephen at the beginning of the passage: Stephen's frown suggests "a perhaps too conscious enjoyment of the danger"; his mother's "glad look," peering "from the *piazzetta* giving upon the flowerclose" exhibits "a faint shadow of remoteness or of reproach." The emotions here are "faint" and subdued. The diction is impressionistic, suggestively descriptive, and static. The whole scene rendered in Pater's style becomes more like a painting than an episode from Bloom's life; it has all the finery of a delicately wrought tableau and none of the emotional substance of Bloom's encounter with Menton. Instead we have a dreamy painting of an 1890s garden-party. Again the context has been transformed and all the specifics within it have been reconstituted.

At this point we might ask quite legitimately whether we could call these two descriptions versions of the same scene. They are in the sense that both descriptions refer to something that occurred at the same time and place. Because some of the details of the passages bear a certain degree of resemblance to each other, we can agree that Pater speaking Bloom and Bloom speaking Bloom are both observing an event on the bowling green at Mat Dillon's one day eighteen years ago. But do the two styles construe the same scene? The principles of focus, organization, and selection, as well as the diction, tone, and effect are completely different.

Joyce's parodies in "Oxen of the Sun" appear to suggest that different styles, as instruments of perception, do not perceive the same things. In other words, Pater speaking Bloom and Bloom speaking Bloom are not simply two ways of seeing the same scene. Rather, the different styles constitute different things that bear varying degrees of resemblance to each other.

Years ago Walton Litz said that in the view of style Joyce developed in the second half of *Ulysses* the artist creates rather than discovers the significance of things through language.[34] Surprisingly, few Joyce critics have pushed Litz's insight to the point of saying that language creates the world not just for the writer himself but for us too insofar as we use his style or styles as instruments of vision.

"Style is the man," Pater was fond of saying, and Joyce, when once asked about politics, said, "I'm only interested in style."[35] These are not the statements of narrow-minded aesthetes. From an epistemological perspective, style not only encompasses everything but constitutes everything, including the nature of our personalities and of our humanity. Things can only be made apparent, that is, made to appear, through one style or another. There is no transparent or neutral style. Derridean indeterminacy notwithstanding, language (as Heidegger has shown) makes things appear, but style, like a scientific instrument, determines how they appear. Oscar Wilde was not simply being outrageous when he said in "The Decay of Lying" that "truth is entirely and absolutely a matter of style" and that "it is style that makes us believe in a thing—nothing but style."[36] Things in themselves, as Kant pointed out, are beyond our ken; and outside of style we can know nothing of them. Style, in other words, is everything, as Joyce and Pater knew and as the "Oxen of the Sun" episode so extravagantly demonstrates.

Pater as a "Moralist"

9

PAUL TUCKER

WHILE PATER'S WORK was the object of severe moral criticism in the author's own lifetime, the tendency of more recent criticism has been to admit its moral seriousness. "Most readers today," wrote David DeLaura twenty years ago, "agree that Pater's aestheticism, for all its confusion of ethics and aesthetics, is essentially a special *morality*—not art for art's sake but art for the sake of a special conception of the perfected life."[1] There are indeed early instances of Pater's being accorded the status of "moralist" by critics, for instance by Vernon Lee in 1895.[2] But there is a marked difference between the way in which the term was applied in the past and the way in which it has been applied since the 1950s. While it used to be claimed that Pater *became* a moralist, he is now said simply to be one, but one evidently uneasy about his chosen morality.[3] The difference reflects an important change in critical attitude towards the moral conflict instanced in Pater's writing, especially in his central work, *Marius the Epicurean* (1885), all but avowedly concerned with reviewing the ethical position put forward in his first book, *Studies in the History of the Renaissance* (1873).

This element of conflict and of crisis was of course tacitly recognized by critics such as Vernon Lee who posited a transition on Pater's part from an early "aesthetic" to a later moral standpoint. But the notion of a smooth and untroubled "progression" from the one to the other

107

shows an excessive readiness to underwrite Pater's own attempts to reconcile the conflicting elements in his thought. It results in a misleadingly indefinite, unproblematic, and over-spiritualized version of his morality, as, for example, an adherence to "the conception of health and congruity in matters of the spirit."[4] Critics are now readier to acknowledge Pater's "confusion between ethics and aesthetics," and acknowledge too that the crisis announced in *Marius* remained unresolved.[5] Thus, Richard Stein has remarked that Pater's later, fictional writings record "a persistent conflict, stemming from a deep ambivalence over his first book and its doctrine of art for art's sake":

> All of Pater's fiction attempts to mediate between aesthetics and morality, to create, while defining a position distinct from Ruskin's, a new "moral aesthetic". . . . Yet his fictional attempt to moralize *The Renaissance* often seems to defeat itself. . . . [N]ew ideas emerge in Pater's late writing and yet remain subordinated within an essentially aesthetic context. . . . The dominant spirit throughout his career is the spirit of art. Pater's new moral aesthetic . . . is an aesthetic before it is a morality.[6]

A similar view has been put forward more recently still by Hilary Fraser. In a study of the relation between aesthetic and religious interests in a number of Victorian writers from Newman to Wilde, she points out how "despite their antagonism towards Ruskinian aesthetics and conventional morality, both Wilde and Pater betray a moral sensitivity in their work and are interested in exploring the possibilities for a redefinition of the moral implications of aesthetic experience."[7] Like Richard Stein, she sees the critical reception of his first book as having been a stimulus to a deepened moral concern in the later work. The decision to omit the offending "Conclusion" to *Studies in the History of the Renaissance* in the second edition (1877), and to restore it (1888) only after he had re-stated its position in *Marius* "shows a moral awareness which one would have not perhaps suspected from a reading of the earlier works, but it is a dimension which makes itself increasingly apparent in Pater's mature work."[8] Pater's is a "special moral aesthetic" derived "from his belief in a natural correlation between the beautiful and the good, and in the fundamental asceticism of human nature." His is a serious attempt "to understand the relationship between aesthetic experience and a moral system."[9] However,

> [f]or Pater, art remains the only way of life, sensibility supersedes morality. Plato's, and indeed Ruskin's, concern is to include aesthetics in an ethical system. Pater's is the assimilation of ethics to aesthetics. Moral virtue is but one beauty among many. . . . Even in his most "moral" works, every ethical principle, every ethical attitude, every religious discovery, is grounded in an aesthetic preference."[10]

And yet, "it is still true to say that Pater did perceive an ethical dimension in art. Although he denied that art bore any moral responsibility or didactic function, he nevertheless conceded that it could have a profound moral effect. . . . Even in *The Renaissance* Pater cherishes many of the deeper ethical values which art should hold for humanity."[11]

I have quoted at length from Hilary Fraser's account of Pater's "special moral aesthetic" because its somewhat tortuous character seems to me illustrative of the limitations that beset even the most recent discussion of the subject. While the element of moral conflict in Pater's position is acknowledged, too little effort is made to define that conflict. There is generally too uncritical a reliance upon key terms or categories such as "moral," "moralist," "ethics," and "ethical," and hence a tendency to replicate them without sufficiently questioning their use. One result of this situation is that it has not clearly enough been shown that the ethical crisis of the 1880s was not extrinsic but rather fully intrinsic to the positions adopted by Pater in the writings of the 1860s and 1870s.

One aim of this essay will therefore be to distinguish the two ethical directives already contained in Pater's early work. But there is another reason for the inadequacy of the common claim that Pater is a "moralist," however it is made, and this is that his aestheticism is not to be explained solely by reference to specifically ethical motives. These need to be distinguished from the theoretical or metaphysical concerns which also inform Pater's writing. This will be the essay's second aim, leading to an examination of the place of art in Pater's early aestheticism—too often taken for granted by critics.

The best way of differentiating, from a specifically ethical point of view, the two ethical directives contained in the early essays is perhaps to consider them as two distinct modes of revulsion from the deductive stringency, or variously "hard and abstract"[12] character of traditional morality. What primarily distinguishes them is that whereas the first, in reacting to the rigour of the tradition, places itself outside the traditional perspective, the second moves from within it. Thus the former objects to the constraints placed by the traditional morality on the self and its free development and opposes itself to the traditional viewpoint; the latter objects to the severity of judgment shown others, on grounds ultimately borrowed from the tradition. Each resultant counter-ethic may be associated with a particular quality or "virtue"; each has its peculiar watchword. Thus, on the one hand we get a "higher morality" of "passion," and on the other a morality of "sympathy."

Let us considert the second of these first, since even if it is the less dominant of the two it is also the more straightforward, being entirely ethical, indeed moral, in its motivations. The term "sympathy" makes its first ap-pearance in Pater's writings in the essay on Botticelli (1870):

> So just what Dante scorns as unworthy alike of heaven and hell, Botticelli accepts, that middle world in which men take no side in great conflicts, and decide no great causes, and make great refusals. He thus sets for himself the limits within which art, undisturbed by any moral ambition, does its most sincere and surest work. His interest is neither in the untempered goodness of Angelico's saints, nor the untempered evil of Orcagna's *Inferno*; but with men and women, in their mixed and uncertain condition, always attractive, clothed sometimes by passion with a character of loveliness and energy, but saddened perpetually by the shadow upon them of the great things from which they shrink. His morality is all sympathy; and it is this sympathy, conveying into his work more than is usual of the true complexion of humanity, which makes him, visionary as he is, so forcible a realist.[13]

However, this morality of sympathy, though not termed such, already forms part of the argument of "Coleridge's Writings," where one element in Pater's defence of the "relative spirit" is precisely that it gives rise to a less unyielding form of moral judgment: "The relative spirit, by dwelling constantly on the more fugitive conditions or circumstances of things, breaking through a thousand rough and brutal classifications, and giving elasticity to inflexible principles, begets an intellectual finesse, of which the ethical result is a delicate and tender justness in the criticism of human life."[14] Pater further instances Coleridge himself as one who would have benefited from a greater indulgence in matters of moral assessment: "all the time his own pathetic history pleads for a more elastic moral philosophy than his, and cries out against every formula less living and flexible than life itself."[15]

From the essay on Botticelli onwards, this same plea for a more tolerant application of moral rules is always made in the name of "sympathy." The term is in frequent use in the essays that separate *The Renaissance* from *Marius the Epicurean*, in which it may be said to come into its own. The following is an instance from the essay on *Measure for Measure* (1874):

> The idea of justice involves the idea of rights. But at bottom rights are equivalent to that which really is, to facts; and the recognition of his rights therefore, the justice he requires of our hands, or of our thoughts, is the recognition of that which the person, in his inmost nature, really is; and as sympathy alone can discover that which really is in matters of feeling and thought, true justice is in its essence a finer knowledge through love.[16]

The term "sympathy" would have had peculiar resonance for readers of the *Westminster* and *Fortnightly Reviews* where these essays first appeared, for it represented the central concept of the ethic with which the French Positivist Auguste Comte (1789-1858) had crowned his philosophical system in the early 1850s. These periodicals were among those directly responsible for introducing Comtean Positivism into Britain in the 1850s and 1860s. Comte had developed his ethics in opposition to "metaphysical" and "theological" ethics, which he rejected as not founded on positive science and essentially individualist in character. Positivist ethics, on the other hand, was grounded in the "scientific" study of man as a biological and social animal and in *knowledge* of the bond of sympathy that naturally binds men together. It essentially regards the opposition between the "egoistic" and the "altruistic" or "sympathetic" instincts in man. While it recognizes that the former are dominant, it insists on the "modifiability" of this naturally given condition, and that the latter are more susceptible of development. In the exercise and development of the altruistic instincts (that is, in ascending order, Attachment, Veneration and Universal Love), Comte saw "the solution to the problem of Humanity."[17] But Comte was not the first philosopher to have pointed to "sympathy" as the source of moral feeling and action. Indeed he himself acknowledged the impor-tance in this respect, given the predominantly "metaphysical" character of eighteenth-century philosophy, of the "Scottish school" of Hume, Smith and Ferguson.[18] Hume, for instance, in his *Treatise of Human Nature* had argued that the distinction between virtue and vice was not derived from reason but from the operation of a "moral taste" and proceeded from "certain sentiments of pleasure or disgust which arise upon the contemplation and view of particular qualities or characters."[19] Sympathy, he maintained, or a natural "concern for society" and its interests[20] was in many instances the principle that motivated that moral taste.

It is to be noted that all instances of the term "sympathy" in Pater's writings prior to *Marius* occur in the discussion of art. It is the works of Botticelli and Shakespeare, of the artists of the Italian Renaissance generally,[21] or of Charles Lamb,[22] which are specifically held up as examples. This is indicative of the fact that the quality is invoked by him there less as a general principle of moral sentiment and action than with specific regard to the problem of the judgment of human character and conduct.[23] While Comtean Positivism itself attributed great importance to art "as a form of 'moral exercise . . . calling sympathies and antipathies into healthy play',"[24] this identification of the moral quality of sympathy with art is more immediately to be associated with the English Romantic tradition, which like Comtean ethics, but more directly, derived from eighteenth-century theorists of sensibility and sympathy as the central concepts of morality. The Romantics regarded art as a truer and more direct means of moral edification than any simple citing of rules. For them art teaches by instantiating rather than instancing goodness. As M. H. Abrams suggests,

> To Shelley, as to Wordsworth and De Quincey, the importance of poetry as a moral instrument lay in its exercising and strengthening the under-structure of moral action, although to his view this is not so much a matter of feeling as of fellow-feeling. It is above all by conveying their power of universal sympathy and understanding that poets, though singing in solitude, become "the hierophants of an unapprehended inspiration" and "the unacknowledged legislators of the world."[25]

This Romantic tradition of a direct service of art to morality through its affective enhancement of the capacity for sympathy survives in Pater's notion of a literally "*poetical justice*," that "finer justice" of which poetry is the prime example by virtue of its genius for observation, its special attention to *circumstance*, above all with regard to human actions: "It is not always that poetry can be the exponent of morality; but it is this aspect of morals which it represents most naturally, for this true justice is dependent on just those finer appreciations which poetry cultivates in us the power of making, those peculiar valuations of action and its effect which poetry actually requires."[26]

The second of the two ethical directives embodied in Pater's early writings is to be identified with the watchword "passion," and may be conceived as a revolt against the constraints of strictly moral prescription and a bid for release into a broader self-fulfillment. The classical expression of this revolt is the "Conclusion" to *The Renaissance*, especially in its first version: "The theory or idea or system which requires of us the sacrifice of any part of this experience, in consideration of some interest into which we cannot enter, or some abstract morality we have not identified with ourselves, or what is only conventional, has no real claim upon us." Against the curtailment of experience imposed by an ethic of sacrifice, Pater vindicates the right of the individual to cultivate and expand the sense of self in accordance with a "higher morality" of sheer tensity of mind and feeling, of intensely experienced sensation, of "a quickened, multiplied consciousness," in short, of "passion"[27]—the perennial antagonist of the ethical tradition, whether as an impediment to the achievement of the inner peace and harmony requisite for individual happiness, or as an obstacle to virtue, but here elevated into an ethical principle.

There is a fundamental ambiguity about this new ethic, manifest in the term "higher morality" itself. More than a right, the term seems to vindicate a duty, and this is evidently an inconsistency in an ethic opposed to the prescriptive exactions of the traditional morality, especially in one that otherwise apparently prefers a classical to a rule-based modern model. As Alasdair MacIntyre suggests: "In general Greek ethics asks, What am I to do if I am to fare well? Modern ethics asks, What ought I to do if I am to do right? and it asks this question in such a way that doing right is made something quite independent of faring well."[28] Pater's "higher morality" of "passion" aligns itself intermittently with both positions. It can be seen as a peculiar morality of duty, one where the concept of duty is divorced, not from that of happiness, but from that of moral virtue itself. But at the same time the spirit of this "higher morality" is unmistakably classical, being concerned as it is with personal well-being. It even defines itself, in a characteristically Greek way, as a form of "wisdom."[29] Wisdom is not the same as knowledge. It is the sort of knowledge acquired, tested and applied in experience, a kind of practical knowledge or expertise. Greek ethics teaches wise or expert living, expertise in the practical art of living. Its criterion for a life lived well is not extrinsic to the actual living of it, effectiveness or, as Pater has it, "success,"[30] rather than merit.

This ambiguity may partly be explained by pointing to what was probably the major source for this new inwardness, the ethical idealism of the German philosopher J. G. Fichte (1762-1814), whom Pater is known to have read in the early 1860s, and from whom he probably took the term "higher morality."[31] It seems likely that the tendency to posit the passionate exertion of the self as a form of duty is an echo of the high ontological status accorded the inner striving of the subject in

Fichte, for spiritual activity and aspiration were the primary truths of Fichte's "turbulent metaphysics of development."[32] They expressed the essential dynamism of reality, which had its absolute foundation and driving principle in the will to self-affirmation of the infinite Ego or subject of being. Fichte viewed objective existence as the product or refraction of infinite self-consciousness. Consciousness of this refracted state was the special privilege of the individual, empirical ego, whose vocation consisted in the unremitting struggle to repair the breach in being signified, by the opposition of subject and object. His power, not to achieve, but to strive towards this end was given him in his moral will: "The endeavour to achieve justice is an objective event; it is a striving to overcome that to which we object, namely, injustice; and in its active expression it is the subject's self-revelation and self-affirmation. In every moral action spirit molds nature as it resists nature, and nature is aroused to manifest spirit; the two are radically, that is, at root, one."[33]

A second organ for the manifestation of spirit in nature was *genius*, embodied in the figure of the *Gelehrte*, the scholar or learned man. In three successive series of lectures[34] Fichte had defined the nature and function of the "scholar" as the "instructor of mankind,"[35] prophet and principal agent of its collective advancement towards complete self-knowledge and self-realization. Pater apparently delivered a talk on "Fichte's Ideal Student" to the Old Mortality Society at Oxford in 1863.[36] This talk has not survived, but the example of the *Gelehrte*'s unceasing dedication to the task of spiritual transformation[37] is clearly discernible in Pater's conception, in "Coleridge's Writings," of "the spiritual element in life" as "the passion for inward perfection,"[38] as well as in the injunction issued in the final paragraphs of the "Conclusion" to maintain a constantly high pitch of spiritual concentration and energy. Moreover, the passage cited from the essay on Coleridge first introduces the notion of a "higher morality":

> Coleridge thinks that if we reject the supernatural, the spiritual element in life will evaporate also, that we shall have to accept a life with narrow horizons, without disinterestedness, harshly cut off from the springs of life in the past. But

what is this spiritual element? It is the passion for inward perfection, with its sorrows, its aspirations, its joy. These mental states are the delicacies of the higher morality of the few, of Augustine, of the author of the "Imitation," of Francis de Sales; in their essence they are only the permanent characteristics of the higher life.[39]

Fichte had used the expression in his *Die Anweisung zum seligen Leben, oder auch die Religionslehre* (*The Way towards the Blessed Life, or the Doctrine of Religion*, 1806), where it designates the third in an ascending scale of "points of view" from which the subject may consider the world. The "true and higher morality" is distinguished from the "regulative" (*ordnendes*), which represents the stage of spiritual development immediately below it, and which Fichte identifies with the concept of moral law as developed by Kant and, in earlier writings (such as his *Sittenlehre* of 1798) by himself. Where the second is "merely negative," in that its task is to maintain a given degree of social equilibrium and tranquillity, the first is "creative," in that its task is not the regulation of an existing order but the creation of one that is absolutely new. It aspires "not just to the *form* of the Idea, but to the very quality and reality of it." Its aim is the transfiguration of mankind, in accordance with its proper destiny and with a faith in the primal reality of "the holy, the beautiful and the true" into "an exact portrait, an image and revelation of its own divine inner essence."[40]

But if the kind of inwardness Pater is promoting in these early essays is indebted to Fichte, it ultimately dissociates itself from the idealism of Fichte's system. This is immediately apparent in the fact that for Pater spiritual "passion" includes sensation. For Fichte, on the other hand, the sensual are the subject's least important faculties: the condition of being sensible is the primary attribute of existence, but is for this reason not worthy of consideration as a mode of knowledge. For what defines existence is at the same time what distances being. A conception of reality which limits itself to what is available to the senses is the lowest of the worldviews in Fichte's scale; and the subject risen to a love of being as such will regard the sensible world merely as the arena for actions inspired by and expressive of that love. But Pater admits the senses as organs of "inward perfection." Already in "Coleridge's Writings" the apology for a new self-signifying spirituality—one neither theologically nor ontologically determined and oriented—is accompanied by an insistence on the primacy of the senses over the speculative intellect.[41] Then in the "Conclusion" the senses are firmly equated with the intellect as a means to achieve the desired inner "ecstasy." Indeed they are so far dominant as to condition the exertion of the intellect: "With this sense of the splendour of our experience and of its awful brevity, gathering all we are into one desperate effort to see and touch, we shall hardly have time to make theories about the things we see and touch. What we have to do is to be for ever curiously testing opinion and courting new impressions, never acquiescing in a facile orthodoxy of Comte or of Hegel or of our own."[42]

But this is where Pater's position ceases to be explainable solely in ethical terms; by which I mean that, as the above passage suggests, sheer inward resonance of being is not the only end contemplated in these essays, for the reason that perceptual experience is not intended there merely as an occasion or mode of "passion," but also as a means to objective knowledge. There is indeed a sort of double imperative embodied in these writings, ethical and theoretical: "A counted number of pulses only is given to us of a variegated, dramatic life. How may we see in them all that is to be seen in them by the finest senses?"[43] They argue not only for "passion," but also for "observation," though in a broader sense than that envisaged by the morality of sympathy:[44]

> The truth of these relations experience gives us; not the truth of eternal outlines effected once for all, but a world of fine gradations and subtly linked conditions, shifting intricately as we ourselves change; and bids us by a constant clearing of the organs of observation and perfecting of analysis to make what we can of these.[45]
>
> The service of philosophy, and of religion and culture as well, to the human spirit, is to startle it into a sharp and eager observation.[46]

There is a positive, though qualified, theoretic thrust to Pater's aestheticism that has commonly been overlooked in favour of the subjectivist

ethic just examined,[47] probably because the anti-theoretical stance of
pieces like the "Conclusion" has been taken too much at face value.
But the actual language of the final paragraphs of the "Conclusion"
reveals a persistent impulse to an objective knowledge of reality.

There are, as David DeLaura has suggested, two distinct groups of
key words here. But these require to be separated a little more rigorously.[48] On the one hand there is the language of "passion," consisting
principally of substantives expressing reflexive mental states and intense
inner sensation: energy, ecstasy, excitement, enthusiasm, pulsations,
consciousness. On the other there is the language of "observation"—a
series of transitive verbs, presupposing, demanding an object: discriminate, see and touch, gather up: "Not the fruit of experience, but
experience itself is the end." The protest is both ethically and metaphys-
ically motivated. The appeal to "experience" comprehends both of its
terms, subject and object—not only the "energy" or "excitement," but
also the "splendour of experience." "Experience" in Pater is not solely
a subjective affect, but includes the experimental,[49] that "experimental,
individual knowledge" held to be the aim of the "true . . . speculative
temper" in "Coleridge's Writings."[50] Under this aspect Pater's
aestheticism presents itself (in accordance with the term's original
meaning)[51] as a sort of metaphysics of perception, a way of affirming the
fundamental reality of experience from within.

This raises the question of the exact relation of the doctrine
enunciated in "Coleridge's Writings" and the "Conclusion" to the
modern scientific and philosophical statements concerning reality and
truth which apparently lend it its premises. For Pater, the fundamental
characteristic of "modern thought" is its relativism. Both of the above
pieces open by making this point. The "Conclusion" paints a particularly graphic picture of the disintegration of the solid world of experience
under the solvent action of modern physiological and epistemological
analysis. The eloquence of this desolating survey of the modern
scientific and philosophical account of reality has certainly contributed
to the commonly held notion that the doctrine which it serves to
introduce was merely negatively determined by that account—in other

words, that the message of the "Conclusion," with its instigation to *experience*, is negatively inferred from the despair of knowledge apparently authorized by the foregoing theoretical description of the world, and that it constitutes a waiving of the whole question of knowledge or truth. On this view Pater's appeal to experience is the expression of a resigned, philosophically redundant scepticism, a mode of compensating for the dissipation of truth apparently brought about by modern science and philosophy, by abandoning these for a life of immediate consciousness. But Pater's scepticism is not so simple, nor his dependence on "the 'relative spirit' " so negative.

He is capable of estimating this positively. In "Coleridge's Writings," for example, there is an unmistakable sense of exhilaration at the spectacle of its subversive force. And there is no disjunction between the attitude of modern science to the world and that which Pater recommends. Indeed, the latter is expressed in language borrowed from the former, the language, as we have already seen, of "observation" and "analysis" and "experimental, individual, knowledge."[52] Not only do the two attitudes share a terminology, they also share an impulse to, and special apprehension of, truth: "not the truth of eternal outlines effected once for all, but a world of fine gradations and subtly linked conditions, shifting as we ourselves change."[53] Pater's turning to experience at the end of the "Conclusion" is not theoretically inconsequential but affirms this same apprehension of truth. It is the expression of a scepticism that tends towards the conservation of truth.[54] And this tendency involves not only the deliverance of reality from the constructions of dogma but its defence against the deliverer, the solvent power of scientific and philosophical analysis.

This positive and at the same time critical thrust to the final paragraphs of the "Conclusion" emerges more clearly if we consider the whole piece in its original context, as the final portion of a review-article on the poetry of William Morris. It has been suggested that its closing pages do not form an organic whole with the rest of the article, or that they were composed independently of, and possibly earlier than the review.[55] Rather, its being an integral part of the essay on Morris explains how the "Conclusion" could come to be extracted and appended to a volume of essays on the Renaissance. The paragraphs in question were originally conceived as a defence of a resurgence of "the pagan spirit" in Morris's more recent Greek poems—this spirit being defined in the formula "the desire of beauty quickened by the sense of death." Pater imagines the inevitable objection to such an attitude, which reprimands those holding it with wilfully ignoring the simple fact that "the modern world is in possession of truths." He takes up the "challenge" issued by this argument, notwithstanding the "strange transition from the earthly paradise" (the title of one of Morris's poems) to "the sad-coloured world of abstract philosophy"; and the final paragraphs answer the question asking "what modern philosophy, when it is sincere, really does say about human life and the truth we can attain in it, and the relation of this to the desire of beauty."[56]

The "argument" of the "Conclusion" is pre-figured in the discussion of the poems, and in particular of the "transition" between Morris's earlier poetry, with its medieval subject-matter, and his later, with its subjects taken from Greek mythology. The earlier poetry treats of a phase of sentiment in which Christianity finds itself rivalled by the "religion" or "cultus" of "imaginative love." The competition between the two is strict: each is penetrated with an equal degree of mysticism, and despite the comparative worldliness of the latter the poetry of both is equally marked by a "wild, convulsed sensuousness," an image of the world lighted up by fervid spirituality. In Morris's later poetry, on the other hand, "there is no delirium or illusion, no experiences of mere soul while the body and the bodily senses sleep or wake with convulsed intensity at the prompting of imaginative love; but rather the great primary passions under broad daylight as of the pagan Veronese."[57] Pater goes on to insist on the emblematic significance of this change:

> This simplification interests us not merely for the sake of an individual poet ... but chiefly because it explains through him a transition which, under many forms, is one law of the life of the human spirit, and of which what we call the Renaissance is only a supreme instance. . . . Complex and subtle interests, which the mind spins for itself, may occupy art and poetry or our own spirits for a

time; but sooner or later they come back with a sharp rebound to the simple elementary passions—anger, desire, regret, pity and fear—and what corresponds to them in the sensuous world—bare, abstract fire, water, air, tears, sleep, silence—and what De Quincey has called "the glory of motion."[58]

Pater is evidently proposing a similar transition to his contemporaries, from the "sad-coloured world of abstract philosophy" back towards the "earthly paradise," a new Renaissance, in the "Conclusion." This is unmistakably a plea for an analogous "simplification" in the apprehension of reality, an analogous "escape to the world without one" from the stifling nightmare world of modern thought, a deliverance not only from the denaturing of experience under the "single sentiment" of metaphysics or of theology,[59] but from the annulment, under the dissolvent spell of epistemological or physiological analysis, of experience itself along with these tyrannies.

I conclude by pointing to a neglected aspect of the function of art in his early writings in order to illustrate the positive theoretic thrust to Pater's aestheticism. The "Conclusion" itself notoriously closes with the recommendation of "the love of art for art's sake" as the most effective stimulus to "a quickened, multiplied consciousness": "for art comes to you professing frankly to give nothing but the highest quality to your moments as they pass, and simply for those moments' sake."[60] On this view the value and significance of art is calculated on the basis of its subjective yield as a pre-eminent record and source of heightened sensation. And this estimation of art corresponds to that aspect of Pater's aestheticism which defines it as an ethic of "passion." Art, of course, acquires a different meaning within Pater's doctrine under its aspect as a morality of "sympathy": it becomes, in its patient and compassionate observation of the world, the token of a more humane phase of justice. Art has a third role in Pater's aestheticism linking it with the latter's cognitive ambition. This role regards the nature of art as a symbolic artefact and its power, in Adrian Stokes's phrase, to "correct abstraction."[61] From this third point of view art betokens an apprehension or representation of reality adequate to its experiential character.

Evidence for such a conception of art is to be found especially in the essay on Winckelmann (1867). This evinces the direct influence of Hegel's *Aesthetic* on Pater's view of art. Hegel had argued for the affinity of art, religion and philosophy as modes of "bringing to our minds and expressing the Divine, the deepest interests of mankind, and the most comprehensive truths of the Spirit."[62] The special vocation of art was, or rather had been, to display "even the highest [reality] sensuously, bringing it thereby nearer to the senses, to feeling, and to nature's mode of appearance."[63] "Had been," because according to Hegel art had been superseded as the supreme mode of knowledge of the Absolute, for the reason that the suprasensuous Idea, which is the content of art, had advanced beyond the stage where it was susceptible of an adequate realization in sensuous form. The mission of art had been, and continued to be, to accompany the Absolute on its way to perfect self-realization, and its destiny was to be transcended as the pure spirituality of the Idea grew steadily more manifest, requiring it to yield its place to abstract thought.

While Pater adopts Hegel's conception of the history of art as the history of the varying relations between sensuous form and spiritual content or thought,[64] the perspective from which he views this history is a different one. He does not share Hegel's faith in the progress of Spirit. His faith is rather in the ability of art to resist or contain the advance of abstract thought. His history of artistic forms follows Hegel's but is very much viewed from the side of sense. He too recognizes the pre-eminent unity of classical art, but he interprets this in terms of an ideal limitation of its spiritual content: "This ideal art, in which the thought does not outstrip or lie beyond the proper range of its sensible embodiment."[65] The interest of modern art for Pater lies not in its tendency to self-transcendence, but in its precarious but enduring hold on its essential identity. This explains the peculiar importance for him of Winckelmann, the man fitted to renew the classical tradition for the modern age through intimate affinity with it, and so to convey the truth of the Greek artistic ideal to his successors, above all to Goethe. It also explains why the essay closes in considering the problem posed to himself by Goethe the *poet*: "Can the blitheness and universality of the antique ideal be communicated to artistic productions, which shall contain the fullness of the experience of the modern world?"[66] Pater concludes that it can. The answer expresses a faith in art as a pledge of a mode of reflection ideally conformed, but at the same time resistant, to modernity.

This faith is amply testified to in the essays on Renaissance art, where an individual work of art is repeatedly presented as an emblem of a certain mode of conceiving the world—one poised between the old religious and metaphysical dogmatism and the modern disintegration of experience.[67] Nothing illustrates this better than Pater's famous interpretation of Leonardo's *Gioconda*. Through the novelty of its expressiveness and its enigmatic resemblance to other images by the artist, through its psychological force and elusive symbolic meaning, and lastly through the history of its own creation, Leonardo's portrait presents itself as an emblem of a mode of thought that evades both ancient and modern forms of prejudice by combining and mutually adjusting them. "Lady Lisa," as repainted by Pater, represents the "embodiment" of the ancient "fancy of a perpetual life, sweeping together ten thousand experiences"—the abstract content of this idea is incarnated and expressed in the person of Leonardo's subject. She is also the "symbol of the modern idea" whereby man is "wrought upon by" and sums up in himself "all modes of thought and life."[68] The essay on Coleridge suggested the annihilating potential of such an idea. But Leonardo's portrait has literally lent a face to a theory of existence that threatens to deprive the individual of all radical initiative in the sphere of experience, while freeing him from subjection to a "perpetual life" above his own. In the human image, in this icon of personal identity, there coalesce two contrasting conceptions of existence—the one subordinating it to a principle that surpasses it in power and scope, and the other to "the intricacy, the universality of natural law."[69] The work of art illustrates the appeal made in the "Conclusion" for a comprehensive culture, the need to "be present always at the focus where the greatest number of vital forces unite in their purest energy."[70] Art is that focus, where the light of thought is neutralized and magnified in the light of sensation.

Visual art owes the pre-eminence accorded to it in the "Conclusion" and in Pater's early writings generally to its capacity to temper and adjust abstract thought, whether religious or metaphysical, through the neutrality of its peculiar medium, the visible. Its power to do this is repeatedly celebrated in the essays contained in *The Renaissance*, where the various instances presented are also examples of the different ways in which adjustment is achieved. The essay on Pico della Mirandola (1871), for example, turns on the ability of the visual art of the Quattrocento to accomplish the effective reconciliation between Christian and pagan traditions which the (in Pater's view) bizarre scholarly efforts of Pico and others were unable to attain, and which would have to await the eighteenth and nineteenth centuries and the rise of the "historic sense" for scientific validation. Painting (Pater cites Michelangelo's *Tondo Doni* as an example) anticipated the resolutions of historicism by combining disparate iconographical elements and so realizing a "picturesque union of contrasts."[71] In the case of Botticelli and his "peevish-looking Madonnas,"[72] the painter's translation of the traditional iconography has humanized its content. His pensive Venus is presented as a historical composite, a Venus born again out of the middle ages, but illustrative of the original complexity of the myth and of the entire "Hellenic spirit."[73] Again, the primordial quality of Michelangelo's images achieves a generalizing of their religious or mythological content. Moreover, the "half-emergent" effect typical of his carved figures, accidental or not, defines a precise formal analogue of the aims implicit in the generalizing treatment of the traditional pagan and Christian representations. The formal tension in Michelangelo's carvings realizes the paradox of a manner of thinking the world not removed from the actual current and specific mode of experience.

Visual art does not retain this pre-eminence in the later writings, due to the aggravation of the ethical conflict which as I have attempted to show was present in Pater's work from the start. But the theoretical motives underlying visual art's early importance are still operative in its eclipse in *Marius* by the (Chrisitian) moral agent, as the latter provides not only a more moral but also a more adequate because living figure of meaning. But this must be the subject of another essay, in which the "ethical crisis" and "confusion of ethics and aesthetics" pointed to by critics in the later writings will be analysed on the basis of the distinctions established here.

Critical Impressionism
as Anti–Phallogocentric Strategy

_____ **10**

RICHARD DELLAMORA

IN RECENT YEARS, it has become something of a commonplace to associate rhetorical strategies in the writing of Walter Pater with deconstruction. In his introduction to *Marius the Epicurean*, for example, Ian Small, without explicitly terming Pater's work deconstructive, notes his resistance to conventional novelistic closure, representation of character, and respect for textual authority.[1] David Shaw has argued that in *Plato and Platonism* (1893) Pater provides a vigorously "deconstructionist" reading of Plato.[2] Pater notes that the "Parmenidean 'One' or 'Absolute' " for which Plato searches, "is after all but zero, and a mere algebraic symbol for nothingness."[3] In *Language and Decadence in the Victorian Fin de Siècle*, Linda Dowling has contended that Pater's resistance to the essentialism of Romantic philology makes his writing deconstructive. Although the discipline parted from the Christian view that had identified language with a divine, centering, and energizing Logos, nineteenth-century philology continued to be logocentric by virtue of identifying language with human reason itself. The foremost exponent of this view during Pater's lifetime was the comparative philologist and mythographer, Max Müller, who taught at Oxford from 1868 to 1875. Pater's affinities, in contrast, are with

Müller's antagonists in the new field of anthropology and with eighteenth-century English epistemology, which, in a revisionary reading of Locke, had acknowledged the arbitrary character of linguistic signs.[4] This rhetorical concept of language matches Pater's sense of its contingent character.

Pater consistently opposes totalizing views of linguistic and other forms of culture. In an early essay, he deplores Samuel Taylor Coleridge's yearning for the absolute and argues instead that "modern thought is distinguished from ancient by its cultivation of the 'relative' spirit. . . . To the modern spirit nothing is, or can be rightly known, except relatively and under conditions."[5] While Pater grounds this view in contemporary science, especially biology, elsewhere in the essay he draws upon the *Symposium* in order to indicate the basis of this proposition in individual experience, especially experience of desire. For "us," "the Greek spirit, with its engaging naturalness, simple, chastened, debonair, τρυφῆς, ἀβρότητος, χλιδῆς, χαρίτων, ἱμέρου, πόθου πατήρ, is itself the Sangrail of an endless pilgrimage."[6] The Greek phrase, quoted from the *Symposium* (Steph. 197D), makes clear that "Greek spirit" is Pater's discreet translation of the term eros.[7] Accordingly, when Pater emphasizes the importance of "know[ing] one's own impression as it really is, to discriminate it, to realise it distinctly,"[8] "impression" is in part erotic.

Nevertheless, critics who have aligned Pater with deconstruction, first and most prominently J. Hillis Miller, ignore or misconstrue the specifically erotic tenor of difference in his writing. Yet male-male desire is as evident a "motive" (to use one favoured term) as it is in the writing of Johann Winckelmann, whom Pater in his first major essay takes as a model of the aesthetic critic. In other early essays on figures like Leonardo da Vinci, Pater again underscores the importance of masculine desire in prompting and shaping cultural activity, an idea that he returns to in his essays on Greek mythology, in *Marius the Epicurean* (1885), and in imaginary portraits like "Denys l'Auxerrois" (1886) and "Apollo in Picardy," this last published in the year before his death. Pater's concept of language is material in character—and "material" in this context includes the relations between language and somatic experience, sexual awareness, and gender-roles. Pater's ambiguous position at Oxford, where he functioned as a member of a male elite at the same time that he subtly polemicized on behalf of a form of desire whose overt expression could occur only at the expense of the moral and practical authority of that elite, placed him in a highly self-conscious relation, at once complicitous and antagonistic, to literary expression. His language is always masculine—both in his inscription within the male institution summed in the word "Oxford" and in his attempt to express masculine difference. When Pater republished his essays in book form in 1873, John Wordsworth, a colleague, objected to Pater's publication under the signature, a "Fellow of Brasenose College, Oxford." Wordsworth was not prepared to tolerate the mixing of nonconformity with Oxford discourse—yet to object on this ground, as Pater himself was painfully aware, was to object precisely to his position at, but in resistance to, Oxford.[9]

In this essay I consider Miller's ambivalent approach to sexual difference in Pater as symptomatic of the subordination of impressionist criticism within a conventionally masculine outlook. Miller's handling, moreover, occurs at the expense of difference in his own practice since the term loses its significance as a marker of differences, both sexual and otherwise. Without differences, however, difference like other critical principles necessarily becomes phallic: abstract, colourless, and rhetorical in a non-deconstructive sense. I also attempt briefly to glimpse Pater's critique of masculinity in high cultural discourse and his own counter-effort to establish a principle of masculine difference.

Later critics did not find it difficult to detect in Paterian impressionism a desire that by century's end could be referred to with the new term, *homosexual.* In a hostile review of the Library Edition of the Works (1910), Paul Elmore More objects in particular to the seductive tenor of Paterian interpretation: "too often his interpretation, when the spell of his manner is broken, will be found essentially perverted."[10] The comment refers both to the canonical text (whose meaning Pater perverts) and to Pater's psychology (which, in More's eyes, *is* perverse).

The *ad hominem* attack contributed significantly to the depreciation of Pater's reputation during the high modernist phase—even though desire between men continued to be a major motive in aesthetic production.[11]

Against this background, it is not surprising that when, in two essays of the mid-1970s, J. Hillis Miller contributes to the recovery of Pater by invoking him as a presiding spirit of allegorical criticism, he does so in a way that relies on but also misrepresents and eventually elides sexual difference in Pater. In "Walter Pater: A Partial Portrait," Miller signs Paterian tradition with the names of a number of men whose homosexuality is notorious: "This line [of criticism] leads from certain aspects of Ruskin through Pater and Wilde to Proust, and beyond Proust to Walter Benjamin and to the rhetorical or 'deconstructive' criticism of our own moment in literary criticism."[12] As Miller observes, Pater's criticism depends on ideas of "difference and discontinuity":

> Meaning or significance in a personality, in a gem, a song, a painting, a piece of music is always defined by Pater as a force, as the power to make an impression. This power is not single, nor is it a harmonious collocation of energies making a unity. A "virtue" always results from antagonistic forces, sweetness against strength in the case of Michelangelo, strangeness against the desire for beauty in Leonardo, and so on. The meaning is in neither of the two forces separately, nor in their sum. It arises in the space between them, out of the economy of their difference.[13]

Later, more categorically, Miller says that in Pater "meaning" is "constituted by difference."[14] In addition to the mention of Wilde and Proust, the artists whom Miller refers to, Michelangelo and Leonardo, are major figures in a tradition of male-male desire. And the conflations that Miller adduces—of sweetness and strength, of strangeness and the desire for beauty—signify, in Pater, different flavours of homoerotic sensibility.

Having emitted these signals, Miller proceeds to dissociate contemporary deconstruction from *being-homosexual*. Taking as an example Pater's description of a painting of Medusa incorrectly attributed to Leonardo da Vinci, Miller observes Pater's use of the image to suggest a liminal state in which the expression of wayward desire overcomes the limits of a rigid gender-identification that subsumes the self in masculin-ist norms, in "the phallus," to use Miller's word.[15] At the same time, however, he suggests that another sort of male-male desire could capture Leonardo/Pater in phallogocentrism. Miller asks: "Was Pater 'phallogocentric,' frozen like Leonardo himself at a Narcissistic or adolescent homosexual stage?"[16] The implicit answer to this question, which endorses Freud's diagnosis of Leonardo's sexuality, is "yes." The male-male desire to which Miller refers exists within a conventional, that is, heterosexual economy as idolization of the father. By specifying this desire as homosexual, Miller associates homosexuality with the logocen-trism of conventional academic discourse while directing attention away from Pater's self-conscious use of masculine desire as one way of surmounting fear of loss of the phallus.

Similarly, in the ensuing discussion of the recurrence of Medusa-imagery in *Marius the Epicurean*, Miller leaves Marius unable to resolve either the castration or the Oedipus complex despite the fact that Miller might easily argue that Marius, who has "no particular dread of a snake's bite, like one of his companions, who had put his hand into the mouth of an old garden-god and roused there a sluggish viper,"[17] over-comes the paralyzing force of these complexes precisely by letting the snake bite. Immediately following this passage, Miller shifts to the expressly theoretical portion of his discussion; in the process, Pater's erotic difference is translated into an "incipient theory of signs."[18] An apt translation but one that should be made without dropping the thread of sexual difference.

At the end of the essay, Miller reduces meaning in Pater to a play of language whose significance is the indeterminacy of linguistic reference:

> His texts lead the critic deeper and deeper into a labyrinth until he confronts a final aporia. This does not mean, however, that the reader must give up from the beginning the attempt to understand Pater. Only by going all the way into the labyrinth, following the thread of a given clue, can the critic reach the blind alley, vacant of any Minotaur, that impasse which is the end point of interpreta-tion.[19]

Miller, choosing to satisfy himself with "A Partial Portrait," assimilates Pater to his own theory of critical interpretation. The partiality of the portrait, moreover, re-situates Miller's discussion within the academic tradition that he consciously seeks to resist. One should not be surprised, then, that in his usage "difference" does not mean sexual difference—either in the way that the phrase is characteristically used to register the categorization of a feminine Other or in the way that I use it to refer to an awareness of desire not cast in the antitheses of what Monique Wittig has referred to as "the straight mind."[20]

The nexus of the Ariadne-Theseus-Minotaur-Dionysus-labyrinth is central to "Ariadne's Thread: Repetition and the Narrative Line." Miller takes as one of three epigraphs to this essay a long passage from "Apollo in Picardy," one of a number of Pater's re-tellings of the myth of Dionysus. In the passage quoted, Pater describes the collapse of the "long and intricate argument" of "the twelfth volume of a dry enough treatise on mathematics, applied, still with no relaxation of strict method, to astronomy and music." The blocked author of this text is the protagonist, Prior Saint-Jean. Pater draws connections between the phallus (the Prior expects to be rewarded upon completion of the work with "well-earned practical reward as superior, with lordship and mitre and ring, of the abbey"), logocentrism (the "method" pursued in the first eleven books), and phallogocentrism (the Prior as author). On the other hand, his breakdown is associated both with "new light" and with the birth, in deconstructive terms, of a decentered subject: the twelfth volume "began, or, in perturbed manner, and as with throes of childbirth, seemed the preparation for, an argument of an entirely new and disparate species, such as would demand a new period of life also, if it might be, for its due expansion." The "new period of life" seems to mean both a new historical period, that is, a Renaissance, since the "new light" perceived by the Prior is his anticipation of Galileo's discovery that the earth moves around the sun, and also a new way of personal living that includes an overtly expressed desire for other males, whether Apollyon, the Apollo/Dionysus figure that the Prior meets during his sojourn at the Grange of Notre-Dame-De-Pratis, or

Hyacinth, another Dionysus figure who, on the literal level, is the attractive adolescent who accompanies the Prior on his journey.[21]

The link between the idea of history as cultural repetition and the avowal of desire is characteristic in Pater and is connected in his mind with new knowledge in the natural and social sciences. Adapting from anthropology the idea of culture as a series of recapitulations of earlier phases with a difference, in *Studies in the History of the Renaissance*, he devises "an evolutionary scheme showing the transmission of pagan elements under the surface of 'Christian' art from medieval France through Pico of Mirandola into the Renaissance in Italy, then back to the France of du Bellay and thence to the eighteenth and nineteenth centuries."[22] In two pioneering essays, one in *Fraser's Magazine* and the other in the *Fortnightly Review*, in 1872 and 1873 respectively, Andrew Lang, a young literary anthropologist who had come up to Balliol in 1865, attacked Müller's theory of the development of mythology as the corruption of an original solar myth.[23] Drawing instead on the work of Benjamin Tylor, Lang argued the survival of primitive residues: "the lower mythology—the elemental beliefs of the people—do survive beneath a thin covering of Christian conformity."[24] Influenced by these essays as well as by Lang's earlier articles on the development of French literature, Pater organized the book to account for the phenomenon of the Renaissance in terms of a sequence of survivals and returns of "pagan tradition."[25] This pattern doubles on the intellectual level the myth of return summed up in Pater's favoured trope of the young body red in the grave, and, as the image suggests, includes the idea that renaissance is possible only in a culture prepared to celebrate desire between men.[26] To these associations, Pater in "Apollo in Picardy" adds mordant observations about desire in male homosocial culture. In homophobic culture, the fantasy of a masculine desire connecting individuals across lines of class—as in the Prior's attraction to Apollyon, whom he takes to be "a serf. . . , a servant of the house, or farm-labourer, perhaps"[27]—necessarily rebounds upon itself. And the sacrifice of youthful male vitality to the needs of older men induces psychosis.

Despite the long epigraph from "Apollo in Picardy," "Ariadne's Thread" includes no discussion of Pater. Instead, taking another epigraph as his point of departure, Miller analyzes the myth of the labyrinth in a strictly heterosexual context. In "Walter Pater," Miller recognizes that the radiant figures of Denys and Apollyon embody alienation in their recurrence in antagonistic, medieval environments: "the tragedy of all these figures is in the incompatibility between the meanings they carry and the material conditions within which they are forced to embody them."[28] Homophobia, however, is one condition that goes unnamed; and Miller misreads the significance of the trope of the "new body."[29] He sees Pater as decorporealizing the body in a set of fugitive traces: " 'a dream that lingers for a moment, retreating in the dawn, incomplete, aimless, helpless; a thing with faint hearing, faint memory, faint power of touch; a breath, a flame in the doorway, a feather in the wind'."[30] But, as Jeffrey Wallen has recently pointed out, the situation is more complex than Miller allows. Pater repeatedly invokes the word "embodiment" to refer to the work of art: the "sensible embodiment" of "thought"[31] remains an ideal goal of art. Although Pater just as regularly registers the "discrepancy between meaning and its incarnation,"[32] the ideal remains. Similarly, Pater repeatedly invokes the idea of a cultural renewal in which the human body will be recognized as an object of desire without neurotic anxiety.[33]

Pater's double attitude helps account for key concepts in his critical theory. In the first place, difference is intrinsic to his position as one schooled in a "normal" masculine outlook at the same time that he knows himself to be different. This self-recognition inflects and in part impels a revisionary view of literary figures such as Plato while fueling skepticism about logocentric interpretations of language and tradition. Pater is altogether aware of the anxieties about desire and the body inherent in such traditions as Neoplatonic interpretation of the Dialogues. His descendental interpretations of writers like Plato and Hegel are part of a polemical project to revalorize desire, especially between males, and to create the conditions in which groups—of women, of homosexuals, of industrial and agricultural workers, of colonial others—might devise alternative forms of discourse, forms that imply in turn a shifting set of relations between new discourses, emergent communities, and hegemonic masculinity. Passages in Pater such as his description of "The Minor 'Peace of the Church' " in *Marius the Epicurean* locate him in that stream of late Victorian liberalism that is drawn towards social democratic politics.[34] On the other hand, Pater attacks the formation of masculinity within Victorian liberalism that both legitimated resistance of the claims of marginal groups after passage of the Second Reform Bill in 1867 and also underwrote the role that young well-educated men would be compelled to play in administering the Empire.

After the Indian Mutiny of 1857, utilitarian and Evangelical rationales for British expansion abroad lost a good deal of their persuasive power. Instead, subject peoples were categorized as racial degenerates. The upshot, as Karl Marx predicted in articles written for the *New York Daily Tribune*, was "a more repressive dominion."[35] When in a lecture delivered at Oxford six years later, Matthew Arnold extenuates the persecution of Christians during the reign of Marcus Aurelius on the grounds that "Christianity appeared something anti-civil and anti-social, which the State had the faculty to judge and the duty to suppress,"[36] he prompts the cynical wit of youthful listeners liable to find themselves as directors of South African mining companies a generation hence. For his part, writing in the overtly imperial Britain of the 1880s, Pater criticizes conventional gender-roles and the institutions that propagate them. In the chapter, "Manly Amusement," at the end of volume I of *Marius the Epicurean*, he uses a scene of gladiatorial combat to attack ideas of masculine self-worth that depend on aggression and physical brutality. Yet more significantly, he criticizes the Stoicism of the emperor, Marcus Aurelius, that authorizes his complicity with the spectacle below. Since Arnold and others typically invoke Aurelius's philosophy as a guide for Victorians, the confusion of high mindedness, *raison d'état*, and privilege in Aurelius's tolerance of abuses of power warrants underlining.

In his double position at Oxford as both a privileged and a subordinated male, Pater was well versed in what today might be referred to as hegemonic masculinity. In an essay in which he challenges social-role models of masculinity, John Lee has used the phrase to mean

> not . . . "the male role" but . . . a particular variety of masculinity to which others—among them young and effeminate as well as homosexual men—are subordinated. It is particular groups of men, not men in general, who are oppressed within patriarchal sexual relations, and whose situations are related in different ways to the overall logic of the subordination of women to men. A consideration of homosexuality thus provides the beginnings of a dynamic conception of masculinity as a structure of social relations.[37]

Despite the basis of Lee's analysis in the study of contemporary behaviour, the statement has implications for a study of nineteenth-century English literary culture. First of all, although Lee emphasizes the central importance to masculinity of the subordination of women, he also adduces the significance for masculinity of the subordination of working-class men, men of colour, boys, and homosexuals. In this way, he indicates symmetries between the structure of male-female relations, on the one hand, and male relations on the other. Without underplaying the fact that male homosexuals at times occupy the hegemonic male position with regard to women, children, and some other males, the structural parallel that Lee adduces indicates the basis in experience of Pater's critique of Oxonian masculinity. In other words, while terms like "homosexual" or "homosexual existence" need to be used with care in order to avoid anachronism, the relational structure described by Lee provoked resistance in 1885 as it continues to do today.[38]

In the pointedly entitled "Manly Amusement," Pater specifically draws the connection between the games and a relational understanding of masculinity by observing that the emperor has organized them in order to celebrate the engagement of his daughter "to a swinish but influential general."[39] Besides touching on the unequal status of men and women in marriage, Pater locates Marcus Aurelius with respect to the debate within the Victorian middle class over appropriate masculine behaviour. In this context and in contrast to Arnold's portrayal of the emperor as "so beautiful a moralist,"[40] Pater's emperor is a figure of the sacrifice of moral sensitivity, bodily well-being, and emotional affect that Arnold's listeners at Oxford were expected to be prepared to make in the service of God and Empire.

Pater supplements his critique of Roman/British logocentrism with an approach, at once rhetorical and material, to the Logos in "The Will as Vision," a chapter that has received a good deal of attention. Although Dowling and others, as I indicate at the outset, argue that Pater abandoned earlier, theologically based views of congruence between self and meaning, on the one hand, and verbal expression on the other, some current commentators argue that a nostalgic pursuit of the authorizing Word motivates his writing. Following Harold Bloom, for instance, Daniel O'Hara has contended that in "The Will as Vision" "Pater expresses . . . a sublime experience of the presence of a divine spirit, a creative Logos, pervading nature."[41] Yet this assertion misses precisely the figural character of the experience of Pater's protagonist as he meditates "in an olive-garden."[42] In a paragraph that begins with a recollection of Marius's two most important friendships, with Flavian and Cornelius, Marius casts his apprehension of divine presence in terms of an analogy with the experience of friendship: he imagines the reality of "*Creator*" "even as one builds up from act and word and expression of the friend actually visible at one's side, an ideal of the spirit within him."[43] The analogy points not to an antithesis—of the friend's physical expressivity versus his "spirit," for instance—but to the basis in bodily awareness of a sense of noumenal presence. The paragraph begins and ends with the experience of male friendship, though friendship of a special character in this novel, in which Pater polemically engages hegemonic masculinity.

Marius's turn at the end of the chapter away from the afternoon's epiphany and back to everyday life indicates the primary importance in Pater/Marius's view of improving the time. Marius wonders: "Must not all that remained of life be but a search for the equivalent of that Ideal, among so-called actual things—a gathering together of every trace or token of it, which his actual experience might present?"[44] The weight of emphasis in the quotation is not on the fugitive character of material actuality but on the need to find equivalences in mundane life for one's needs, desires, and apprehensions. Both sides of the equivalence remain within the range of human experience. Marius's search is varied; he attempts to overcome self-alienation, including alienation from the body; he searches lifelong for intimate male relationship; he seeks a community infused, to use anachronistic terms, with democratic and communitarian values. In the novel's historicizing rhetoric, he looks toward "the 'new city'," "some celestial New Rome" brought within scope of the temporal imagination.[45]

Because O'Hara fails to see the class and gender politics of the novel that join Pater with members of other groups subjected to hegemonic masculinity, he glides over the qualifications that Pater makes and which bind him to a world of immanent struggle. Given O'Hara's blindness, one is not surprised to find him later belaboring Pater for being apolitical:

> Pater in the end falls prey to his own beautiful idealizations, becomes *victimized by his impossible dreams*, and so appears as the perfect object of attack, awash in the sea of *his own fantastic impotence*. For when one asks what idea of society and of the individual's relation to society does this vision of the creator reinforce, one finds that the answer involves a rationalization, exquisitely phrased, of *the need to capitulate* to the structures of power at work in the world whatever the historical epoch.[46]

Ascribing to Pater a logocentrism that he consciously resisted, O'Hara also commits the indignity of imposing upon him the stereotype of the *fin-de-siècle* aesthete, fiddling while Rome burns. One could scarcely worse misread Marius/Pater's endorsement of "Christianity in its humanity, or even in its humanism, in its generous hopefulness, for man, its common sense, and alacrity of cheerful service, its sympathy with all creatures, its appreciation of beauty and daylight,"[47] an endorsement that we should remember is based on Marius's attachment to his "half-known friend."[48]

If a new form of male friendship provides one counter to the ideological construction of masculinity in Victorian high culture, Pater's contingent approach to cultural artifacts provides another. Pater attempts to theorize difference within culture: for example, in the figures of interpretation that he deploys in a variety of texts: in "the lover of strange souls" who tries to define "Leonardo's genius" or the "I" who pieces together the fragmentary remains of Denys's existence in "Denys l'Auxerrois."[49] Further, Pater positions the subject in cultural production in the theory of *Anders-streben*, which he proposes in the essay, "The School of Giorgione," published in a journal in 1877 and not added to *The Renaissance* until the third edition in 1888. Pater uses the term to refer to music conceived as the paradigmatic artistic medium to which other nineteenth-century artistic forms aspire.[50] More generally, *Anders-streben* is the tendency for work in any medium to exceed the limits of the medium in the search for greater expressiveness:

> Although each art has thus its own specific order of impressions, and an untranslatable charm, while a just apprehension of the ultimate differences of the arts is the beginning of aesthetic criticism; yet it is noticeable that, in its special mode of handling its given material, each art may be observed to pass into the condition of some other art, by what German critics term an *Anders-streben*—a partial alienation from its own limitations, through which the arts are able, not indeed to supply the place of each other, but reciprocally to lend each other new forces.[51]

Further, and as Miller has observed, *Anders-streben* refers to language and critical impression themselves: "The moment, it turns out, though unique, is not single. Each 'impression' is in fact 'infinitely divisible.' . . . It is divisible because it is self-divided, an *Andersstreben* [sic], or striving to be other than itself."[52] In art, "alienation," or what Miller refers to as self-division, is implicit within the very limits of the medium itself.

The term locates as well the producer or receiver of the form as a subject of desire limited by the conditions of material existence. In the nineteenth century, music is often regarded as the medium par excellence of excess, of passion, usually between a man and a woman. But music has a further valence in both revisionary masculine and specifically homosexual tradition, where it is associated—as by both Shelley and

Pater—with the rebellious flute-player, Marsyas.[53] Robert Martin has argued that in *Redburn* (1849) Herman Melville uses the image of Carlo's "hand organ" to signify the various pleasures of music-making, of the free play of fantasy, of masturbation, and of desire between men.[54] Melville associates Carlo with Dionysus.[55] Pater's "Denys l'Auxerrois" begins with the narrator's discovery of representations of Denys/Dionysus in stained glass and tapestry: "the figure was that of the organ-builder himself, a flaxen and flowery creature, sometimes wellnigh naked among the vine-leaves, sometimes muffled in skins against the cold, sometimes in the dress of a monk, but always with a strong impress of real character and incident from the veritable streets of Auxerre."[56] In "Apollo in Picardy," the Prior, precipitated into crisis by inability to complete his treatise on music, is taught by Apollyon's "power of untutored natural impulse, of natural inspiration" to hear "the singing of the planets: he could hear it, and might in time effect its notation."[57]

Miller hears a different music in Pater. In his essay on the writer, Miller refers to the myth of Ariadne and Dionysus in the passage cited earlier, in which he says that Pater's "texts lead the critic deeper and deeper into a labyrinth until he confronts a final aporia. . . . Only by going all the way into the labyrinth, following the thread of a given clue, can the critic reach the blind alley, vacant of any Minotaur, that impasse which is the end point of interpretation."[58] In the myth, the hero Theseus is saved by the love of a young woman, Ariadne. He is saved *from* being devoured by a monster, half man/half beast at the center of the labyrinth. In Miller's abbreviated version, the Minotaur is not encountered; rather, following Ariadne's (Pater's, in context) thread, the critic learns that the monster does not exist; he is a figment. What is at the centre is—an aporia. In "Ariadne's Thread," Miller uses the myth as a figure of deconstruction generally. Commenting on the essay in the course of a discussion in which she attempts to locate "the relations between deconstruction and feminism as practiced in the United States,"[59] Nancy K. Miller has argued that Hillis Miller erases feminine/feminist difference by conflating Ariadne's thread with his own critical practice. In a footnote, however, the feminist critic suggests a more radical view of how masculinity functions in Miller's use of the myth: "the masculist critic uses Ariadne to negotiate his encounter with the woman, perhaps in himself, the monstrous self the male critic might meet at the heart of the maze of heterosexuality."[60]

Reading the myth as Hillis Miller presents it, I notice that a woman's love "saves" the hero in his encounter with a male/monster that recalls the demonic representations of men sexually involved with other men that have long characterized Western culture. In "Walter Pater," in which Pater substitutes for Ariadne, a *feminized* homosexual enables the hero to play his role. Accordingly, Miller is free to leave nominally unanswered the question as to whether Pater is "frozen" at an "adolescent homosexual stage." (In the psychological economy of O'Hara's essay, Pater's "impotence" enables a contrasting display of vigour on O'Hara's part. Hence, ignoring Pater's complex politics is not fortuitous but necessary since otherwise the categories of serious-ness, political relevance, and masculine self-assertion would be mingled with a weak, that is, a specifically homosexual approach.) Neutralized by O'Hara or domesticated as Ariadne-*manqué*, Pater's thought becomes useful to the male deconstructionist who, now able to thread the maze, can show that the monster does not, after all, exist. The Minotaur is an aporia. At this moment, the process of subordination and elision serves yet another function in enabling an implicit fantasy of release (into aporia) from the bonds of conventional masculinity. Yet the setting aside of male homosexual difference has a number of large, unforeseen consequences. For one thing, if the specificities of gay male (not to mention, feminine) and other differences are to be excluded, then what exists within aporia? Or does it become a "blind alley"? In "Ariadne's Thread," the sexual mingling described in the opening interpretation of the myth is superseded, in the turn to theory, by a statement of "nine areas of linear terminology"[61] in terms of a strictly literary taxonomy.

At the end of the essay, however, gender returns in the form of expressly male anxieties when Miller moves to the third text from which he has drawn the epigraphs, Elizabeth Gaskell's *Cranford*. This final section deals with fears of genealogical extinction since, in Cranford, an "effeminate or effeminizing doubling"[62] threatens to lower the birth-rate to zero. While Miller wittily invokes these anxieties, conjured by a female writer, in order to dispel them, in face of the absence of other differences the attempt miscarries and what is reinscribed is continuing anxiety about the legitimate exercise of cultural authority within an alienated male intellectual elite. In its refusals, gaps, and reversals, Miller's writing signals the importance of those who, like Pater, have tried to write masculinity differently. In that process, deconstructive criticism has a significant part to play—as it does, for example, in recent work by Joseph Boone and Lee Edelman;[63] to play that part, however, requires an approach that recognizes both rhetorical contingencies and continual analysis of the assumptions of hegemonic masculinity within the academic practice of deconstruction itself.

"The Last Thing Walter Wrote": Pater's "Pascal"

_____ **11**

HAYDEN WARD

WALTER PATER DIED ON Monday 30 July 1894, the day he had been scheduled to give a University Extension lecture on Pascal.[1] Six months later, in refusing his offer to buy the manuscript, Clara Pater wrote to Edmund Gosse: "We could not possibly part with the Pascal manuscript for money. It is the last thing Walter wrote and was writing even during his illness, and so is precious to us."[2] However, Clara and Hester Pater did allow Gosse to edit the manuscript for publication in the _Contemporary Review_ for February 1895; subsequent to Charles Shadwell's publication of it in October in _Miscellaneous Studies_, the sisters gave it to Gosse.[3] After his death in May 1928, the manuscript was sold at auction (on July 30, thirty-four years to the day after Pater's death). It was sold again in 1942, as part of a Red Cross fund-raising drive, and finally acquired for the the Bodleian Library in 1945.

The essay on Pascal, although unfinished, is sufficiently complete and revised to be an important part of the Pater canon, not only because in writing of Pascal's last years, when he was composing the _Pensées_, Pater offers, by implication, some hints concerning his own late religious views,[4] but also because Pater here recapitulates several leading

143

themes of his earlier writings or presents them in new relations to one another.

These themes are the importance of "expressiveness" as an intellectual and moral force at critical moments of historical change or conflict; the struggle of philosophical and religious absolutism to retain its credibility against the pressure of an advancing moral and psychological relativism that is, in Pater's view, the principal salutary consequence of Renaissance humanism and the emergence of the modern romantic spirit; and the centrality of the aesthetic appeal in both the Primitive Church and Modern Christianity. In relation to all three of these themes of Pater's work, Pascal is an ambiguous and ironic figure, at different stages of his life the model of the diaphanous or transparent expressiveness that, from the beginning of his career, with "Diaphaneitè" (1864), Pater regards as the principal attribute of the perfected literary style, and at the same time the most obsessive example of devotion to the Augustinian or puritanical beliefs and practices that Pater regarded as inimical to human fulfillment as enacted in the harmonious aesthetic life.

Pascal is mentioned in several different contexts in Pater's earlier work.[5] In the 1871 essay on Pico della Mirandola, for instance, Pater contrasts the silent infinitude of Pascal's vision of the universe with the cosmos of coded correspondences elaborated by Pico at the onset of the Renaissance humanist's effort to develop syncretic thought out of a vast new range of experience, still sure of his ability to decipher the divine plan. By contrast, Pascal's wretched little man hovers over the abyss, crying out to a "hidden God"—for Pater, a precursor of the spiritual crisis of modern humanity, similarly placed between infinity and nothingness.

In his 1886 essay on Sir Thomas Browne, Pater speaks approvingly of Pascal's "great resolution" to define and enact the life in God, in contrast to Sir Thomas's more limited religious aspirations and whimsical anthropology. Pascal is the exemplar of "faith"—Browne, of "piety."[6] A year earlier, in the "New Cyrenaicism" chapter of *Marius the Epicurean*, Pater invokes the antagonism of Pascal to Montaigne, who, by historical analogy, is a kind of sponsor for the philosophy of "select sensation" that the youthful Marius, at an early stage in his spiritual quest, is discovering. Pater notes that Pascal calls the kindly and temperate wisdom of Montaigne "pernicious for all those who have any natural tendency to impiety or vice."[7]

Still another allusion to Pascal occurs in Pater's 1886 review of Mrs. Humphry Ward's translation of the *Journal Intime* of Henri Frederic Amiel, a work that by virtue of its fragmentary, occasionally aphoristic musings on morals and religion, prompts superficial comparison with the *Pensées.* Pater remarks that, in contrast to the lonely and sterile Amiel, mired in the still-rigid Calvinism of nineteenth-century Geneva, Pascal was fortunate to come to rest in "the large hopes of the Catholic Church." This statement has ironic implications by the time Pater writes of Pascal in 1894, when he describes the Jansenists of Port-Royal, with whom Pascal had "taken refuge" in his last years, as "the Calvinists of the Roman Catholic Church."[8]

Even in these scattered references in his earlier work, one can foresee the shadow of the tragic figure Pater will make of Pascal in his final essay. This late Paterian Pascal contrasts with the famous Leonardo of Pater's essay of 1869, who in his youth was already a masterful investigator of the laws of nature and of the abstruse, abstract systems of mathematics. The young Pascal was also a brilliant scientist and mathematician. Further, he was a superb polemicist, endowed with wit and pith, capable of expressing his ever-enlarging thoughts precisely and fully, moved by intense intellectual pride and courage to engage himself in the leading religious controversy of his day on the side of the oppressed party. Ironically, as Pater interprets him, he was drawn by irresistible emotional needs and the relentless logic of his own evolving convictions into a futile sacrifice of his own full humanity. In Pater's view, Pascal became "a solitary prisoner of his own dream of a world," abnegating the sensibility sketched in the "Conclusion" to *The Renaissance,* his last years amounting to "an inversion of what is called the aesthetic life."[9]

However, Pater begins the essay not with the inversion but with the triumph of the aesthetic life. He places Pascal at the center of the quarrel between the Jesuits and the Jansenists, between the adherents of the doctrine of "sufficient grace" and those of "necessary grace." In the early part of the essay, Pater emphasizes not Pascal's commitment to Jansenist theology but his powers as a stylist, a writer whose expressive power reveals as never before "the genius of French prose," just as Pater had said, in *Gaston de Latour*, that Ronsard and the other members of the Pléiade had revealed in the century preceding Pascal's the genius of French poetry. One might remark that, even in his late years, Pater's conception of literary and philosophical history remained Hegelian: the diaphanous or aesthetic hero is destined to bring to formal realization the latent but still inchoate style or gestalt of an artistic school, a religious movement, or a political order. Further, he characteristically does so not by imposing upon the resisting zeitgeist the irresistible force of his dominant will—as with Carlyle's heroes, for instance—but by possessing what Pater calls, in "Emerald Uthwart," the "genius of submission," the gift for taking into his own "transparent" (and malleable) nature the representative forces of his age and letting them shape him into the type of their conflict and, sometimes, in the happiest cases, of their resolution.

The witty play of the early *Provincial Letters*, like his work as a prodigy in mathematics and experimental physics, makes Pascal seem, at this stage in his career, a seventeenth-century continuator of the spirit of Renaissance humanism revelling in an exploration of the challenging variety of new knowledge, in revolt against the stultifying and corrupt authority of an outmoded scholasticism. Pater leaves implicit the irony of the fact that this scholasticism is defended not by representatives of the medieval Church but by spokesmen for the newly-created Jesuit order whose teachings are informed by the very skepticism that was one of the elements in Pascal's own later struggle for faith, a struggle that turns on Pascal's effort to repudiate the secular skepticism of Montaigne. In 1656, however, in beginning *The Provincial Letters*, Pascal is the diaphanous man engaged in aesthetic play. As Pater writes: "He took up the pen as other chivalrous gentlemen of the day took up the sword."[10]

In *The Provincial Letters*, with the perfect "expressiveness" of the diaphanous man, endowed with the "nicety with which words balance or match their meaning, and the writer succeeds in saying what he *wills*,"[11] Pascal enacts the aesthetic morality of Pater's essay on "Style," in cheerful but increasingly earnest combat with the logic-chopping equivocations of the Jesuits. The target of his criticism is the divorce of words from consistent or serious meaning that violates the true aesthetic morality. In this endeavor, Pater informs us, Pascal is of the genial company of Rabelais and Montaigne, of Molière and Voltaire, of Socrates and Newman, able to dissect the weaknesses of his opponents' argument so adroitly that he can afford to be gay and serious at the same time. In Letter XI, Pascal himself, quoting Tertullian, defines the tone of his writing against the Jesuits: "It is the proper privilege of truth to laugh, because she is gay, and to ridicule her enemies, because she is sure of victory. It is true that one must be careful to see that the gibes are not cheap and unworthy of truth, but, apart from that, where there is a chance of using them skillfully, it is our duty to do so."[12]

Pater says that Pascal was carried beyond this playful attitude by his deepening awareness of "those awful encounters of the individual soul with itself which are formulated in the eternal problem of predestination."[13] In the opposition of the Jesuits' expedient theology for the convenience of the mediocre many (turning upon the crucial but elusive concept of "sufficient grace") to a Jansenist principle of necessary and "irresistible grace" (defined in Cornelius Jansen's own *Augustinus* [1640], which traces the origins of the doctrine back to not only Augustine but to St. Paul), Pascal discovered an opposition between the futile, self-serving pragmatism of a politicized contemporary religion and the enduring truth of historically "developed" Church.[14]

His brief account of the Jansenist doctrine of freedom of the will to which Pascal gives his allegiance, as contrasted with the "Molinism" of Jesuit teaching, leads Pater to a reflection that helps to place his account of Pascal's sifting of rival doctrines in a nineteenth-century context that recalls Pater's earliest and most radical formulation of the issue: "There are moments in one's own life, aspects of the life of others, of which the conclusion that the will is free seems to be the only—is the natural or reasonable—account. Yet those very moments on reflexion, on second thought, present themselves again, as but links in a chain, in an all-embracing network of chains."[15] The "chains" of this passage were the "elements," the "fibres," of the "Conclusion" to *The Renaissance*, whose protean and evanescent forms were to be the objects of watchfulness and analysis in a "life of eager observation," lest they dwindle into nothingness before our eyes.

For Pascal, the intense commitment to the Jansenist doctrine of free will is, in Pater's view, the ironic first step in the assault on skepticism that was to result in the *Pensées* and in his gradual withdrawal from the world (as was, in Pater's mind, the case with Newman). The problem for Pascal, as apparently for Pater himself in his last years, was the inability totally to overcome the appeal of skepticism and to achieve a truly settled faith. Pater writes that Pascal "is not a sceptic converted, a returned infidel, but is seen there [i.e., in the *Pensées*] as if at the very center of a perpetually maintained tragic crisis, holding the faith steadfastly but amid the well-poised points of essential doubt all around him and it. It is no mere calm supersession of a state of doubt by a state of faith; the doubts never die, they are only just kept down in a perpetual *agonia*."[16]

The diaphanous clarity and poise that Pascal exhibited in *The Provincial Letters* are clouded in the *Pensées*, as Pater interprets that work, by a "malady" of body and soul. "In his soul's agony, theological abstractions seem to become personal powers," and these "powers" destroy his ability to take joy in the concrete human reality that is, for Pater himself, the basis of genuine religious sentiment. (In this respect, Pascal is more like Coleridge, as Pater describes him, than like Newman, who, as Pater says elsewhere, always had his faith rooted in a love of the "visible church.")

Pater evidently derived most of his information about the opposition of the Jansenists, and of Pascal, to the philosophy of Montaigne and of

Molière, "la Morale des l'honnêtes gens," from Book III of C. A. Sainte-Beuve's *Port-Royal*.[17] That philosophy makes the "natural man," in Richard Chadbourne's words, "a self-sufficient source of moral order and happiness," and derives from the teachings of the ancient Stoics, Skeptics, and Epicureans.[18] Such a philosophy is in direct conflict with the Jansenists' belief in "necessary grace," and therefore, as Pascal himself writes in the *Conversations with M. Saci* (1655), confuses and disillusions ordinary men who would believe in the mysteries that inspire true religious faith.

In refuting Montaigne, Pascal begins, according to Alban Krailsheimer,[19] with the same assumption as Montaigne and Socrates, that the end of man is to know himself. Thus, he preserves, at first, his allegiance to the historical role of diaphanous man, which is to be open to the whole range of possibilities in the search for truth and not to be bound or limited by undue adherence to "abstract" philosophies. But Pascal does not accept Montaigne's disavowal of reason in that search, since such a disavowal leads to intellectual inertia and moral relativism, and hence to indolence and hedonism. With reason operating not alone but under the influence of God's grace, man could break out of the false dilemma of skepticism and dogmatism, and achieve true faith, freed from the alienation from God that afflicts him when the evidence of his thought and senses tells him only that the world is hopelessly fallen and corrupt.

For Pascal, as Krailsheimer notes,[20] the goal was to transcend the dualism of mind and matter; that transcendence (which for Pater's diaphanous man, in his aesthetic morality of style, is the *fusion* of form and content in "perfect expressiveness") is only possible, according to the Jansenism that Pascal for the most part embraced, by the intervention of grace. Pascal's version of Montaigne believes that humanity is without that necessary grace.

So, too, is Pater's Montaigne, as he appears in the chapter of *Gaston de Latour* called "Suspended Judgement." Writing near the end of his own life, Pater attributes to Montaigne a philosophy that strongly recalls Pater's ideas in the "Conclusion" to *The Renaissance* and the

"New Cyrenaicism" chapter of *Marius*: "The priceless pearl of truth [lies], if anywhere, not in large theoretic apprehension of the general, but in minute vision of the particular; in the perception of the concrete phenomenon, at the particular moment, and from this unique point of view—now, but perhaps not then."[21] Here, in Pater's own words, is the "relativism" that Pascal fears. Beyond its relativism, Pater notes that the New Cyrenaicism possesses a "somewhat antinomian" cast: antinomianism is akin to the fideism of Montaigne. Pascal, in rejecting Montaigne, then, rejects a heretical doctrine that, by the time he wrote *Marius*, Pater recognized as latent in his own philosophy of the aesthetic life, in diaphanous openness and expressiveness. That is, he came to see that implicit in modern humanism is the temptation or danger of disregard for moral law. Pascal's renunciation of worldly involvement is, of course, a repudiation of humanism (of the "aesthetic life," says Pater, equating the two terms). That kind of about-face was impossible for Pater himself, it seems, and so he set out, as he had in *Marius*, to demonstrate that, by interpretation, harmony could be made to exist between the apparently conflicting strands, the changing "organic filaments," of his philosophic web. He sought to demonstrate the compatibility of the moral law and the life of disciplined, diaphanous receptivity and expressiveness, in the lectures on Plato and Platonism.[22]

Plato is Pater's late model of diaphanous man. He joins to the sensuous felicity and openmindedness of Montaigne a firm belief in the need for intellectual rigor, physical discipline, and perseverance in the pursuit of the higher truth. To Pascal, on the other hand, Pater assigns no such admirable status but stresses instead the melancholy and eventual morbidity that he perceives to be the consequence of Pascal's effort to synthesize reason and faith.

To understand Pater's view, incompatible as it is with the interpretations of Pascal offered by modern scholars much more intimately conversant with Pascal's writings than Pater was, one must go back to the review of Mrs. Ward's *Robert Elsmere* that Pater wrote for the *Guardian* of 28 March 1888. There, he describes what he calls a large class of minds which cannot be sure that the sacred story is true. It is philosophical, doubtless, and a duty to the intellect to recognise our doubts, to locate them, perhaps to give them practical effect. It may also be a moral duty to do this. But then there is also a large class of minds which cannot be sure it is false—minds of various degrees of conscientiousness and intellectual power up to the highest. They will think those who are quite sure it is false unphilosophical through lack of doubt. For their part, they make allowance in their scheme of life for a great possibility, and with some of them that bare concession of possibility (the subject being what it is) becomes the most important fact of the world. The recognition of it straightway opens wide the door to hope and love; and such persons are, as we fancy they always will be, the nucleus of a Church. Their particular phase of doubt, of philosophic uncertainty, has been the secret of millions of good Christians. . . .[23]

This "philosophic uncertainty," nurtured by "the scientific spirit which is for ever making the visible world fairer and more desirable in mortal eyes," is in an inimical relation to the "Augustinian" doctrine of Original Sin that so darkened the consciousness of Pascal that he was unable to live with the mere "possibility" of God's redemptive grace. To "wager" on God was to reject a morality rooted in fallen nature, based upon presuppositions about the inherent goodness or self-sufficiency of humanity.[24]

Pater's "hopefulness" is not a full-blown skepticism or agnosticism (like that, say, of Leslie Stephen, who wrote an essay on Pascal contemporaneous with Pater's[25]), but a more tentative "hedging" of the bet that in the appeal of the "visible world" (i.e., of philosophical materialism) may lie some dim but consoling spiritual element to be found in the bond of human community rather than in the impossibility of a lonely, transcendent communion of the individual with God. That "transcendent" element is what makes Pater reject Pascal's religious thought, with its "Calvinist" dimension, as the basis of the Christian life.[26]

Pater begins his analysis by commenting that the *Essais* of Montaigne are "the under-texture" of the *Pensées*; indeed, Montaigne offers a "compte rendu" of the experience of the world as Pascal, too, has known it. However, because of his Augustinian theology, Pascal is filled with terror by the vision of life that inspires merely a complacent skepticism in Montaigne. The "nothingness" of being fallen away from God is unendurable to Pascal; he must strive for its antithesis, sanctity. In Pascal's moral logic, says Pater, there can be no "middle terms."

Pater focuses on the apparent contradiction of Pascal's assertion that the truth of revelation must be based on evidence interpreted by the integrated powers of reason and imagination, and his assertion that the imagination only deceives the truth-seeker.[27] Pater suggests that by denying himself the use of the imaginative part of imaginative reason, Pascal failed to achieve "true peace within the Catholic Church." The last words of Pater's essay say that the imagination was simply in "active collusion" with Pascal's physical illness.

One cannot read these last pages of Pater's essay without being put in mind of Matthew Arnold's famous dictum in "Pagan and Mediaeval Religious Sentiment": "The poetry of later paganism lived by the senses and understanding; the poetry of mediaeval Christianity lived by the heart and imagination. But the main element of the modern spirit's life is neither the senses and understanding, nor the heart and imagination; it is the imaginative reason."[28] Arnold's dialectical formulation coincides neatly with Pater's own, in his earlier work, in which he discusses the pattern of medieval Christian asceticism giving way to the gradual enlargement of humanist sympathies in the Renaissance. It would seem, as Pater thinks of it at any rate, the Pascal enacts a reversal of this dialectic. He begins, as in *The Provincial Letters*, as a diaphanous advocate of a "fresh current of ideas" against the corrupt vestiges of scholasticism and expediency in Church and State, but ends his life by returning himself to the most rigorous practices of the old Church, which in its decadence, he had done so much to discredit. The irony of his career is that, in clearing away the debris of the degenerate modern Church, he became a victim (in Pater's view, at least) of an eccentric revival of the debilitating Augustinian theology of the Patristic Church.

Invariably, in applying to Pater's views on Pascal the paradigm of historical change that Arnold proposes and that Pater qualifies, one is led to think of Newman, whom Pater presents initially as comparable to Pascal, at least in the latter's early diaphanous phase.

One finds in the fragmentary text of Pater's evidently early essay on Newman, now in the Houghton Library, a contrast of Newman and Pascal.[29] Newman is joyful and confident once he has entered the Catholic Church, while Pascal is anguished in body and spirit, unable to see what Pater calls, in the Pascal essay, "the beauty of holiness." Newman's attraction to the Primitive Church and to Roman Catholicism is rooted in his desire for a historical continuum of religious community, in his desire for a "visible Church," as Pater calls it in *Marius* and elsewhere. Marius himself feels this Newmanesque longing at the end of the novel. Newman's "assent" is comparable to the faith attained by the adherents of the Primitive Church, as Pater describes it in the chapter of *Marius* called "The Minor Peace of the Church." The Newman of Pater's early essay is clearly diaphanous and remarkably undogmatic, a thinker disinclined to give undue weight to the claims of philosophy or theology as against allegiance to the claims of human life in this world. It is what he takes, arbitrarily and very selectively, to be the tranquillity and poise of Newman in the Catholic Church, not the Catholic "influence" and the theologian, that Pater finds attractive, that his entire essay, even in its scattered state, plainly expounds and endorses.[30]

Pater takes Newman perhaps too much at his word in believing that, after 1845, he never had a single doubt. For Pascal, by contrast, the doubt and melancholy persisted until the end. While Pater had ambivalent feelings about the intellectual triumphs and the human sacrifice of Newman's career, he felt, at the last, no such ambivalence toward Pascal, who, such as Pater draws him in this final essay, is diaphanous man in defeat and despair.

The Historiography
of *Studies in the History*
of the Renaissance

_____ 12

J. B. BULLEN

THOUGH PATER'S *Studies in the History of the Renaissance* appeared in 1873, his interest in the Renaissance dates from as early as 1864. Within this decade the concept of "renaissance" was historiographically unstable and its status as a historical myth extremely problematic. Was it a historical period at all, and if so how did it stand in relation to the Middle Ages? Was it characterized by the sum total of its works in art and literature or was it more specifically a set of ideas, attitudes and values? Was it located geographically in Italy or did it extend to France and the rest of Europe? The most pertinent question, however, and the one which gave most trouble, was its relationship with modern culture. Was it, as Ruskin in England and Rio in France would have it, the source of modern materialism, infidelity and pride extending, as Ruskin put it, "from the Grand Canal to Gower Street," or was it, as Quinet and Michelet would have it, an ontological, antinomian revolution which laid the foundations for modern rationalism and free thinking? All those who addressed themselves to the issue were agreed that the Renaissance was in some way a subversive movement; they were united in the belief that it was in conflict ideologically with the period that

155

preceded it, that it anticipated periods which followed, and that its influence was felt strongly in the present. Where they differed was in their interpretation of the nature of that subversion. Some saw it as destructive, others read it as creative. So when Pater applied himself to Renaissance history, the discourses available to him were highly polemicized. Whether he had chosen to side with Ruskin or with Renan, with Gautier or with Arnold, it was incumbent upon him to assess the period not only in terms of its own values, but more importantly, it was imperative for him to account for the way in which the Renaissance had contributed to the religion, the art, and the general culture of the nineteenth century.

"History," as Lévi-Strauss pointed out, "can never completely divest itself of myth,"[1] and in drawing on the contemporary myth of the Renaissance, Pater exploited those aspects of it which held most significance for the present. I want to show how Pater arrived at this view of the Renaissance and how in two of the early studies—studies of Leonardo da Vinci and Sandro Botticelli—he adopted a mode of writing which was not simply descriptive of the past but actually acted out, within the text itself, a response to the past which was essentially modern.

In a key passage in his essay on style Pater described the activity of the historian. "Your historian," he says, "with absolutely truthful intention, amid the multitude of facts presented to him must needs select, and in selecting assert something that comes not of the world without but a vision within." "So," he goes on, "Gibbon . . . Livy, Tacitus, Michelet . . . each, after his own sense, modifies—who can tell where and to what degree? and becomes something else than a transcriber . . . he becomes an artist, his work *fine* art."[2] There are two important elements here which bear directly upon *Studies in the History of the Renaissance*. First, Pater suggests that historiography is not a matter of recording facts; for him it is an integral act of self-expression. Second, true historiography is not a mechanical task; it is a fine art.

As to the first point, Roland Barthes quotes Nietszche as saying: "here are no facts *as such*. We must always begin by introducing a meaning in order for there to be a fact."[3] In the same context Barthes comments that the modern historian is "one who collects not so much facts as signifiers and relates them i.e. organizes them in order to establish a positive meaning and to fill the void of pure series."[4] In Pater's view, the historical fact—the signified—is of less importance than the "vision within." For Pater the chain of signification, or the form of historical discourse, takes precedence over the signified, the historical fact or the content of historical discourse. Pater's view on historical writing is further clarified by another remark from Barthes where he suggests that frequently in historical discourse there exists what he calls a second level, "that of a signified transcending the entire historical discourse transmitted by the historian's thematics, which we are thereby entitled to identify with the form of the signified."[5] This second level of signification must surely be associated, in Pater's case, with what he calls "the vision within" or the personal imprint of the historian within his own work. Of all recent writers it has been Gerald Monsman who has shown how pervasive is the Paterian "self" within the writings, and when he points out that "Pater modifies his reader's conceptions of the past and creates his precursors anew in his own image"[6] Monsman lends further weight to the notion that it is indeed that "self" which exists at the second level of signification within Pater's historical discourse.

Pater's second point, that true historiography is fine art, follows logically from the first as I have interpreted it. Fine art, as Pater understood it, is an expression of self. He says in *Marius the Epicurean* that to write well one must know, first of all "the true nature of one's impression . . . a true understanding of one's self being ever the first condition of genuine self."[7] But for Pater art is also a system where form takes precedence over matter, or alternatively where the signifier takes precedence over the signified. Thus Pater exploits the contemporary stress between past and present in Renaissance historical discourse by making his historiography an art-form. As Pater employs them, the details of Renaissance history become a chain of signifiers which point at one level to the past, i.e., to the historical period itself, and at the second level to the present where the "present" is defined most pertinently by the contemporary "self" of the writer.

Studies in the History of the Renaissance fulfills both criteria which Pater set out for the writing of history. It is the expression of a personal "self" and it is also a highly wrought work of literary art. Yet its early readers objected to it as orthodox history since it appeared to them to be disjunctive, incomplete and insubstantial. This feeling of light-weightedness derives in part from the high coefficient of selectivity in choice of subject and partly from the absence of primary and secondary material to lend weight and substance to the text. Readers of Hallam's *Middle Ages*, Sismondi's *History of the Italian Republics* or Ranke's *History of the Popes* must have been disappointed by *Studies in the History of the Renaissance*; Pater's response was to change its title.[8]

The problem lay in the relationship between what Barthes calls the syntagm and the system. Stephen Bann in his excellent work on nineteenth-century historiography uses Barthes's terms to distinguish between the narrative text of historical discourse—the syntagm—and the "series of associated fields" out of which it grows—the system. As Bann convincingly demonstrates, different kinds of historical writing can be attributed in part to the articulation of syntagm and system. In the work of a historian like Hallam the discursive mode is primarily epical. The syntagm proceeds logically and chronologically, while the system— the "storehouse of parallel and overlapping texts which the historian has drawn upon"[9]—is indicated in the elaborate network of footnotes. Pater, however, does not write like this. The size and complexity of the system in Pater's work is manifestly apparent in the huge supplement to *Studies in the History of the Renaissance* provided by both Billie Inman and Donald Hill. But Pater goes out of his way to give priority to the syntagm by weaving the system directly into the texture of the narrative.

Pater further stresses the importance of the narrative as narrative by a refusal to adopt the epical mode. Chronological sequence is replaced by a series of affinities. Periodization is dissolved. The text is reduced to a spare sequence of studies in temperament extending from the Middle Ages to the eighteenth century and beyond, each of which is metonymically linked to a set of Renaissance ideas and attitudes. Furthermore, and perhaps most important, the relationship between past and present is problematized. The demarcation between what is now and what was is persistently foreshortened, partly by linguistic devices—the use of the verbal imperfect and present rather than the perfect—partly by a panoply of intertextual references which generate an exchange between past and present—references to the work of Goethe, Heine, Browning, Arnold, Rossetti and so on—but mainly by implying an affinity between the perceiving consciousness of each of the Renaissance personae and that of the author. So, for example, Botticelli's painting is located referentially within the system of the neo-classical appreciation of Raphael and the more recent romantic appreciation of Fra Angelico. Botticelli's Madonnas, Pater writes, "often come back to you when the Sistine Madonna and the Virgins of Fra Angelico are forgotten."[10] But at the level of the syntagm Pater's sympathetic reading of the *Madonna of the Magnificat* acts simultaneously as an emblem of Botticelli's theological disinterestedness—"the high cold words have no meaning for [the Madonna]"[11]—and Pater's personal indifferentism. Furthermore what Barthes calls in another context the "excess of signification"—here it is the white light in the picture which Pater describes as being cast up "hard and cheerless from below, as when snow lies upon the ground, and the children look up with surprise and wonder"[12]—serves to intensify the presence within the text of the sensitive Paterian "self."

What I wish to suggest is that there is an intimate connection between Pater's highly personal mode of historical discourse and his choice of the Renaissance as the subject of his writing. I want to stress that the evolution of the historical Renaissance as a central topic in Pater's early essays is intimately linked to a personal renaissance, and a process of self-discovery in the context of historiography.

It is characteristic therefore that the very first time that Pater alludes to the Renaissance it appears as a function of temperament. This occurs in "Diaphaneitè" of 1864 where Raphael is described as being "in the midst of the Reformation and the Renaissance, himself lighted up by them," though he yields "himself to neither."[13] The Renaissance contributes one element to Coleridge's writings in the essay of 1866. What Pater calls "the dawn of the Renaissance"[14] in the thirteenth century is the first indication of his interest in the Renaissance, not so much as a period, but as a process—a process which is explored more fully in the difficult and rebarbative essay on Winckelmann in the following year. What took place at the dawn of the Renaissance is rehearsed in Winckelmann's rediscovery of classical culture, this time in the eighteenth century. What is especially interesting for us in Pater's account of Winckelmann's work is his persistent collapse of historicity. The distant past—the Renaissance—the early eighteenth century and the immediate present are foreshortened with an urgency and an energy previously absent from Pater's writing:

> Filled as *our* culture is with the classical spirit, *we* can hardly imagine how deeply the human mind was moved when at the Renaissance, in the midst of a frozen world, the buried fire of ancient art rose up from under the soil. Winckelmann here reproduces for *us* the earlier Renaissance sentiment. On a sudden the imagination feels free. How facile and direct, it seems to say, is this life of the senses and the understanding when once *we* apprehend it! That is the more liberal life *we* have been seeking so long, so near *us* all the while. How mistaken and roundabout we have been in *our* efforts to reach it by mystic passion and religious reverie; how they have deflowered the flesh; how little they have emancipated us![15]

The first person plural, "us," and the possessive, "our," both draw the early Renaissance and the work of Winckelmann into the present and establish the centre of the discourse firmly within the shared identity of reader and writer. The essay is charged with similar moments of self-realization, and it is this sense of self-realization which becomes the principal subject of his next essay on the poetry of William Morris. Once again the first person singular dominates at points of crux. Modern identity, or selfhood, is defined by Pater as part of a process of historical evolution:

> The composite experience of all the ages is part of each one of *us*; to obliterate any part of it, to come face to face with the people of a past age, as if the

middle age, the Renaissance, the eighteenth century had not been, is as impossible as to become a little child, or enter again into the womb and be born. But though it is not possible to repress a single phase of that humanity, which, because *we* live and move and have *our* being the life of humanity, make us what *we* are; it is possible to isolate such a phase, to throw it into relief. . . . *We* cannot conceive the age; *we* can conceive the element it has contributed to *our* culture. . . .[16]

The Morris essay is pivotal in Pater's treatment of history. Here Pater principally employs two modern texts—"The Defence of Guenevere" and "The Life and Death of Jason"—as emblems of contemporary shift in mental awareness—a shift which he had already detected within the matrix of history.

The earlier poem represents the "mystic passion and religious reverie" which he had, in the Winckelmann essay, identified with the culture of the Middle Ages. It is the poetry of "reverie, illusion, delirium" in which "the things of nature begin to play a strange delirious part."[17] The later poem represents the reawakening of the mind to "the body of nature for its own sake, not because a soul is divined through it."[18] But it is the shift itself or the process enacted in the term "renaissance" which concerns Pater. In two modern texts, he finds a principle or a "law" as he calls it, which transcends temporality and period. "It explains," he says, "through [Morris] one law of the life of the human spirit, and of which what we call the Renaissance is only a supreme instance."[19] Pater had reached this point by a slow process of indirection over a period of some four years; but within the interstices of two contemporary texts he had at last clinched the personal significance for him of "past ages" as he found them embedded in the texture of the present.

The famous closing paragraphs of the Morris essay are organically linked to this discovery. The first part of the Morris essay identifies the self as the creation of a historical process; the second part identifies fine art as the consummate expression of the self. Structurally these two sections anticipate Pater's remark on historiography in his essay on style. The historian discovers himself in history, he asserts something that comes of the "vision within" and in articulating that self "he becomes an artist, his work *fine art.*" The first element in this structure represents the signified, the meta-subject of Pater's future work, the process called the "renaissance"; the second element represents the mode of signification—history as fine art. The essay on Morris appears at the end of *Studies in the History of the Renaissance*. The material on Morris, however, was removed by Pater and all the essays in the series took its place. The structural relationship, nevertheless, remains intact.

I think that we can safely say that it was at this point Pater established for himself a methodology and a system for the writing of the remainder of his Renaissance essays. After his essay on Morris the whole tenor of his discourse changes and it is at this point he makes a transition from the writing of history as analysis to the writing of history as enactment. The change can be expressed, in part, as a shift from metaphor to metonymy. Previously Pater's historiography had been largely metaphoric. The temperament and work of Winckelmann and the poetry of Morris metaphorically embodied central aspects of the Renaissance spirit as Pater conceived it. "Winckelmann . . . reproduces for us the earlier Renaissance sentiment" and "the simplification" in Morris's poetry is interesting because it "explains . . . one law of the life of the human spirit." In many of the Renaissance studies which follow, Pater adopts a predominantly metonymical approach. Leonardo da Vinci is but a fragment, a supreme instance of one aspect of the Renaissance, and his art represents in turn highly concentrated and refined examples of the more general tendency of his mind. The very title of the volume, *Studies in the History of the Renaissance*, has a metonymic ring to it. It suggests neither epical history nor metaphorical history but indicates instead an accretion of parts—hence the contemporary criticism of its inadequacy as "history."

The shift from metaphor to metonymy is most vividly registered in Pater's treatment of works of visual art. His intertextual use of visual artifacts prior to the Leonardo essay of 1869 are few and when they occur are frankly illustrative and ostensive. In the Winckelmann essay, for example, he uses Fra Angelico's *Coronation of the Virgin* as a

metaphor for the inability of medieval art to adequately convey immediately apprehended sensuous experience: "Take, for instance, a characteristic work of the Middle Ages, Angelico's 'Coronation of the Virgin,'
at San Marco, in Florence. In some strange halo of a moon sit the
Virgin and our Lord, clad in mystical white raiment, half-shroud half
priestly linen. . . . Certainly it cannot be said of Angelico's fresco that
it throws into sensible form our highest knowledge about man and his
relation to the world."[20]

Pater contrasts this with the Venus de Milo, which he says, "is in no
sense a symbol, a suggestion of anything beyond its victorious fairness."
The *Westminster Review*, in which the essay first appeared, carried no
illustrations, but the comparative method—"look on this and now on
this"—gesturing to that which lies outside and beyond the text calls out
for the illustration which feels entirely appropriate in Donald Hill's
edition. This method had been brought to a high pitch of refinement
by Ruskin who frequently employed visual images as cultural metaphors.

Pater's treatment of Leonardo's works, however, is very different
from his account of Fra Angelico's *Coronation*. I have suggested
elsewhere that Pater's account of the *Gioconda* is an accretion of
symbols which relate directly to his interpretation of romanticism[21] and
taken in isolation it is possible to interpret Pater's account as primarily
symbolical or metaphoric. Within the discourse of the essay as a whole,
however, the treatment of the *Gioconda*, as of the other works of art by
Leonardo, is primarily metonymic. It is, Pater tells us, "the revealing
instance of his mode of thought and work."[22] Within the single
fragment, the painted picture, are gathered up the elements which
constitute Leonardo's special temperament, focussed, refined and
concentrated in one image. In comparing the Fra Angelico and the
Venus de Milo, Pater adopts an ostensive mode. The objective
properties of the visual artifacts are stressed, and the signified takes
precedence over the signifier. In his account of the *Gioconda*, however,
the signified, the physical properties of the work of art itself fade from
view and the highly encrusted prose, the signifier, takes precedence. The
shift from the method of the Winckelmann essay to the Leonardo essay

can be seen in terms of a shift from an allegiance to the methods of Ruskin to those of Swinburne.

Swinburne's account of Leonardo's studies in the Uffizi is well-known: "fair strange faces of women full of dim doubt and faint scorn; touched by the shadow of an obscure fate."[23] So, too, is Pater's acknowledgment of a debt to Swinburne. Swinburne's "Notes on Designs of the Old Masters at Florence" is an essay which deals with nearly three dozen artists and is a veritable taxonomy of responses. Swinburne prefaces his notes, however, by various remarks which locate those responses firmly within the perceiving consciousness of the author. "For guide," Swinburne writes, "I have but my own sense of interest and admiration . . . [and] I have aimed at nothing further than to cast into some legible form my impression of the designs. . . ."[24] Swinburne suppresses the descriptive and stresses the affective and in casting into "legible form" his "impression" he has written himself into his own text. Swinburne's essay was published in July 1868; Pater's essay on Leonardo appeared in November 1869, and in Swinburne's work Pater discovered a means by which the transformation of the visual sign into the verbal sign might act as an expressive vehicle for the temperamental mode of the authorial self.

It is possible to say that in the essays which preceded the piece on Leonardo, Pater employed works of visual art illustratively. In the essays on Leonardo and Botticelli he seizes upon a discourse developed by Swinburne which shifts the locus of representation from illustration to perception and interpretation. In other words, the paintings which are signified within the text are no longer metaphors of historical ideologies; they are instead the focus of a perceiving consciousness. Pater's method, however, is much more ambitious than Swinburne's. Whereas Swinburne is writing only a series of what he calls "Notes on Designs," Pater locates the art works in a larger historical framework. Within that framework the works function on two levels. At one level they act as the paradigmatic modes of perception of the subjects of each essay. The *Gioconda* is the "most revealing instance of [Leonardo's] mode of thought" and *The Birth of Venus* is the "most complete expression"[25] of Botticelli's classical sentiment. At a second level, however, they are also the expression of Pater's own perceiving consciousness, what Swinburne called "the legible form" of his "impression." In Pater's verbal rendition of visual objects these two levels unite and dissolve one within the other. "The consciousness of author and character" as Monsman puts it, "become inextricably interwoven."[26] There are no illustrations in *Studies in the History of the Renaissance* and rightly so. Priority is given to the chain of signifiers, "the animalism of Greece, the lust of Rome, the mysticism of the middle age"[27] while the signified, the portrait of Gioconda which hangs in the Louvre, fades into insignificance. So it is with *The Birth of Venus*, and with the other works of art in the *Studies*.

But Pater extends this technique from the art works to the artists, painters, sculptors and writers who form the subjects of *Studies in the History of the Renaissance*. So as he handles the "legends" of his historical characters, as he picks and chooses among the myths associated with them, he creates a syntagm which is related to, but independent of, the system of historical reference. In writing history, Pater, in his own words, is concerned "not with the world without but with a vision within." The first duty of the aesthetic critic, as he points out in the "Preface," is to identify the nature of his own impression. Like Swinburne he puts into "legible form" the "impression" and in doing so he becomes "something else than a transcriber . . . he becomes an artist and his work *fine* art."

As we know, art—and particularly literary art—was given high status in Pater's hierarchy of values. In the "Conclusion" to *The Renaissance* he describes art as the repository of intensified experience, a bastion against the flux of the material world and the flux of the sensational world. Art also is an expression of the self; it serves to disengage the permanent self from the disturbing and dissolving aspects of consciousness. The historian, according to Pater, is an "artist and his work fine art" and as Monsman correctly says, "Pater envisions himself . . . as a figure of multiple selfhood . . . a web of cultural relationships and the individual to be the visible image of an infinite companionship of like-oriented selves that pervade and shape the personality."[28]

In this way we can see that *Studies in the History of the Renaissance* is in essence a work of modern art, and what modern art has to do "in the service of culture," as Pater says at the end of his essay on Winckelmann, "is so to rearrange the details of modern life, so to reflect it, that it may satisfy the spirit."[29] Consequently his attempt throughout the book is to make sense of the present in terms of the past.

The reasons why Pater committed himself to a modern work of historiography based upon Renaissance subjects in or around 1868 is now a little clearer. The system within which Pater was working at this time, as Billie Inman's book on Pater's reading makes clear, was dominantly French. And when we examine the texts of Michelet, Quinet and Gautier, the figure of Leonardo emerges as "tout moderne."[30] The creation of the modern myth of Botticelli, on the other hand, was essentially an English phenomenon. Arthur Symons pointed out that *Studies in the History of the Renaissance* "has many affinities with the poetic and pictorial art of Rossetti, Swinburne and Burne-Jones"[31] and by 1868 it is certain that Pater knew of the high reputation of Botticelli among these artists.

Pater's studies further enhance the "modernity" of these historical figures. Throughout his writing about them he persistently casts off the debris which made them subjects of what he calls "mere antiquarianism." Moreover, they are given a contemporary existence through the vitality of their works of art which transcend the passage of time and within which their personalities are inscribed. As Pater describes them each becomes a kind of cultural burning glass, "present . . . at the focus," in Pater's words, "where the greatest number of vital forces unite in their purest energy."[32] Each of them, true to the "vision within," wrests from the flux of historical change, images of intensity and vitality which are vested in the permanent forms of art. The essay on Winckelmann is a discursive and analytical account of this process; the essays which follow the Morris article are an enactment of the process in these, Pater himself becoming the final link in the chain of that process; he himself is "focus" where the vital forces of his own culture unite. His ostensible subject is a metonymic study of the Renaissance embodied in the life and works of certain individuals; but these in turn are transformed and become a secondary system in a work whose meta-subject is Pater himself. Just as Leonardo or Botticelli focused the essential components of their culture in their works of art, so Pater re-enacts that process in *Studies in the History of the Renaissance*. We can see that Pater's realization in 1868 that "the composite experience of all the ages is part of each one of us" led him to create a historical text which was "fine art" developed out of a "vision within" and a sensibility which was exclusively modern.

Pater's Mythic Fiction:
Gods in a Gilded Age

13

M. F. MORAN

THE DISCUSSION of Pater's mythological fiction has been governed by two predominant strains in Paterian criticism. One is the autobiographical and psychoanalytic perspective; critics employing this approach have focused on the hidden selves obliquely embedded and disguised in Paterian texts. Among recent analyses of "Denys L'Auxerrois" (1886) and "Apollo in Picardy" (1893) have been readings of these short stories as coded references to Pater's homosexuality and, as in Gerald Monsman's sophisticated *Walter Pater's Art of Autobiography*, an oedipal drama linked to "the theme of artistic self-consciousness."[1]

Alternatively, these tales have been considered from a thematic and structural viewpoint which emphasizes Pater's concern with opposing abstract philosophical positions. In an important 1961 essay, for example, R. T. Lenaghan identifies a Hegelian dialectic permeating Pater's fiction. The pattern he detects is based on an essential opposition between two human tendencies: the spiritual Apollonian "ideal human development" signifying order, sanity, and balance, and the Dionysian power of "massive vitality external to man" which emphasizes the physical, sensuous, and freely mobile.[2] For Lenaghan, Pater's fiction explores the continued recurrence of these impulses, suggesting

169

"the possibility of synthesis" at certain cultural moments, or division at others. Thus, "an enduring symbolic significance" may be attributed to the old gods who are refashioned in Pater's two stories.[3]

Other critics have followed this lead. Sloane Frazier, for instance, examines the oppositions inherent in Pater's Denys and Apollyon; he suggests these godlike characters have a "timelessness" in their "spiritual isolation" so that readers are carried "above and outside of history" to investigate conflicting spiritual impulses.[4] Wolfgang Iser, more simply, sees the tales as presenting both Pater's "longing for unity" and its disappointment, while Steven Connor's recent investigations reveal an elusive temporary synthesis of the contradictions of myth.[5]

Moreover, from time to time, critics have also seen Pater's transformations and displacements of myth as strategies for cultural analysis. Pater adopts diachronic as well as synchronic approaches to myth, but both indicate his concern with relationships between myth and culture. His chronological study of myth's development through time and his reincorporation of mythic elements in a range of fictions have prompted readers to interpret the stories "almost as a series of essays examining different *Zeitgeists*."[6] On the other hand, the displacement of gods to an alien medieval environment provides an ahistorical base for the construction and interpretation of mythic narrative. In so far as essential characteristics of the gods remain embedded in their human counterparts, Pater is able "not just to show how the world has changed, but to show also, in the continued vitality of the old myths, how it has not changed."[7] From both perspectives, however, there is an underlying assumption that Pater's treatment of myth is closely tied to a belief that mythology expresses the experience of a culture—past or contemporary.

Certainly, the study of Victorian theories of mythology suggests that this view of myth as expressive of a society was well-established and widespread in the period. James Kissane, for example, highlights the pervasive influence of George Grote, who argued that myth was based on the "prevalent emotions of the public."[8] In *Studies of the Greek Poets* (1873), Edward Tylor made the same connection between myth and self-expression of a community or society: " 'myth is the history of its authors, not of its subjects; it records the lives, not of superhuman heroes, but of poetic nations'."[9] Similarly, Janet Burstein has demonstrated that the Victorians saw myth as a symbolic discourse revealing ideas and feelings about the external world as it related to the self. She convincingly links Pater particularly to the work of Grote and Tylor, and the folklorist Edward Clodd, all of whom shared a view of myth "as a dense and highly complex mode of thought and expression."[10]

It lies beyond the scope of this essay to explore in depth the ways in which Pater's myth-making can be translated into his experience of the culture of the Victorian age. However, a study of Pater's own reworkings of mythic characters in the light of his views on the cultural significance of mythology lends further support to current critical interest in Pater's definition of the modern sensibility emerging in his period. "Denys L'Auxerrois" and "Apollo in Picardy" dramatize the development of a modern spirit resistant to the imaginative syntheses which classical myths traditionally offered: syntheses of life and death, of flux and stability, even of the earthly and transcendent, the material and the unseen. Focus on Pater's mythography and transformations confirms his interest in a modern consciousness divided against itself: a theory of personality which Paterian scholars have deemed a "commonplace in Modernist literature."[11] But more radically, the mythic fiction highlights a particular manifestation of this divided modern spirit located in critical practice itself. At the same time as the tales express a "reading" of the modern cultural dilemma, their form and narrative strategies call into question traditional concepts of "reading," of the process of ascribing meaning, of the practice and nature of interpretation.

Pater's view of myth-making as an interpretive act can be traced in his essays on the development of Greek mythology. He suggests, for example, that the imaginative and creative process underpinning all stages of a myth's transformations is intimately bound to a community's attempt to understand and articulate its experience. In "The Myth of Demeter and Persephone" (1875) Pater attributes the origins of the myth to "no single person, but the whole consciousness of an age," suggesting myth expresses shared cultural perceptions, however "faintly-felt."[12] Again, in the 1876 essay "A Study of Dionysus: The Spiritual Form of Fire and Dew," Pater describes the "thought of Dionysus and his circle" (for the Greeks) as "a sacred representation or interpretation of the whole human experience, modified by the special limitations, the special privileges of insight or suggestion, incident to their peculiar mode of existence."[13] This view of the expressive and culture-specific nature of myth also lies behind his discussion of the evolution of Dionysian myth from its first primitive form as generalized "tree-worship" to its poetical humanization and eventual connection "to ethical culture, to the perfecting of the moral nature."[14] Pater focuses on the ways in which the changing events and characters of the myth attempt to explain a society's view of itself and its relationship to forces which are not wholly comprehensible in terms of other available discourses, nor even clearly identified. While Pater asserts that the "element of natural fact . . . is the original essence of all mythology," the myth of Dionysus which gradually takes shape in Greek art and poetry is rather more than crude natural history, becoming instead "the projected expression of the ways and dreams of this primitive people, brooded over and harmonised by the energetic Greek imagination."[15]

Like many Victorian mythographers, Pater views myth in broad terms as subjective in origin, expressive of the changing perceptions of a culture and gradually transformed as the world is re-structured or reinterpreted by a culture's changing consciousness. The figure of the god becomes a single form "comprehending, as its animating soul, a whole world of thoughts, surmises, greater and less experiences."[16] Pater embraces the idealist view of myth as a symbolic process, part of—in Viconian terms—"the story of man making himself, man recreating his own spirit and subjective being"; it is a "language of the imagination," a "communal expression."[17] In manner and matter myth for Pater has a "cognitive function . . . as the representation of the inner vision of a people."[18] It is itself an act and art of interpretation, ascribing shape, explanation, or meaning to diverse, inchoate experiences, intuitions, and feelings. It is not thus surprising that Pater's re-inventions of myths for his own age deal explicitly and implicitly with the art of interpretation: not only do they construct a new reading of the modern temper but they deconstruct the "myth" of interpretation and deny the possibility of a stable, identifiable meaning.

Pater's treatment of the modern sensibility in both "Denys L'Auxerrois" and "Apollo in Picardy" is particularly revealing when considered in the light of his earlier analysis of the temper and imagination responsible for the classical manifestations of Dionysus and Demeter. In the first place, Pater foregrounds the ways in which all stages of these myths reveal a cultural consciousness capable of accepting and fusing experience of both physical phenomena and "unseen powers beyond the material veil of things."[19] The early phase of the Demeter myth, for example, which Pater likens metaphorically to childhood with its undifferentiating grasp of the external world, is one of unconscious instinct and empathy, a spontaneously affective response to both realms: "[T]he mental starting point . . . [is] some such feeling as most of us have on the first warmer days in spring, when we seem to feel the genial processes of nature actually at work; as if just below the mould . . . there were really circulating some spirit of life, akin to that which makes its energies felt within ourselves."[20] Pater's stylistic qualifications—"some such feeling," "most of us," "seem to feel," "as if . . . there were really circulating"—emphasize the subjectivity of this representation of the external world, which presents a community's feelings about its environment, not an objective empirical analysis of it.

Similarly, his assertion that at the root of Dionysus's characterization lies a "world of vision unchecked by positive knowledge"[21] confirms his view of the imaginative structuring of experience offered in myth. But the comment points to a further belief in myth as an embodiment of the transcendent or numinous intuitions of its creators. By referring variously to the "unseen forces," "visionary places," "hidden ordinances"[22] which underpin the conception of Dionysus, together with the more homely and physical culture of the vine, Pater presents the classical temper as one open to the Numen, that "*wholly other*" nonrational, non-moral "Presence uniting mystery and transcendence with energy, vitality, force."[23] And, as the physical beauty of the god comes to represent the *"spiritual form* of fire and dew,"[24] so the act of forging and developing a mythic narrative becomes a way of externalizing and accommodating a human sense of difference, an awareness of the co-existence of both the self and the unfamiliar Other: "a certain mystical apprehension . . . of unseen powers beyond the material veil of things."[25]

Even his treatment of the malign or demonic forces of Dionysian myth—its blood-lust and insanity—or of the sorrowing mother figure of Demeter, conveys something of Pater's sympathy for the Greek ability to embrace "certain shadowy places" of foreboding and corruption in life, at least in the context of a mythic narrative.[26] The Other may seem evil and threatening; but the Greek imagination which can creatively respond to such difference is saluted as "a unifying or identifying power, bringing together things naturally asunder."[27] The growth of self-consciousness in Greek culture results not in an exclusion of difference, but in its acceptance and incorporation into a re-creation of the myth "made by and for sorrowful, wistful, anxious people."[28]

Moreover, the extent to which Dionysus, like Demeter, is typified by Pater as a dual god, reflecting "a certain darker side" of nature[29] demonstrates Pater's interest in ancient myth as a conciliatory language which momentarily holds in suspension the complex polarities and contraries in human experience. Poised between the finite perfection of the human form and intuitions of a fluid and free natural life-force, myth expresses a mediation between transcendent and mortal, expansion and regulation, between a centrifugal dynamic ("teeming, still fluid") and a centripetal impulse to intelligent order and discipline, a manifestation of the definite and concrete, the "perfectly conceivable human forms."[30] Myth for Pater unites these two seemingly irreconcilable perspectives; beneath the concrete sensuous form still lies that "restless idealism, inward vision"[31] which is constantly re-expressed as the conscious and unconscious perceptions of a culture change.

Indeed fluidity itself becomes a dominant characteristic of each myth which Pater considers in *Greek Studies*. Myth may capture and represent, in a coded way, a society's idealized and internalized dreams of itself. But the idealized "reading" of human nature and potentiality encoded in myth remains an expression of desire only, the resolution offered indefinite and elusive: "the visible embodiments of the *susceptibilities* and *intuitions* of the nobler kind of souls."[32] And the insights thus expressed remain vision or dream only; as an interpretation of a community's sense of itself, it will be continually re-created in keeping with changing cultural needs and perceptions.

Recently, Pater's similarity to other Victorian mythographers who identify a clear three-stage evolutionary process within mythologies has been called into question. Pater's revisions of his essays on myth might, as Steven Connor effectively argues, indicate his growing preference for a dynamic of development based on the dialectical oscillation of "instinctive within conscious ways of knowing."[33] Nonetheless, what is clear is that Pater relates the process of myth-making to the history of a culture and its changing conception of its own experience. His theoretical writings also indicate that he finds myth a creative and interpretative narrative art.[34] The many transformations of a given mythos chart a society's attempts to "make" itself, to construct an identity (moral, spiritual, emotional, even national), to offer a reading of the connection between objective and subjective phenomena, between conscious perceptions and unconscious intuitions.[35] But in his emphasis on the constant refashioning, refining, and re-creating of myths to accommodate new versions of the ideal, Pater also implicitly suggests something of the relative and unstable nature of the process of interpretation itself. A myth is never static. Each "interpretation" of experience which a myth expresses will become outmoded and unrelated to the new vision which a society has of itself and must be re-interpreted in turn. There is no single, permanent ideal vision or myth with one, single, and stable meaning.

Pater's own refashionings of mythological narratives to represent the new sensibilities and values of a modern culture seem in subject-matter alone to highlight this very fluidity. The pagan gods of antiquity are displaced to the alien environment of the "spiritualized" Middle Ages. They are caught in a period of transition and cultural instability,[36] when an earlier sensuous and passionate temper closely bound to the movement of nature has not yet been wholly supplanted by a new rigorous rationality and asceticism. Nevertheless, Pater's mythological fictions resist any easy appropriation of classical values by the modern spirit; the interaction of the exiled figures with their new environment proposes no nostalgic return to a Golden Age.

In the first place, Pater's definition of the modern spirit is wholly at odds with the cultural ambience which he links to the production and reception of those old myths. Dionysus and Apollo are products of a worldview which acknowledges the individual's connection to the physical environment and which holds in awe a powerful, transcendent Other, the cosmic source of energy and vitality. But the worlds of Denys and Apollyon, characterized by a curious single-mindedness and inflexibility, are presented as directly opposed to this classical sensibility. In the medieval societies of both "Denys L'Auxerrois" and "Apollo in Picardy" there is a marked emphasis on a coldly reasonable and ordered relationship between the individual and the world beyond. Rigid discipline rather than creative energy generates the products of this culture. The eleven volumes of Prior Saint-Jean's "dry" treatise on mathematics seek to pinpoint exact and precise truths through the application of "strict method" and "long and intricate argument."[37] The religious rituals of Auxerre ludicrously celebrate the spiritual freedom of redemption through a game of ball played on Easter Day like a funeral rite by pompous self-important canons who act "solemnly," "gravely," with "decorum."[38] Analytical scientific or scholastic discourse, like that of the Prior, or the mechanized, superstitious rituals of the people of Auxerre, become ways of structuring the disorderly, irrational, and individualistic element of experience to keep it under conscious control. Indeed the repression of difference which Pater explores in the texts might be read as another important feature of the modern (not just medieval) temper. Tactics of authoritarian control and the irrepressible drive of the unconscious form important themes in both stories, and might well signal the potential clash between "order" and "anarchy" in Victorian capitalist England, entering in its late phase an uneasy transitional stage not unlike the worlds of Denys and Apollyon.[39]

Pater's own suspicion of these techniques of repression can be seen in his narrative description of such approaches. All reek of death; the Prior's privileging of intellect and logic is connected to a life which is rigidly compartmentalized and suffocating, whatever its material rewards. He is literally incarcerated by the monastic walls with little "breathing-space." His massive scientific treatise is designed to conclude the rigidly organized progress of his career, "by drawing tight together the threads" of the argument.[40] The exhumation of the saint in Auxerre is an attempt to control the malevolent forces which the townsfolk fear are at large. But the rite quite literally reveals a stagnant culture in love with death, as the unprepossessing mummified shrunken body is placed in an elaborately jewelled shrine amidst the stench of "mouldering human remains."[41]

Such rituals suggest a world which can scarcely accommodate mythic vision, as Pater conceived it in *Greek Studies*. This world lacks a sense of vital and sympathetic connection to a living, external environment. Moreover, the societies which Pater depicts are marked by a secularized consciousness. Despite the grand churches and elaborate religious liturgy of Auxerre, there is little sense of the transcendent in the ceremonies. Monks like Hermes "study and experiment," not in order to reaffirm mankind's participation in the vital cosmic life-force, but to wrest nature's secrets from her, even, as in the case of the Prior in "Apollo in Picardy," to gain material reward in the form of promotion.

This emphasis on a self-centred and intellectualized perspective is coupled with a further privileging of authority and hierarchy as tools of power and control. The monastic communities and feudal system as presented in the stories marginalize the common people. The laity are usually simply passive onlookers at religious ceremonies; for most of the narrative they are silent, and their resentment at the luxury and power of those above them only obliquely suggested. The monastic pigeon-house in "Apollo in Picardy" is a striking example of the deathly nature of the feudal structure.[42] Described as "a feathered brotherhood" the pigeons are likened metaphorically to the monastic system itself. The tower's white exterior excludes the dangerously different and unacceptable (the never-named "creeping things"), and the "common people" are forbidden "so much as [to] ruffle" a single bird. The birds, though ostensibly a "community," are compartmentalized, "each in its little chamber," so that the term "brotherhood" becomes an ironic misnomer for both birds and the monastic order they exemplify. The entire group is given to preening "self-content"; though, indulgent as this may seem, the birds themselves seem to the narrator as pampered "inmates" bred and cossetted to form "the daintiest fare" at the monastic table. In miniature, then, the pigeon-house reveals the ultimate danger of the stagnant self-satisfaction of a corrupt society. In protecting itself through mental structures of control, it renders itself prisoner. It is a community divided and fragmented and, as such, self-destructive; the feathered brotherhood are (somewhat cannibalistically given the metaphor) devoured by their human counterparts.

While the modern spirit which Pater represents in these stories seems far from the consciousness which developed the myth of Dionysus, his views on the function of myth as a mediating vehicle which accommodates opposed readings of experience seem initially to be dramatized in the narratives. Denys and Apollyon each provide a positive image of that Other which the modern sensibility has repressed rather than accommodated. Both are associated with nature, not culture. Apollyon the shepherd inhabits a grassy, fertile valley, an idyllic pastoral world where even thunder resembles music and lightning a "soft aurora." Denys is similarly associated with the vitality and fertility of the natural world, as can be seen in his market stall with its succulent melons and pomegranates. The sensuality of both characters is also allied to a definition of freedom which opposes the control and rationality seen as characteristic of the modern environment. Denys's transformation of the Easter ball game into a carnivalesque experience overturning the solemn and disciplined hierarchy is a good example. The clergy's collectively grave demeanour is replaced by "the delightful glee" of both ecclesiastical and lay persons who are all inspired and released from repressive self-consciousness to participate in what is suddenly "really a game." Similarly, Apollyon's association with games and play is defined explicitly by the narrator as "the power of untutored natural impulse, of natural inspiration"[43] set against the rules and regulations which govern the lives of the Prior and Hyacinthus.

The principles of artistic freedom are also re-defined through the characterization of Apollyon and Denys. They privilege not reason and logical structures but imagination and the fanciful individuality associated with unconscious intuition. The artistic products which they inspire are marked by unique inventiveness, the expression of a self intimately bound to the physical order of sense, underpinned by an awe for the transcendent and intangible. Apollyon's unearthly, fascinating music inspires the builders and stonemasons so that a new temper modifies their work. Architectural structures take on organic form; they "blossomed gracefully."[44] Large, potentially dehumanizing buildings become domesticated and cosy. Denys too inspires "by kind of visible sympathy," enabling artists to draw on unconscious and previously suppressed intuitions to produce work "in many an enduring form of exquisite fancy."[45] Indeed the stages of artistic composition inspired by him are akin to Pater's stages of cultural development identified in his examination of the evolution of particular myths in *Greek Studies*. Undifferentiating empathy with nature and the unseen gives way to self-conscious acknowledgement of the dark places of experience and hence ethical insights:

> There was first wild gaiety, exuberant in a wreathing of life-like imageries . . . [then it passed] into obscure regions of the satiric, the grotesque and coarse . . . [then] a well-assured seriousness . . . as if the gay old pagan world had been *blessed* in some way. . . .[46]

Pater's narratives seem not so much fanciful tales about the return of the gods themselves, but new myths to posit the return of those powers of thought, feeling and imagination which found their expression in the creation and transformation of classical mythology and which might, it would seem, have a role to fulfill in the modern age once again.

Pater's tales proposing the return of mythic modes of thought, intuition and their expression thus serve to highlight two opposing ways by which the human consciousness structures or interprets its experience: the synthesizing approach of the classical myth-makers who fuse conscious and unconscious, physical and spiritual experience; and the modern "scientific" spirit of rational and materialistic segregation, exclusion and control. The polarization between protagonist and society signifies a split in the human consciousness which can so differently make sense of itself and its environment. And this division is further developed by an analogous division within the central protagonists themselves. Employing a strategy similar to that of doubling or mythic "decomposition,"[47] Pater identifies even his gods as beings of divided consciousness, caught between death and life, guilt and joy, the sensual and the spiritual. For all Denys's fresh youthfulness and association with the fertility of the vine, he is, like his counterpart Dionysus, coupled with a darker Otherness, exotic, even sinister. Returning from the east where he "trafficks" with strange civilizations, he "ate flesh for the first time, tearing the hot red morsels with his delicate fingers in a kind of wild greed."[48] Even the lexical opposition here—"tearing . . . wild greed" and "delicate fingers" establishes a disjunction within the character. Moreover, Denys the hunter is also the hunted, suffering scapegoat. But this is not the simple opposition established in the classical "splitting" of Dionysus; Denys suffers the guilt of a self-conscious modern, reduced to a "subdued, silent, melancholy creature" with a morbid taste for relics and a self-destructive desire to "restore his popularity."[49]

The treatment of Apollyon even more forcefully indicates Pater's reading of the modern spirit as a divided one, incapable of recovering its previous capacities of insight and imagination. The Hyperborean Apollo's healing and orderly nature is modified in response to the rigid and sterile environment. He offers a refreshing alternative to the Prior's theoretical abstractions for he conveys a liberating sense of the physical. But his impulsive cruelty is foregrounded as in his torturing games with the wild creatures that flock to him and in his savage destruction of the pigeon-house. And he too admits to guilt for his misdeeds. His meek appearance at the church "like any other penitent" reveals a new spiritual consciousness which modifies his character.

In some ways this double nature of Apollyon and Denys enables them to be read as the mediating term between the oppositions Pater identifies. Like Lévi-Strauss's "trickster" figure they occupy a "position halfway between two polar terms [retaining] . . . something of that duality—namely an ambiguous and equivocal character."[50] Insofar as they promise synthesis, they represent the culture's idealized aspiration towards cosmic order and psychic unity. Certainly, on one level such harmony is provided by the interaction of Pater's protagonists with their societies. These re-creations of the pagan gods with their liberating commitment to sensuousness, imagination, and individuality become the visible embodiment of all that the modern environment would repress or rigorously curtail. Their return heralds a reassessment of perspectives and qualities previously deemed evil, if acknowledged at all. And as the community comes to tolerate the difference of Denys or Apollyon, so its members are brought to self-knowledge and maturity, expressed in personal, social, and artistic terms.[51]

The Prior, Hyacinthus, and the people of Auxerre seem initially to experience an enlargement of heart and mind. Such growth is likened to a rite of passage or rebirth. The Prior physically journeys out of darkness into a golden, summery world; his fading health is restored. Hyacinthus discovers "his true self for the first time" as if previously trapped by a false vision or assessment of his nature, place, and value. Denys too seems to encourage restoration and renewal: "the sight of him made old people feel young again." He is also associated with communal disruption and renewal which seems to unite opposing social poles—the excluded and the powerful. Suddenly in the community youth gains precedence "yet as if with the consent of their elders, who would themselves sometimes lose their balance, a little comically."[52]

The feudal structure is temporarily eroded so that the mute and marginalized common man is given voice and place: "one man engaged with another in talk in the market-place; a new influence came forth at the contact . . . a new spirit was abroad everywhere."[53] Even works of art produced under the auspices of Apollyon and Denys demonstrate a fusion of contraries or the accommodation of what was formerly denied, as in the Cathedral of Auxerre with its "broad masses" and "delicate lines," its individualistic irregularities encompassed in a traditional form; the Prior's twelfth volume is like "a violent beam, a blaze of new light, revealing, as it glanced here and there, a hundred truths unguessed at before."[54]

Yet such cultural rejuvenation is neither continuous nor unambiguous in these fictions. If classical myth stems from and dramatizes visionary capacity to accommodate and synthesize difference, Pater's mythic fictions suggest such fusion is no longer possible for the modern mind. His god-surrogates remain divided and guilty. Denys, unlike Dionysus, is not reborn. The return of the repressed ultimately creates discord and, paradoxically, its own defeat, given the twisted and distorted modern sensibility. Denys's inspired townsfolk soon pass from liberated joy to riotous frenzy and uncontrollable passion indiscriminately indulged. While the inspiration of the god releases natural passions, it is the old falsely spiritualized and superstitious desire for controlling rites to exclude the inexplicable, that reasserts itself and results in Denys's death. The final episode begins as a superstitious folk-custom, a remnant of some primitive pagan rite designed to ensure the renewal of the natural order—"a somewhat rude popular pageant, in which the person of Winter would be hunted blindfold through the streets."[55] But the ritual and relic-seeking become intensified to actual sacrifice and dismemberment. The irony underlines Pater's reading of the modern temper. Rather than accommodate difference, that which is excluded is momentarily released to serve the desire for repression and control, to banish strangeness and destroy what is thought "unholy." And the brutality of such suppression reinforces a belief that the idiosyncratic Other deserves nothing better than extinction.

Similar ironies underpin "Apollo in Picardy," and again suggest Pater's view of the disabling and self-defeating modern spirit. Apollyon ultimately thwarts creativity and causes destruction. The death of Hyacinthus in the very act of the play which signals his youthful renewal seems ironically cruel; but even more disturbing is the way in which only this sacrifice restores that "half-extinguished" deity's "proper immensity, its old greatness and power."[56] The divided nature of the god is itself healed solely by the destruction of the very beings his power would restore. Perhaps even more significantly, the apparently liberating vision which he inspires can be neither understood nor articulated by the community he has affected. No sense is made of the "mazy borders," the "long spaces of hieroglyph," "winged flowers, or stars with human limbs and faces" which form the Prior's final volume symbolizing how his vision divided "hopelessly against itself the well-ordered kingdom of his thought."[57]

In this subversion of the mediating terms within the narratives, Pater's tales of the gods' return offer a new myth for modern man, suggesting a further stage in "the history of the dynamics and evolution of the mind."[58] Unlike the classical myths of Dionysus and Demeter with their reconciliation of polarities, their emphasis on a continual cycle of growth-death-rebirth, and their celebration of natural and transcendent spheres of experience, Pater's mythic transformations seem to assert the inevitability of division, destruction, and repression in the modern world. The culture which can produce and read these "myths" is one marked by duality. Such mythic narratives speak of a world where individuals are thwarted in their attempt to reconcile opposing tendencies, fragmented in consciousness, haunted by powerful forces they would repress but which they cannot control. Clinging to intellect and reason as a means of structuring experience, the culture's analytical, authoritarian, and hierarchical procedures stifle creative synthesis and eventually overwhelm the idealized mediation of polarities traditionally proffered in myth.

Yet the very processes and strategies by which this reading of the modern sensibility is presented in the short stories signify a further paradoxical element in Pater's personal myth-making. These tales ultimately undermine confidence in their own sure expressiveness, their own mythic status as part of "a system of communication . . . a message."[59] On the one hand, they seem to signify a bleak interpretation of the modern individual as a creature of divided consciousness; but on the other, their equivocal and evasive methods of signification establish that meanings are always absent, interpretation itself never a secure process. Interpretation—and mythic narratives as a metalanguage of interpretation—can be no more than a self-conscious hovering between polarized signs: and it is this postmodern belief that Pater's mythic fictions ultimately enact.

Certainly, much of the interest and significance of these mythic tales stems from the ways in which the societies depicted read themselves, their world, their products. To this end these narratives might be considered to be explicitly about the practice of interpretation and the extent to which the "meanings" attributed to experience are culturally determined. The very ambiguity of the protagonists—central to their potential mediating function—depends upon equally plausible but conflicting interpretations of their nature and actions. Denys's instinctive sympathy for the alien or outcast, "for [the] oddly grown or even misshapen" might be read as a liberating and mature acceptance of difference: "He taught the people not to be afraid of the strange, ugly creatures . . . nor think it a bad omen that they approached."[60] But this very ability to attract and defend the "unacceptable" arouses "a deep suspicion and hatred" from the spiritualized and repressed community. While this evaluation of Denys may serve initially to reveal simply the restricted vision of medieval Auxerre, it is called back into play when the town descends into "coarseness" and "satiety," into suicide and murder. Embracing the excluded becomes a morally equivocal act, resistant to evaluation in a single way.

Interpretation of the characters is also seen to be a problematic enterprise in the tales. Rumours abound, but are rarely conclusively supported by fact. Apollyon's association with murder and other illicit actions, with disease and destruction, is based on the Janitor's surly gossip and suppositions, not on any experienced truth. Satisfying "meaning" even evades Pater's sophisticated contemporary, for the Victorian tourist misreads the relief of Apollyon on the gable: "King David, or an angel?"[61] Such ironic and unanswered questions are another way in which the rhetoric of the text self-consciously dramatizes Pater's rejection of certainty.

The ambiguous or open endings of these fictions also deny the fixing of meaning associated with closure. Denys's death seems to preclude possibilities of renewal; but even more provocatively, Hermes, by burying his friend in the church beneath a cross falsely Christianizes him. What is excluded by this poignant "blessing" are the pagan qualities which the tale foregrounds as vital to a renewal of a corrupt society whose Christianity is dry, mechanical, and superstitious. The action suggests something of Denys's effect on members of his community, stirring the affection and loyalty of a few sympathetic and noble souls; but simultaneously it points to the extinction and ineffectiveness of the vital pagan energy which should regenerate. Similarly, the circularity of "Apollo in Picardy," with the Prior once again in his cell, deprives the reader of the consolation of completion for this Prior is confused and impotent, dying without decisive understanding or action. His affection for the dead Hyacinthus might suggest an element of growth, of loss of selfishness, and hence of the value of the introduction of a "pagan" perspective into his experience. Yet even this certainty is undercut. The Prior weeps not for his companion, but for a vague muddle of hazy "blue distance," "blue flowers" and the "colour of Holy Mary's gown . . . the colour of hope."[62]

The destabilizing of any fixed and recoverable certainties within the tales is increased by the way in which both evade generic classification. The close identification of both protagonists with supernatural deities, the suggestion of inexplicable and marvelous events, the polarization of characters and settings: all are standard conventions of the romance. But the framing devices of each tale—the discovered manuscripts, the sophisticated traveller's interest in the "discriminate collection of real curiosities," even the assertion that Denys "seemed to have been a real resident at Auxerre"[63]—are all strategies of formal realism, devices used to insist on the empirical truth of the fiction which follows.

Such oscillation between rumour and fact, between closure and ambiguous irresolution, between modes of realism and romance, is also parallelled by the process of narration and the treatment of technical point of view. In "Denys L'Auxerrois," for example, the experienced wanderer who opens the tale and assesses the architectural splendours of France with a practised eye, who begins to piece together the artistic relics of Denys's return with the finesse of the connoisseur, might well be relied on as an author-surrogate, an authoritative interpreter capable of establishing truth, of guiding the reader confidently through the ambiguities of the narrative with the objectivity of historical distance. But in a matter of pages the narrator loses both detachment from and control over his story. He asserts the tale "shaped itself" based only on "a fancy in my mind," as if rising unbidden from his unconscious. From initial detachment he becomes a curious participant in the events of the tale itself; when gazing at the transported tapestry figures in the priest's house, he hears "some of them shouting rapturously to the organ music." And the critical distance which supports authoritative, clear judgment is further eroded by the sympathetic shifts to the focalization of the protagonist—though even these give rise to no single, exclusive interpretation of the events of the story. Denys "could but wonder" if he was indeed guilty of the vineyard murder, for example.[64]

The collapse of the chronology and narrative levels within the stories frustrates attempts to identify a single, secure moral standpoint. Sympathy for the protagonists is gained by immersing the reader in the chronological present of both tales, and in the narrator's identification of the positive and lasting effects of the protagonists; but almost immediately this seeming validation of the character is qualified. Apollyon is typified as a competent herdsman; such literal details seem to slide effortlessly into a Christ-like metaphor. He is a good or "affectionate shepherd" who "seemingly loved his sheep." Yet immediately the narrator slips silently into an alternative and contradictory evaluation of the character: "if Apollyon looked like the great carved figure over the low doorway of their place of penitence at home, that could be but an accident, or perhaps a deceit."[65] The authoritative narrator's assessment and that of the nervous and confused Prior become indistinguishable, and the reader is left with only a continuous, irresolvable oscillation between Apollyon's healing qualities and his duplicitous nature. In "Denys L'Auxerrois" the character's "sad ending" is juxtaposed with his "pleasant" stimulation of his society and his sponsorship of "a *sort of* golden age."[66] As the narrative proceeds, the efficacy of Denys's regeneration of the modern world is constantly called into question: "The golden age had indeed come back for a while:—golden was it, or gilded only, after all?"[67] Not only is the effect of Denys's intervention transitory; the use of "gilded" points to the equivocal worth of this renewal, as if the community has been seduced by the showy trappings of a plausible but dangerous trickster. But the use of the rhetorical question mockingly undercuts *any* attempt to fix on a decisive understanding of Denys's role. The tale resists all efforts to fix meaning. It continually evades and destabilizes the process of its own interpretation.

Even Pater's treatment of symbolic details and imagery deconstructs fixed categories and renders any moral evaluation of attributes unstable and ambivalent. Those terms or perspectives set against each other— pagan and Christian, sacred and profane, order and chaos—are revealed as interchangeable and in effect self-cancelling. The Christian communities with their rigid discipline and superstitious, ungodly rituals lack all the compassion, charity, and transcendent vision which one expects. Those qualities are, ironically, the property of the "unholy" pagan protagonists whose reverence for and delight in the vital plenitude of the natural world contrast strikingly with the profane neglect and fear of God's creation which marks the often materialistic monks. Yet the imagery which would support this inversion turns in on itself on many occasions as if to destroy any certainties. In particular metaphors drawn from the natural world seem initially to validate the pagan perspective. Under Apollyon, for example, buildings "blossom gracefully," but the same image of fecund nature is also used to describe the self-destructive and sinister mental confusion of the Prior under Apollyon's tutelage: "Somewhat later they [flowers] and the like of them seemed to have grown into and over his brain."[68]

With such continual doubling back of the tales on themselves, Pater's mythic fictions become doubly suited as new myths for a modern age. They dramatize a new version of man divided within and against himself, no longer capable of mythic consolations. But the fractured consciousness is not the only division which these narratives explore and "mythologize." They are equally myths about the process of interpretation itself. In terms of narrative structure and strategies these short stories explore the gap between the desire for meaning and certainty and its unattainability. By deconstructing fixed terms of identity and definition, by subverting mediation, resolution, and synthesis, by denying authoritative viewpoints and control, Pater's tales explode the false myth of interpretation as the recovery of a stable, fixed meaning accepted by consensus. At the best interpretation is revealed as a process of provisional negotiation, a series of oblique attempts—by myth and metaphor, by constant re-creation—to name the gap, but never to bridge it.

Pater and Architecture

_____ **14**

BERNARD RICHARDS

ARCHITECTURE was not the most important of the arts for Pater because, for the most part, it was not figurative. Nevertheless it is an aspect of his taste that cannot be ignored, and it is one of the last remaining areas in Pater studies awaiting detailed research. This essay concentrates on Pater's view of Gothic architecture, since, by a strange paradox, this was the style to which he was principally drawn. Classical and neo-classical buildings had their appeal for him, but it was the works of the Middle Ages that stimulated his imagination more forcefully.

Transition is the theme that dominates Pater's writing on architecture. Buildings seem to be stable, monolithic and immutable; in this sense they are at the other end of the spectrum from the evanescent and wayward subjective experiences of which Pater was a connoisseur, experiences which painting and literature are more adept at capturing. But although Pater is able to respond to the solidity and finality of buildings he is also able to see them as indicative of fluid historical movements. To the subtle and penetrative eye the transition from classic to gothic, from religious to secular, from gloomy to brilliant, from fantastic to rational, is detectable in buildings, so that they too exist in a continuum, admittedly moving in slow motion if one compares the process with psychological states. They are subject to patterns of

189

weaving and unweaving, thesis and antithesis. All this is only to be understood by the analytical and abstract mind, holding history in its head; but there is a more sensory version of the provisional nature of building, and this is observed when Pater lovingly records the varied lighting effects to which structures are subjected, so transforming as to make us question their absoluteness and their solidity. Pater's picture of transition and even fleetingness is the one I wish to concentrate on here.

It is in the study of Winckelmann that Pater considers the early evolution of architecture, and he realizes that it is not the most expressive of the arts:

> Architecture, which begins in a practical need, can only express by vague hint or symbol the spirit or mind of the artist. He closes his sadness over him, or wanders in the perplexed intricacies of things, or projects his purpose from him clean-cut and sincere, or bares himself to the sunlight. But these spiritualities, felt rather than seen, can but lurk about architectural form as volatile effects, to be gathered from it by reflexion. Their expression is, indeed, not really sensuous at all.[1]

And then, in an important passage, he reveals that architecture does not represent the human body, is not figurative, and so, by implication, will not appeal to him as much as the arts of sculpture and painting, which deal "immediately with man":

> As human form is not the subject with which it deals, architecture is the mode in which the artistic effort centres, when the thoughts of man concerning himself are still indistinct, when he is still little preoccupied with those harmonies, storms, victories, of the unseen and intellectual world, which, wrought out into the bodily form, give it an interest and significance communicable to it alone. The art of Egypt, with its supreme architectural effects, is, according to Hegel's beautiful comparison, a Memnon waiting for the day, the day of the Greek spirit, the humanistic, spirit, with its power of speech.[2]

Pater did not visit Egypt, but he would have known something about Egyptian architecture via works such as Owen Jones's *The Grammar of Ornament* (1856) and the various reproductions of Egyptian buildings in international exhibitions and the like.[3] He would have known that the system of the classical "orders" did in part descend from Egyptian traditions.

I am not sure that Pater found classical architecture especially exciting, and in this sense he is a child of his time. His "Postscript" to *Appreciations*[4] is one of the nineteenth century's fullest and most interesting discussions of the difference between Classicism and Romanticism. Immediately we recognize a characteristic strategy in Pater, when he shows himself reluctant to use the labels as exclusive modes of identifying specific historical periods, since to do that would be to lay himself open to partiality for one or the other. He prefers to consider the terms as indicative of enduring and perennial principles in the artistic temperament, so that any one could surface at any time, and make the writing of architectural history a very flexible activity. In the "Preface" to *The Renaissance* Pater also expresses a reluctance to promote one mode in preference to another, since to do so would possibly limit the full range of aesthetic experience: the aesthetic critic "will remember always that beauty exists in many forms. To him all periods, types, schools of taste, are in themselves equal."[5] This statement is as far away from Ruskin's position of partiality and commitment to particular epochs and styles as it is possible to get. Still, Pater says much less about ancient architecture than about medieval, and he does quote Stendhal in the Postscript to *Appreciations*: "Romanticism is the art of presenting to people the literary works which, in the actual state of their habits and beliefs, are capable of giving them the greatest possible pleasure; classicism, on the contrary, of presenting them with that which gave the greatest possible pleasure to their grandfathers."[6] What Pater appreciated in romantic art was its "strangeness," its grotesqueness even, and it was summed up, in almost caricature form, by "that Germany which, in its quaint old towns, under the spire of Strasburg or the towers of Heidelberg, was always listening in rapt inaction to the melodious, fascinating voices of the Middle Age."[7]

However, when we turn to *Marius the Epicurean* we discover that although the buildings are classical, there is actually no such thing as a monolithic classicism, and romantic strangeness and grotesqueness are to be detected even in this world, if one is sensitive enough to recognize it. Marius finds in Rome buildings which speak of "eariler ages" and are "immeasurably venerable." Pater is, I think, excited at the prospect of finding a tendency in any work of art opposite to the obvious or ostensible one, since when he perceives such a thing his originality, independence and perceptiveness as a critic are more on view.

In *Marius* a number of buildings, real and imaginary, are described. They are not there simply as background, but as part of the psychic geography of the novel, since for Pater buildings in which people lived were expressive of human agency and intention, and key factors in the moulding of personality and the provision of mental furniture. The buildings of the late Roman Empire, like other features of the cultural life, adumbrate, in some of their features, the Christian Middle Ages, especially when one regards them with the wisdom of hindsight. Pater is not particularly good at dealing with passionate interpersonal experience, but one of his fortes is establishing the intense interrelation between the inner and outer in a psychic life. The buildings in *Marius* take on a resonating symbolic and an atmospheric status, and some of the descriptions are very long and detailed, almost mini-essays. Chapter XI is an elaborate tour-guide evocation of Rome's palaces and shrines.

Pater is sensitive to the charms of classical architecture, and he evokes it well, but he was, after all, a child of the nineteenth century, a century dominated by the Gothic revival, and he must have found it difficult not to be influenced, in some measure, by Ruskin's influential chapter "The Nature of Gothic" (originally published in Volume II of *The Stones of Venice,* 1853). It has often been claimed as one of the most important and persuasive pieces of Victorian prose. Ruskin urges the case for Gothic as an architecture developing from liberal and enlightened social conditions, expressive of freedom and individual vision, flexible and responsive to human demands. Classicism, on the other hand, is overdetermined and inflexible, and requires not the intelligence and initiative of the individual artisan, but his subservience and manual skill. It is, so Ruskin thinks, "helot architecture," and symptomatic of illiberal regimes. Pater did not subscribe to all aspects of this thesis, but when he describes Romanesque architecture the influence of Ruskin's interpretation is felt, and he suggests that Gothic is only able to develop when the yoke is shaken off. It was because the process could actually be observed in operation in the monastic church at Vézelay in Burgundy that he devoted so much attention to that building in the second of his essays "Some Great Churches in France" (1894), reprinted in *Miscellaneous Studies*:

> It is . . . the grandest Romanesque interior in France, perhaps in the world. In its mortified light the very soul of monasticism, Roman and half-military, as the completest outcome of a religion of threats, seems to descend upon one. . . . [I]t is here at Vézelay, in this iron place, that monasticism in its central, its historically most significant purpose, presents itself as most completely at home. There is no triforium. The monotonous cloistral length of wall above the long-drawn series of stately round arches, is unbroken save by a plain small window in each bay, placed as high as possible just below the cornice, as a mere afterthought, you might fancy.[8]

Pater was born into a century that was obsessed by Gothic architecture, and in the "Battle of Styles," which occurred in his childhood, it was Gothic that took the field. Insofar as the Victorian period attempted to evolve a style of its own the basic originating matrix, as J. Mordaunt Crook has shown, was Gothic.[9] Pater drunk this in, as any child of the age would. There was, it seemed, something natural and inevitable and admirable about the emergence of Gothic architecture. A key statement is to be found in chapter XXII of *Marius*, "The Minor Peace of the Church":

> The aesthetic charm of the Catholic church, her evocative power over all that is eloquent and expressive in the better mind of man, her outward comeliness, her dignifying convictions about human nature:—all this, as abundantly realised centuries later by Dante and Giotto, by the great medieval church-builders, by the great ritualists like Saint Gregory, and the masters of the sacred music in the

middle age—we may see already, in dim anticipation, in those charmed moments towards the end of the second century.[10]

But the evolution of a humanized and relatively cheerful Gothic did not come overnight, and there were "those troublous intervening centuries" known as "the Dark Ages."[11]

Pater was always inclined to take an ambitious overview of the sweep of history. We see evidence of this in his earliest important work, *The Renaissance*. Whenever he looks in detail at a particular epoch he cannot but help register the adumbrations of a following one. It is an almost instinctive reaction in him to consider a style, whether in literature, painting or architecture, both as a quintessential absolute and as something that will eventually modulate into its opposite. Buildings are the most significant and large-scale cultural statements available, and for a interpreter such as Pater they cry out to be noticed and analyzed. The Gothic, for the Victorians, was not a single monolithic style but the combination of a number of styles, ranging from the primitive and austere to the sophisticated and elaborate, and whenever Pater considers a building he first of all instinctively tends to place it fairly precisely on some kind of stylistic spectrum. So in "Denys l'Auxerrois" Sens is grave, severe and northern, "cool and composed, with an almost English austerity,"[12] whereas Troyes is more strange and florid: it has an impressive "breadth of proportions internally," and the porch, with its "surprising height and lightness," is a "kind of wildly elegant Gothic-on-stilts."[13] Auxerre, appropriately for the story in which the culture of the south meets that of the north, is the "perfect type of that happy mean between northern earnestness and the luxury of the south," both in its architecture and its surrounding countryside. In *Plato and Platonism* he thinks that Doric architecture might be compared with chaste Cistercian.[14] One of the most sensitive pieces of writing on the differences between the various types of Gothic must be his essay on Vézelay. It is a Cluniac building, and hence representative of an austere form of monasticism. Pater likes to believe that the religious and architectural tradition of Cistercianism is "a reaction against monasticism itself,"[15] and though chaste and austere, emanating from a state of mind almost aesthetic: asceticism for asceticism's sake one might describe it as. He may not approve altogether of Vézelay, certainly it represents a repression of spirit from which the Renaissance freed Western man, but he responds to it in fine and evocative prose. Vézelay, like so many Gothic buildings, was not built all at once to a single unified design; it was modified through the ages. So that at the east and west ends of the church a dramatic stylistic change takes place; the process of evolution and transition that so intrigued Pater is actually visible:

> [T]he Pointed style, determined yet discreet, makes itself felt—makes itself felt by appearing, if not for the first time, yet for the first time in the organic or systematic development of French architecture. Not in the unambitious *facade* of Saint-Denis, nor in the austere aisles of Sens, but at Vézelay, in this grandiose fabric, so worthy of the event, Viollet-le-Duc would fain see the birthplace of the Pointed style. Here at last, with no sense of contrast, but by way of veritable "transition," and as if by its own matured strength, the round arch breaks into the noble curve, *les arcs brises*, with a wonderful access of grace. And the imaginative effect is forthwith enlarged.[16]

He responds to the drama and contrast in the interior of Vézelay very well, and it is as if the transition from one mode of the human spirit to another is accomplished within the building:

> [T]he long, tunnel-like, military work of the Romanesque nave opens wide into the exhilarating daylight of choir and transepts, . . . with a vault rising now high above the roof-line of the body of the church, *sicut lilium excelsum*. The simple flowers, the *flora*, of the early Pointed style, which could never have looked at home as an element in the half-savage decoration of the nave, seem to be growing here upon the sheaves of slender, reedy pillars, as if naturally in the carved stone.[17]

The transition is compared to the dramatic progress in the great church of Assisi from the dark crypt, "through the gloomy 'lower' church, into the height and breadth, the physical and symbolic 'illumination,' of the church above."[18] This architectural sequence speaks of the passage of time, of the distinctiveness of periodicity, but at other instances Pater responds to concepts of timelessness, as at Vézelay: "[I]n strictly monastic Vézelay you have a sense of freshness, such as, in spite of their ruin, we perceive in the buildings of Greece. We enjoy here not so much, as at Amiens, the sentiment of antiquity, but that of eternal duration."[19] The difference alluded to here is between a diachronic and a synchronic experience of architecture, with the latter finding favour for the moment.

As Gothic developed it became lighter and airier, and there was an almost inevitable logic in the reduction of the wall and the enlargement of the window. Pater's knowledge of actual Gothic buildings was accurate and extensive enough, so that he had no difficulty, when the need arose, of creating imaginary buildings, such as the church in *Gaston de Latour*, a church which undergoes, as many actual buildings did, a gradual transformation in time. When Gaston as a youth enters the chapel of Saint Hubert, his heart sinks, since it is so dark and sepulchral within, and the light is like that in Chartres, with "only an almost angry ray of purple or crimson, here or there," crossing "the dark roomy spaces."[20] When he alters and grows older he changes it all, and banishes the Gothic darkness and heaviness, to produce something that sounds like flamboyant architecture:

> A thicket of airy spires rose above the sanctuary; the blind triforium broke into one continuous window; the heavy masses of stone were pared down with wonderful dexterity of hand, till not a hand's-breadth remained uncovered by delicate tracery, as from the fair white roof, touched sparingly with gold, down to the subterranean chapel of Saint Taurin, where the peasants of La Beauce came to pray for rain, not a space was left unsearched by cheerful daylight.[21]

Pater finds it natural and inevitable, in writing fiction, to provide appropriate architectural settings. These settings are not "background," since in their intensely realized characters they represent the psychic history of the actors; indeed, to a large extent they are that history. Pater's entry into the states of mind of people who lived in previous centuries is principally made by sharing in experiences available to both past and present, experiences of natural phenomena, of sculpture and painting, of literature and of building. Hence in *Gaston de Latour* a whole chapter, entitled "Our Lady's Church," is devoted to Chartres, not just as Gaston knows it in its full glory, but as *we* know it, ravaged and despoiled.

Amiens was of course also an important building for nineteenth-century architectural writing, since Ruskin devoted a complete book to it, *The Bible of Amiens*, and Pater a whole essay. It is interesting that Pater boldly follows a thesis about the secularity of medieval cathedrals whereas Ruskin preferred such an idea to remain implicit. In the early 1850s Ruskin still retained his religious faith, but in "The Nature of Gothic" he tends to weaken the effect of Gothic architecture as an exclusively religious statement, since he encourages us to read Gothic buildings as evidence of the freedom and untrammelled expressiveness of the societies and the workmen that produced them. He is encouraging, whether he is aware of it or not, a certain secular interpretative mode. Pater lost his religious faith at an earlier age than Ruskin, and maintained an essentially secular outlook on life (which does not mean he is axiomatically unsympathetic to the contribution made by the religious spirit). This cast of mind causes him to stress the secularization in thirteenth-century France, and to interpret Amiens cathedral, in his essay of 1894, as a secular building, built on the human scale and indicative of humanistic tendencies in the age: "The great and purest of Gothic churches, Notre-Dame d'Amiens, illustrates, by its fine qualities, a characteristic secular movement of the beginning of the thirteenth century."[22] It "concurred . . . with certain novel humanistic moments of religion itself."[23] There is "no mystery" in the design, and it reassures the intelligence and keeps "one's curiosity . . . continually on the alert."[24] Here he does not see eye to eye with the Ruskin of *The Bible of Amiens*, even though Ruskin is aware that there might be secular and humanistic elements entering into the construction of a work as religious as a cathedral.

Often, the awe Pater feels in the presence of Amiens is not religious exactly, but technical: he is excited by it as a civil engineering problem solved, as an architectural feat worth achieving, architecture for architecture's sake one might call it:

> Here . . . you are conscious restlessly of that sustained equilibrium of oblique pressure on all sides, which is the essence of the hazardous Gothic construction, a construction of which the "flying buttress" is the most significant feature. Across the clear glass of the great windows of the triforium you see it, feel it, at its Atlas-work audaciously. . . . Those who built it might have had for their one and only purpose to enclose as large a space as possible with the given material.[25]

One cannot imagine Ruskin writing that; he would have wished to stress the symbolic importance of admitting the light of God into the interior, and would have been most reluctant to encourage the view that a cathedral may be viewed as the successful solution of civil engineering problems.

Ruskin and Pater are both struck by the expressive naturalism of the choir stalls at Amiens, but whereas Ruskin surrounds the woodwork with a religiose aura, Pater prefers to believe that such naturalism grows from lay traditions, from confederated labour and from "communistic sentiment."[26] He takes the view that "older cloistral workmen" "had but fed their imagination in an embarrassed, imprisoned, and really decadent manner, or mere reminiscence of, or prescriptions about, things visible."[27] In his essay on Vézelay Pater devotes considerable attention to the sculptures: "The minds of those who worked thus seem to have been almost insanely preoccupied just then with the human countenance, but by no means exclusively in its pleasantness or dignity. Bold, crude, original, their works indicates delight in the power of reproducing fact, curiosity in it, but little or no sense of beauty."[28] He seems to believe that the sense of beauty and the exercise of primitive faith are not quite reconcilable. It requires more sophisticated minds to introduce notions of style and treatment into the exercise of art— perhaps of religious practices too.

Pater was fascinated by the later evolutions of Gothic architecture, in which classical motifs are starting to appear. It was particularly visible in the Loire Valley. He lends his perceptions to Gaston as he travels south from La Beauce: "Frequently, along the great historic stream, as along some vast street, contemporary genius was visible . . . in a novel and seductive architecture, which, by its engrafting of exotic grace on homely native forms, spoke of a certain aspiration to be what was not but might become—the old Gaulish desire to be refined, to be mentally enfranchised by the sprightlier genius of Italy."[29] This passage is typical of the movement of Pater's mind; even as the hero looks at what might appear to be solid and unchangeable buildings he has a view of cultural journeys in time and space: transitions.

Pater had alluded years earlier, in his essay on Giorgione, to the charm of the chateau architecture of the Loire, which is capable of modulating into poetry, so that solid architecture is transformed to something more flexible: "Architecture . . . often finds a true poetry, as in those strangely twisted staircases of the chateaux of the country of the Loire, as if it were intended that among their odd turnings the actor in a theatrical mode of life might pass each other unseen; there being a poetry also of memory and of the mere effect of time, by which architecture often profits greatly."[30] This is a case of where an apparently solid art proves to be fluid and flexible by aspiring "out of the hard limitation" of its form.

There are two areas worth considering in which Pater is different from Ruskin. First, he is more concerned with the function of buildings in everyday life; and secondly, he is more responsive to lighting effects. He is aware that buildings are for men and women to live in, to worship in, and that they are the indicators of freedom or restriction, optimism or pessimism, acceptance or rejection:

Our susceptibilities, the discovery of our powers, manifold experiences—our various experiences of the coming and going of bodily pain, for instance—belong to this or that other well-remembered place in the material habitation—that little white room with the window across which the heavy blossoms could beat so peevishly in the wind, with just that particular catch or throb, such a sense of teasing in it, on gusty mornings; and the early habitation thus gradually becomes a sort of material shrine or sanctuary of sentiment; a system of visible symbolism interweaves itself through all our thoughts and passions; and irresistibly, little shapes, voices, accidents—the angle at which the sun in the morning fell on the pillow—become parts of the great chain wherewith we are bound.[31]

A chain of necessity, yes, but of potentially pleasurable necessity, in which architectural surroundings are capable of administering to the sense of pleasure. Merely to move in well-lit space is, for Pater, entrancing experience which is capable of counteracting the tragedy of life. Imagination needs and responds to its local habitation.

We find many of Pater's characteristic attitudes to architecture in his treatment of the great barn in "Apollo in Picardy." It is almost classical, and it is associated with an Apollonian revival. Northern Europe and southern Europe are, once again, locked in an interesting contest with each other. This is, of course, an imagined building, and I do not know whether Pater saw anything exactly like it, but some of the magnificent Cistercian barns in France must have given him a suggestion. The Prior Saint-Jean goes to recuperate in a country district, which, Pater tells us, is something like "Prospero's enchanted island."[32] While he is there a barn is built, under the guidance of a mysterious figure who has come from the classical world, and whose presence is at once life-giving and baneful. Unlike a church it is set north and south, but it has aisles, and stone pillars reminiscent of ecclesiastical architecture:

> [It has] a sort of classical harmony in its broad, very simple proportions, with a certain suppression of Gothic emphasis, more especially in that peculiarly Gothic feature, the buttresses, scarcely marking the unbroken, windowless walls, which rise very straight, taking the sun placidly. . . . The great northern gable is almost a classic pediment. The horizontal lines of plinth and ridge and cornice are kept unbroken, the roof of sea-grey slates being pitched less angularly than is usual in this rainy clime. A welcome contrast, the Prior thought it, to the sort of architectural nightmare he came from.[33]

It is built to music played by Brother Apollyon, as if aspiring, in the fashion of the best art, to the state of music: "Mere audible music, certainly, had counted for something in the operations of an art, held at its best . . . to be a sort of music made visible. That ideal singer, one might fancy, by an art beyond art, had attracted beams and stones into their fit places."[34] The spirit of these passages is very close to the chapter on "Plato's Aesthetics" in *Plato and Platonism*, where he thinks that Greek music is very like Gregorian, and both "call to mind the kind of architecture, military or monastic . . . , that must be built" to it. The stern and hieratic Doric architecture seems to him close in spirit to Cistercian Gothic, purged of the kind of barbaric ornament we saw on the capitals at Vézelay:

> It seems a long way from the Parthenon to Saint Ouen "of the aisles and arches," or Notre-Dame de Bourges; yet they illustrate almost equally the direction of the Platonic aesthetics. Those churches of the Middle Age have . . . their loveliness, yet of a stern sort, which fascinates while perhaps it repels us. We may try to like as well or better architecture of a more or less different kind, but coming back to them again find that the secret of final success is theirs. The rigid logic of their charm controls our taste, as logic proper binds the intelligence: we would have something of that quality, if we might, for ourselves, in what we do or make; feel, under its influence, very diffident of our own loose, or gaudy, or literally insignificant, decorations.[35]

In diminishing the importance of architectural decoration Pater has travelled further along the road to the abstract purity and formalism of effective architecture than Ruskin did.

The other principle governing the building is human proportion and human scale, versions of which take us into mystical mathematics of various kinds, both for Gothic and Classical buildings. The brooding narrative presence in "Apollo in Picardy" reflects: "And is not the human body, too, a building, with architectural laws, a structure, tending by the very forces which primarily held it together to drop asunder in time?"[36] As we saw at the outset of this essay Pater regarded architecture as non-figurative, and yet he has a tendency to keep introducing the human figure into architectural contexts.

Mention must be made of Pater's concentration on lighting effects. He is a votary of the ephemeral and the transient. To some extent the Heraclitean vision of the world in flux alarmed and perturbed him, but he managed to make himself psychologically at home in that vision, and although, in certain moods, the physicality, the materialism, the solidity of a building are a satisfying antidote to evanescence, in other moods their inert identity weighs heavily on his soul. Varying effects of light flickering over a building have the result of making it seem more evanescent and ephemeral than it actually is, and reducing the impression it conveys to a state of fluctuation and uncertain visual identity. At this point it challenges the aesthetic consciousness to notice and record its rare epiphanic manifestation, and the response to that challenge is eminently satisfying. At the end of his essay on Du Bellay in *The Renaissance* Pater records the satisfaction of this kind of experience: "A sudden light transfigures some trivial thing, a weather-vane, a wind-mill, a winnowing fan, the dust in the barn door. A moment—and the thing has vanished, because it was pure effect; but it leaves a relish behind it, a longing that the accident may happen again."[37] "Sudden light" is an evocative phrase: it is the title of a Rossetti poem which expresses the magic of a visionary moment—a moment, though, in which human beings engage with each other rather than buildings.

Finally we have to consider whether Pater's knowledge of and interest in architecture influenced his style and his theories of style. It seems to me always difficult to make sound analogies between architectural construction and prose style, though many people have tried to do so. The critical rhetoric of such exercises always sounds plausible and impressive, but it does not always bear close scrutiny. Pater's best known venture into this parallelistic rhetoric is in his essay "Style" (1888):

> For the literary architecture, if it is to be rich and expressive, involves not only foresight of the end in the beginning, but also development or growth of design, in the process of execution, with many irregularities, surprises, and after-thoughts; the contingent as well as the necessary being subsumed under the unity of the whole. As truly, to the lack of such architectural design, of a single, almost visual, image, vigorously informing an entire, perhaps very intricate, composition, which shall be austere, ornate, argumentative, fanciful, yet true from first to last to that vision within, may be attributed those weaknesses of conscious or unconscious repetition of word, phrase, motive, or member of the whole matter, indicating, as Flaubert was aware, an original structure in thought not organically complete.[38]

This elaborate parallel between text and building is very suggestive, but it does bring problems in its train, since very few literary artists actually find that they have much "foresight" of what the completed work will be like, when they begin. But Pater does recognize that "surprises" and contingencies will occur as the work progresses. He does not state it here, but the kind of building he has in mind seems to be more Gothic than Classic, since much more foresight is required to erect a classical building, and once the ground plan is established almost everything follows with a kind of preordained inevitability. Not so with a Gothic building, which can develop with much more flexibility, and even accommodate a new style of architecture once it has been begun. Most Gothic buildings give some impression of unity, but on closer investigation many elements are difficult to reconcile with each other, or with any overall concept.

Pater, almost instinctively reached for art analogies when he described the process of producing prose. In the "Postscript" to *Appreciations* he makes his famous plea for eclecticism:

> [T]he scholar will still remember that if "the style is the man" it is also the age: that the nineteenth century too will be found to have had its style, justified by necessity—a style very different, alike from the baldness of an impossible "Queen Anne" revival, and an incorrect, incondite exuberance, after the mode of Elizabeth: that we can only return to either at the price of an impoverishment of form or matter, or both, although, an intellectually rich age such as ours being necessarily an eclectic one, we may well cultivate some of the excellences of literary types so different as those: that in literature as in other matters it is well to unite as many diverse elements as may be: that the individual writer or artist, certainly, is to be estimated by the number of graces he combines, and his power of interpenetrating them in a given work.[39]

What is interesting about this passage is that Pater readily assumes, in the phrase "in literature as in other matters," that there will be parallels between the arts. There was a desire in the nineteenth century to find styles unique to the time, and it applied to all the arts. J. Mordaunt Crook has told the story of architecture in *The Dilemma of Style*, and indeed, he quotes this passage.[40] Interestingly the Elizbathan revival was "incorrect, incondite and exuberant" whether in architectural contexts—one thinks of Anthony Salvin's Harlaxton, Lincolnshire (1831-37) and Thoresby, Nottinghamshire (1864-75), Edward Blore's Merevale, Warwickshire (1838-44), Lewis Vulliamy's Westonbirt, Gloucestershire (1863-70) and G. F. Bodley and Thomas Garner's Hewell Grange, Worcestershire (1884-89)—or literary (predominantly Browning). But however "bald" the Queen Anne Revival might have been in Austin Dobson's *Proverbs in Porcelain* (1877), only a certain amount of Queen Anne Revival building is "bald." One thinks of Norman Shaw's Bedford Park, Philip Webb's Clouds, Wiltshire (1879-91), E. W. Godwin's houses in Tite Street, Chelsea and J. J. Stevenson's 27 Banbury Road, Oxford (built for T. H. Green in 1881); generally it was more likely to be flamboyant and generously decorated, as in Norman Shaw's New Zealand Chambers in Leadenhall Hall Street, London (1871-73, now demolished) or Lowther Lodge, Kenginston Gore (1872-75).[41]

One needs a little caution in pursuing parallels between Pater's theory of prose style and his architectural tastes. Pater is anxious for literary works to have structural design and "constructive intelligence," but there are a number of ways in which, attractive as the architectural parallels seem to be, they do not function particularly well. They gave Pater a kind of moral support, but finally his prose style had to be evolved without the detailed help and suggestivity that architecture seemed to offer.

The Crystal Man:
A Study of "Diaphaneitè"

———————————— **15**

ANNE VARTY

"DIAPHANEITÈ," composed probably early in 1864 and published only posthumously in 1895, is notoriously difficult to elucidate.[1] It tempts the critic by seeming to offer a kind of manifesto for Pater's subsequent work ("A majority of such would be the regeneration of the world")[2] but it does not easily yield its meaning. Perhaps the critic should not be too concerned by this; the essay is the earliest piece in Pater's corpus, he never revised it for publication himself (the manuscript is in Shadwell's hand),[3] and the internal evidence of the piece suggests that it was a collection of notes rather than a sustained argument. Pater, in writing about the inner perfection of man, was himself most inward in his utterance. However we know that he delivered the piece (or some version of it) to the Old Mortality Society in February 1864[4] and that many fragments of the essay are worked into "Winckelmann," first published three years later in 1867 and continuously revised until 1893.[5] "Diaphaneitè" therefore provided Pater with a body of thought to which his imagination continually resorted.

The essay describes a certain type of ideal man and calls for a renaissance of the type. In the 1867 version of "Winckelmann" Pater warns himself as much as his reader against abuse of the term "ideal":

" 'Ideal' is one of those terms which through a pretended culture have become tarnished and edgeless. How great, then, is the charm when in Hegel's writings we find it attached to a fresh, clear-cut conception! With him the ideal is a *Versinnlichen* of the idea—the idea turned into an object of sense."[6] Having reminded himself of the desirability of "objects of sense" as anchors, or indeed instantiations, for the ideal, and putting that into practice effectively in "Winckelmann," Pater deleted these sentences from all subsequent versions of the essay. In "Diaphaneitè" exemplars of the ideal are less readily distinguishable, but they are there, if submerged nonetheless. The "objects of sense," illustrations of the ideal type, in "Diaphaneitè" are of two kinds: images and individuals. On the one hand we are given the images of crystal and sculpture; on the other hand, the historical figures Raphael and Goethe. While these two kinds of *Versinnlichen* function as independent constellations of ideas in the essay, they can also function conjointly. Raphael is described indirectly in terms of sculpture, Goethe in terms of crystal.

"Over and over again the world has been surprised by the heroism, the insight, the passion, of this clear crystal nature," Pater announces.[7] The crystal image itself is not a common one in Pater's subsequent work, despite the fact that other British aesthetes, under the influence of Gautier and Baudelaire, came to write about gems and precious stones as artifacts which elude the cycle of decay and death, and Pater's own attitude of mind is characterized by the "hard, gem-like flame" of the "Conclusion."[8] It is not until *Plato and Platonism* (1893) when describing Plato, who came to occupy the position of ideal man in Pater's mind, that he uses the crystal image again directly: "For [Plato], as for Dante, in the impassioned glow of his conceptions, the material and the spiritual are blent and fused together. While, in that fire and heat, what is spiritual attains the definite visibility of a crystal, what is material, on the other hand, will lose its earthiness and impurity."[9] This use of the image represents a development in Pater's thought since "Diaphaneitè" because here it is not the mind of Plato which is "crystal," but what, in the furnace of his visionary imagination, his mind sees and makes manifest for others.

Two instances of the crystal metaphor as characterization of an individual occur in material by Carlyle which Pater had read before the composition of "Diaphaneitè."[10] The first, in the chapter "The Hero as Poet" in *On Heroes* (already shown to be significant for the composition of "Diaphaneitè")[11] reads: "Of [Goethe] too you say that he *saw* the object; you may say what he himself says of Shakespeare: 'His characters are like watches with dial plates of transparent crystal; they show you the hour like others, and the inward mechanism also is all visible'."[12] The second occurs in *The French Revolution* and concerns not Charlotte Corday (a passage about whom is quoted in "Diaphaneitè"), but another woman of the Revolution, Madame Roland de la Platrière:

> Reader, mark that queenlike burgher-woman: beautiful, Amazonian—graceful to the eye; more so to the mind. Unconscious of her worth (as all worth is), is her greatness, of her crystal clearness; genuine, the creature of Sincerity and Nature, in an age of Artificiality, Pollution and Cant; there, in her still completeness, in her still invincibility. . . .[13]

The first passage is about seeing and being seen; both Goethe and his creations reveal their inner lives through their outer manifestations, like transparent crystal. It is significant that Carlyle transfers an appreciation of subjects in art to a subject in life, as though aesthetic criteria were as applicable to life as to art. The second passage is about personal integrity and moral worth, where again the inner life is seen as congruent with the outer and a radiant example in an unenlightened age, presented in aesthetic rather than moral terms. These two examples of the "crystal" self, one a poet, the other a revolutionary, may have fused in Pater's mind, to emerge as an abstract picture of "revolutionism . . . softened, harmonised, subdued."[14]

The association of Goethe with the crystal image had also been made by G. H. Lewes in his *Life of Goethe*, the second edition of which appeared in December 1863 (marked 1864 on the title page).[15] Lewes uses the metaphor as follows:

> All men of genius go through this process of crystallisation. . . . The diamond, it is said, can only be polished by its own dust; is not this symbolical of the truth that only by its own fallings-off can genius properly be taught?

> He was crystallising slowly; slowly gaining the complete command over himself.

> The crystallising process which commenced in Weimar was completed in Rome.[16]

Lewes uses the verb "to crystallise" to describe the action which the mind of genius performs upon itself as it matures to perfection, turning outward circumstances to its advantage. Pater uses the noun/adjective "crystal" to denote the already completed product of this process. When Lewes announces that "the crystallising process which commenced in Weimar was completed in Rome" he refers to the fact that it was on Goethe's journey to Italy, and in particular during his sojourn in Rome, that he encountered the writings of Winckelmann. These made a new dimension of experience vivid to him (that of ancient sculptural form) and determined the direction his creativity was to take. A major aspect of Pater's interest in Winckelmann is the effect which the scholar's imagination had on the poet.

It may even be Goethe's response to Raphael, evoked by the Italian journey, and reported by Lewes as follows, which qualified the painter as a subject for "Diaphaneitè": "if Raphael were to paint peasants at an inn he could not help making them look like Apostles, whereas Teniers would make them look like Dutch boors; each artist working according to his own inborn genius."[17] In Pater's essay Raphael is likened to antique sculpture by juxtaposition rather than direct allusion. The reference to "Raphael . . . even in outward form a youth . . . yet surprising all the world" is followed immediately by reference to the "sexless beauty" of "the Greek statues."[18] The juxtaposition is startling and abrupt, as the long central paragraph of the essay about the desirable approximation of life to art sweeps to a close. It is best understood in the context of Hegel's teaching about the significance of ancient Greek sculpture in the *Aesthetics*, which Pater was reading in 1863 and to which he confesses his debt in "Winckelmann."[19]

In the introduction to the *Aesthetics*, Hegel discusses how the terms "art" and "beauty" are to be understood. As an idealist he defines art as the expression of the highest ideas in sensuous form, and beauty as the material representation of the Spirit. But he also speaks more conventionally in terms of the form and content of a work of art. He argues that in a good work of art the form must contribute something essential to the content, and the content must justify the form in which it is treated. Hegel's account of how the reciprocity of form and content creates beauty uses imagery of light, shining and radiance which anticipates that by Pater in "Diaphaneitè":

> the spirit and the soul shine through the human eye, through a man's face, flesh, skin, through his whole figure, and here the meaning is always something wider than what shows itself in the immediate appearance. . . . According to this view, to sum up, we have characterised as the elements of the beautiful something inward, a content, and something outward which signifies that content; the inner shines in the outer and makes itself known through the outer. . . .[20]

This congruence of "inward" and "outer" form accords with the way Pater had found and redeployed his crystal imagery. Hegel, like Pater after him, transfers an account of physical human beauty to aesthetic beauty, describing the latter in terms of the former. Hegel introduces the human individual to his argument simply as a way of illustrating how the unity of aesthetic form and content may be understood. An individual exemplifies the union of "inner" and "outer" (soul and body), which is like the union of form and content in the aesthetic domain which Hegel is establishing. In Pater's work this distinction between the argument and the illustration is discarded.

In "Diaphaneitè" Pater isolates moments or aspects of life as they are arrested by historiography or the imagination and he applies aesthetic criteria to them. Hegel does likewise. The very passage from the *Aesthetics* which Pater translates in "Winckelmann" shows Hegel doing just this:

> They are great and free, and have grown up on the soil of their own individuality, creating themselves out of themselves, and moulding themselves to what they were and willed to be. The age of Pericles was rich in such characters: Pericles himself; Phidias, Plato, above all Sophocles, Thucydides also, Xenophon and Socrates, each in his own order, without the perfection of one being diminished by that of the others. They are ideal artists of themselves, cast each in one flawless mould—works of art which stand before us as an immortal presentment of the gods.[21]

However, whereas Hegel had confined his endeavours to find human lives susceptible of aesthetic appreciation to figures of fifth-century Athens, Pater plunders more recent history for such figures and selects, for instance, Raphael.

Hegel's commentary on the significance of Phideian sculpture develops his account of the relation between aesthetic form and content. This kind of sculpture "forms individuals whom it treats and shapes in their objective spiritual character as complete and perfect in themselves, in independent repose, exempt from relation to anything else."[22] He concludes: "what must be brought before our eyes in undimmed clarity is the eternal element in gods and men, divested of caprice and accidental egotism."[23] By the time of "Winckelmann," Pater regarded these features of Hellenic art as a kind of absolute ideal expression of human perfection and perfectibility which reveals itself recurrently through art (and sometimes life) across history. He moves towards this view in "Diaphaneitè" by declaring that ideal man is "like a relic."[24] In the implied likeness between Raphael and such a work of art, Pater offers sexuality as a metonym for individuality and individual desire. The ideal man requires nothing to complement or complete him. He, like a Greek statue, is entirely self-composed and stands outside natural cycles. In "Winckelmann" he states this more clearly. Phideian sculpture "unveils man in the repose of his unchanging characteristics. Its white light, purged from the angry blood-like stains of action and passion, reveals not what is accidental in man, but the god, as opposed to man's restless movement. It records the first naive, unperplexed recognition of man by himself."[25]

The compatibility, even the blending, of the metaphors of sculpture and of crystal, as Pater uses them to indicate the congruence of inner and outer lives which reveals something archetypal about man, can be demonstrated by the metamorphosis of a statement from Lewes's *Life of Goethe* in "Diaphaneitè" and again in "Winckelmann." Lewes, introducing the subject of Goethe's relationship with Frau von Stein, wrote: "It is a silver thread woven among the many-coloured threads which formed the tapestry of his life. I will here detach it, to consider it by itself."[26] Pater retains the image but, eclipsing the solid Frau von Stein, alters its significance in terms that are too similar to be coincidental. Pater, writing about what for him was ideal or archetypal about Goethe, stated that "[i]t is a thread of pure white light that one might disentwine from the tumultuary richness of Goethe's nature."[27] In "Winckelmann" this became: "Through the tumultuous richness of Goethe's culture, the influence of Winckelmann is always discernible, as the strong, regulative under-current of a clear antique motive."[28]

An examination of the contexts in which sentences from "Diaphaneitè" are redeployed in "Winckelmann" reveals that the early essay is applied as much to ancient Greek sculpture as to Winckelmann himself, indicating their interchangeability in Pater's mind. So, for instance, when in "Diaphaneitè" the ideal temperament had been the subject of the sentence "[i]t is like the reminiscence of a forgotten culture . . ." in the later essay it is "he [Winckelmann]" who "seems to realise that fancy of the reminiscence of a forgotten knowledge."[29] And when, in "Diaphaneitè," it had been the ideal man of whom Pater had said, "[l]ike all the higher forms of inward life this character is a subtle blending and interpenetration of intellectual, moral and spiritual elements," in "Winckelmann" it is of the youths depicted in the Parthenon frieze and of the *adorante* that Pater declares:

> This colourless, unclassified purity of life, with its blending and interpenetration of intellectual, spiritual, and physical elements, still folded together, pregnant with the possibilities of a whole world closed within it, is the highest expression of that indifference which lies beyond all that is relative or partial.[30]

One simile in "Diaphaneitè" had prepared the way for this two-fold application of the early essay. There Pater had written: "[s]uch a character is like a relic from the classical age, laid open by accident to our alien modern atmosphere."[31] And in "Winckelmann" Pater states that Winckelmann's own nature was "itself like a relic of classical antiquity laid open by accident to our modern atmosphere."[32] Already in the opening lines of "Winckelmann" this simile had become a metaphor. Goethe, Pater states, "classes him with certain works of art."[33] Pater goes on to insist that Winckelmann unifies himself with his object of study: "[h]e is *en rapport* with it; it penetrates him, and becomes part of his temperament."[34] This identification of the individual with his subject anticipates the use to which Pater put his crystal metaphor in relation to Plato.

It is a feature of Pater's portrayal of ideal man that ethical and aesthetic categories of judgment are merged, so that the aesthetic subsumes the ethical. What is beautiful is good, and nothing can be good unless it is beautiful. Goethe classes Winckelmann as a work of art, Hegel classes Pericles as a work of art, Pater classes Raphael, Goethe and Winckelmann as works of art. Each one is to be admired, and their form of life emulated. No doubt Pater had taken note of Goethe's dictum, cited by Carlyle in "The Hero as Poet," that "The Beautiful is higher than the Good; the Beautiful includes it in the Good."[35]

Looking forward to the imaginary portrait "Duke Carl of Rosenmold" we can see that these early standards of taste continued to affect Pater's mature imagination. Raphael, Winckelmann and Goethe, the diaphanous triumvirate, all appear in the portrait as standards against which the achievements of Duke Carl are measured. The portrait provides a fairy-tale setting for an account of the development of eighteenth-century taste in Germany. The narrative voice chooses to call it an account of "*Enlightening*" in the closing paragraphs.[36] Here Pater announces, in the first person, that Duke Carl has been a prophet for Goethe, preparing the way for one who appears "like a son of the gods."[37]

Duke Carl's own "enlightening" begins when he escapes from the perpetual "candle-light" of the Rosenmold court into the "broad day" of an attic lumber room.[38] There he finds the *Ars Versificandi: The Art of Versification* by Conrad Celtes, and his aesthetic education begins. The transition from artificial to daylight is a symbolic move. We remember from "Diaphaneitè" the allusion to Dante's ascent to Purgatory: "[h]e who is ever looking for the breaking of a light he knows not whence about him, notes with a strange heedfulness the faintest paleness in the sky."[39] In "Winckelmann" this has become, "Dante, passing from the darkness of the *Inferno*, is filled with a sharp and joyful sense of light."[40] It is stated to illustrate Winckelmann's enthusiasm on moving to Rome where he encountered the Hellenic light of antiquity. Duke Carl then, is in the attic sunlight, and in the intellectual light of the discovered Hellenic culture shed by Celtes's book. He wants to bring Apollo, the god of light, to Germany. He sets up a naive and amusing cult of Apollo in Rosenmold, and soon his courtiers are telling him that he is the Apollo he has told them of.

But Pater ironizes their belief and Carl's earnest endeavours. Duke Carl is far from an Apollonian figure. To indicate how far short of this measure Duke Carl falls, Pater introduces the work of one of his exemplary figures to Rosenmold, and tests Carl's sensitivity to it. Raphael arrives in Rosenmold:

For ten thousand marks—day ever to be remembered!—a genuine work of "the Urbinate," from the cabinet of a certain commercially-minded Italian grand-duke, was on its way to Rosenmold, anxiously awaited as it came over rainy mountain-passes, and along the rough German roads, through doubtful weather. The tribune, the throne itself, were made ready in the presence-chamber, with hangings in the grand-ducal colours, laced with gold, together with a speech and an ode. Late at night, at last, the wagon was heard rumbling into the courtyard, with the guest arrived in safety, but, if one must confess one's self, perhaps forbidding at first sight. From a comfortless portico, with all the grotesqueness of the Middle Age, supported by brown, aged bishops, whose meditations no incident could distract, Our Lady looked out no better than an unpretending nun, with nothing to say the like of which one was used to hear. Certainly one was not stimulated by, enwrapped, absorbed in the great master's doings; only, with much private disappointment, put on one's mettle to defend him against critics notoriously wanting in sensitivity, and against one's self.[41]

This account is a parody of the events which took place in 1754 when the *Sistine Madonna*, purchased by Augustus III, arrived in his Dresden court, and was displayed on the throne for want of a better place to put her. The anecdote is told by Passavant in his 1839 study of Raphael which, as a contemporary work about the artist, Pater may well have consulted.[42] The cost of the purchase was noted by Winckelmann in a letter to Berendis on 17 September 1754.[43]

Duke Carl's immaturity is marked by his failure to respond to Raphael's painting. The date of this failure is significant. It was not until 1755 that Winckelmann published his *Gedanken über die Nachahmung der Griechischen Werke in der Malerei und Bildhauerkunst*. On 4 June 1755 Winckelmann wrote to Berendis to describe the king's favourable reception of the work, despite the criticism of his own taste.[44] Winckelmann lists five features of the work which he believed to be innovative. The third of these is his promotion of Raphael: "the first bringing to light of the virtue of the ancients and of Raphael, whom nobody has hitherto recognized."[45] Carl, though exhibiting "a really heroic effort of mind at a disadvantage,"[46] is possessed by the spirit of the age and needs the insight of a Winckelmann before he can transcend the atmosphere of decaying medievalism which prevails in Rosenmold.

In "Winckelmann" Pater had explained what purpose this culture served: "By hastening the decline of art, by withdrawing interest from it, and yet keeping the thread of its traditions, it has suffered the human mind to repose, that it might awake when the day came with eyes refreshed to those antique forms."[47] Carl experiences the period of awakening from this repose. He suffers a sense of displacement in Rosenmold culture. He entertains the fancy that "he must really belong by descent to a southern race," and like the diaphanous type, he seems to have "the imperfect reminiscence of something that had passed in earlier life."[48]

Gradually he anticipates events which passed in both Goethe's life and in his fiction. Like Goethe, he spends time in Strasbourg admiring the Gothic features of the cathedral there. As Goethe had later scorned the taste which he extolled in *Von Deutscher Baukunst*, so the narrative voice tells us that Carl's stay in Strasbourg was "one long mistake."[49] But Carl can also exclaim in a moment of insight, "For you, France, Italy, Hellas, is here!" as Wilhelm Meister was to learn to say in *Wilhelm Meisters Lehrjahre* (1795), "*Hier oder nirgend ist Amerika!*"[50]

Carl's very posturing as Apollo had been as anticipation of Goethe. Lewes presents Goethe as an Apollo figure when he describes what the poet was like in 1774:

> Those . . . who think of him as the calm stately minister the old Jupiter throned in Weimar, will feel some difficulty perhaps in recognising the young Apollo of this period. But it must be remembered that not only was he young, impetuous, bursting into life, and trying his eagle wings with wanton confidence of strength; he was, moreover, a Rhinelander, with the gay blood of that race . . . not a Northerner muddled with beer.[51]

"Duke Carl of Rosenmold" closes with an episode from Goethe's life, in which Goethe is seen by Pater as the *Resurgam* of Carl.[52] The episode which Pater cites was the subject of an engraving by Wilhelm Kaulbach. It depicts the poet in the posture of a latter-day Apollo Belvedere. The engraving is called "Goethe in Frankfurt," and was made to illustrate *Goethe Galerie. Goethes Frauengestalten* (Munich, 1862). It was published in Britain in 1867, with a new commentary by Lewes, as *Female Characters of Goethe. From the Original Drawings of Wilhelm Kaulbach. With Explanatory Text by G. H. Lewes.*[53] The book was certainly available to Pater, and the engraving may have impressed him. For there was an image of his ideal man, dressed in eighteenth-century costume, but posing as the god of light and poetry, a historical figure conforming to the pattern of classical sculpture, there to "regenerate the world" as Duke Carl had hoped to.

Nineteenth–Century Responses to Montaigne and Bruno: A Context for Pater

16

JANE SPIRIT

MANY OF PATER'S CRITICS have identified in his fiction Pater's response to the intellectual and historical debates of his day.[1] More recently, writers have indicated its appeal both to a wider conventional audience and to an elite readership capable of discerning those carefully veiled references which effectively undermine the apparent moral conformity of the text.[2] Both these approaches have enabled commentators to regard Pater's presentation of historical figures as further evidence of a deliberate ambivalence, of those "strong but fluctuating identifications" which inform his writing.[3] In the light of such research this paper provides an outline of the British context in which Pater created his portraits of Montaigne and Bruno. In particular, I note how, despite a continuing debate over their moral worth, both were increasingly celebrated during the second half of the nineteenth century for the freedom of thought they were seen to represent. By reference to the published and manuscript portions of *Gaston*, I discuss both Pater's sympathetic response to Montaigne and Bruno and his doubts concerning the moral and aesthetic consequences of their philosophies of indifference. In addition, they are associated in the manuscripts with a decadence which simultaneously repels and attracts.[4] I should like to suggest that Pater manipulated this ambivalent response to form an ironic comment on the duplicity of later nineteenth-century society which had come to associate Montaigne and Bruno with its own moral and liberal self-image.

Donald Frame indicates how Romanticism led to a revival of French interest in Montaigne, but one which attended to his personality rather than to his ideas.[5] The enthusiasm in France described by Frame is also evident in England. In 1827, for example, *The New Monthly Magazine and Literary Journal* published an article discussing passages marked by Byron in his copy of Cotton's translation of the *Essays*. The article examines the link between Byron and Montaigne and particularly defends Montaigne against the charge of "egotism" by finding this "term very ill applied to the self-reflections of such men."[6] In 1828 Landor's fictional portrait of Montaigne appeared; in it Montaigne converses with Scaliger and shows him around his house. The reader thus overhears the servants praising God for the kindness and thoughtfulness of their master. The image here is of a man with Epicurean tendencies, whose wit and tolerance outfaces Scaliger.[7]

Such early British admiration for Montaigne's tolerance and self-criticism must be balanced against the evident disapproval of a supposed moral indifference. Carlyle's entry on the essayist, written for Brewster's *Edinburgh Encyclopaedia* (1820-23), exemplifies an ambiguity of tone which British writers continued to adopt up to the end of the century. Carlyle found it possible to excuse Montaigne for his apparent egotism because "a modern reader will not easily cavil at the patient and good-natured, though exuberant, egotism which brings back to our view 'the form and pressure' of a time long past."[8] However, Carlyle could not equate Montaigne's apparent religious scepticism with the pious death recorded in the biographies. Nor could Carlyle accept those sections of the *Essays* in which Montaigne indulges in a discussion he finds needlessly crude, and he concludes that Montaigne "deserves the bad pre-eminence in love at once of coarseness and obscenity."[9] This mixture of responses continues among late nineteenth-century commentators. Pater would have been aware of a strong body of moral criticism which existed alongside an increasing admiration for Montaigne as a freethinker who demonstrated tolerance in an age of bigotry.

Writing in the 1920s Irene Cooper Willis complained that Montaigne's whole moral outlook had been undermined by the excessively scrupulous Victorians.[10] This kind of outlook can be seen in an extreme form in the writings of Alexander Vinet, who reaches the simplistic conclusion that atheism leads to immorality. His essay of the 1830s was published in English in 1850, his translator also attacking Montaigne with the claim that "God was often on his lips, as in his writings, but not in his thoughts, above all, not in his affections," and thus adding hypocrisy to Vinet's charge of immorality.[11] Again, writing in 1857, the Oxford theologian R. W. Church suggested that Montaigne's scepticism was his own fault, being the result of that same weakness of character that displayed itself in the crudities of his work.[12] The persistence of this rather prudish view is demonstrated by John Owen's inclusion of a footnote dismissing Church and defending Montaigne in his book on sceptics of the French Renaissance published as late as 1893.[13]

Despite an evident dislike of what was regarded as crudeness and moral laxity on Montaigne's part, a fascination with his personality, initiated by the Romantics, developed into an alternative view of him as a perplexed and modern man. This was combined with attempts to understand Montaigne as a character and thinker in the context of his complex age rather than to judge him by nineteenth-century standards. The result was a more generally sympathetic viewpoint. F. D. Maurice, for example, described Montaigne as being no common observer of human nature. He discussed Montaigne within his social context, as an aristocrat believing that moral principles "might be safely trusted to the instincts and cultivated sense at least of gentlemen than to the judgement of professional sages of any school."[14] So, although Maurice did not approve completely of Montaigne, he provided an historical explanation of what others read as a deliberate and arrogant flouting of traditional religious values. In 1858 Bayle St. John published the first book on Montaigne in English and the first extended life of him in any language.[15] St. John found in Montaigne's supposed egotism the source of nineteenth-century empathy with him: "Ordinary selfishness repels; but the selfishness of Montaigne seems to make him more amiable. There is something feminine about it; but, more than this, we feel it to be a flattered portrait, that will bear public exhibition, of our own cruel indifference to the wants and sufferings of our fellow-creatures."[16] In 1865 W. E. H. Lecky also used the term "indifference" in connection with Montaigne, not to describe him as callous, but to praise him for his neutrality and refusal to become embroiled in the contentions of his day.[17]

Arnold's response to Montaigne was similarly approving. In his 1861 essay "On Translating Homer" Arnold had spoken of Montaigne as the epitome of the ideal critic, referring to the "ondoyant et divers" (undulating and diverse) being of Montaigne.[18] In 1863 he cited Montaigne as one of "the excellent markers and recorders of the traits of human life," placing him in the same category as La Bruyère and Addison.[19] Perhaps the most significant remark of Arnold's on Montaigne, in terms of the new approach it embodies, is his comment in an 1877 article that rescues the essayist from the still pressing charge of immorality, by redefining moral behaviour and by setting Montaigne alongside other artists. Morality, Arnold argues, cannot be judged according to changing standards of action, but according to a common motivation. Thus Arnold acknowledged a link between Montaigne and Shakespeare: "The master-pressure upon their spirit is the pressure exercised by this same thought: 'Let the good prevail.' And the result is that they deal with the life of all of us—the life of man in its fulness and greatness."[20] It is this overall restoration of Montaigne's reputation that lies behind such popular accounts as that given by Lynn Linton in 1894 in which Montaigne is characterized as kind, honest, and as "one of the acutest thinkers the world has ever seen."[21]

Pater's image of Montaigne in the published parts of *Gaston* owes more to the approving tone of Arnold than the moralistic approach of Carlyle. Pater stresses not Montaigne's coarseness, but his wonderful "fineness of sensation"[22] and praises Montaigne for maintaining basic moral decency which is "better than any kind of heroism, in an age whose very virtues were apt to become insane."[23] Even his link with the later "immodesty of French literature"[24] shows him in a favourable light, as an artist making a serious contribution to modern style, while his scepticism may be regarded as a prelude to the acknowledgement of faith as a "certain great possibility, which might lie among the conditions of so complex a world."[25] Although criticism may be detected in the way Pater presents Montaigne's friendship with de la Boetie as the one experience that breaks through Montaigne's indifferent and controlled emotional life, Pater's depiction enhances the earlier Romantic use of Montaigne as a symbol of devoted male friendship which yet retained respectability.[26]

However, sympathy for Montaigne's relativistic philosophy is matched by doubts about its moral implications. Pater's account also acknowledges how the "suspended judgement,"[27] which leads to Montaigne's tolerance, is based upon egotism; the "one subject always in prominence—himself."[28] While such self-reference may be acceptable as a moral basis, it is itself undermined by the impossibility of fixing any permanent image of the self amidst flux. Instead Montaigne presents us with images of the "disparate . . . men who keep discordant company within each one of us."[29] Montaigne's relativism as the "proper intellectual equivalent to the infinite possibility of things"[30] leads both to egotism and to a loss of that sense of identity which ensures moral order. The tapestries depicting Circe that hang on the walls of Montaigne's tower represent not only the enchanting atmosphere there, but also the interweaving of good and evil inherent in Montaigne's philosophy.[31] Similarly, while the progression of *Gaston*, such as it is, leads the protagonist away from the relativism of Montaigne and towards the absolutism of Bruno, in the decadent atmosphere of Valois Paris, their distinctive voices merge for Gaston, just as his presence becomes indistinguishable in the text. The "opportunist" philosophies of Montaigne and Bruno complete a circle of indifference;[32] their apparent reasonableness inevitably subsumed into Valois decadence.

Pater's interest in Bruno reflects a contemporary resurgence of interest in "the Nolan" as James Joyce was to call him,[33] associated with the Risorgimento and culminating in the unveiling of a statue in Rome on 9 June 1889 to mark the place where Bruno had been burnt as a heretic in 1600. Controversy over the memorial epitomized the late nineteenth-century Italian reaction against what was perceived as the anti-scientific and anti-intellectual Roman Catholic church.[34] In August of the same year Pater's article "Giordano Bruno, Paris: 1586" appeared in the *Fortnightly Review*. The revised version of this article forms chapter seven of *Gaston*.

Analyzing the adulation of Bruno in the last century, Frances Yates traces it back to the publication of Domenico Berti's book on Bruno in 1867.[35] This biography opened the way for the use of Bruno as an heroic figure by liberals and intellectuals during the 1870s. Of course earlier writers had also discussed Bruno and may have influenced Pater directly as well as have moulded general opinion to which he also responded. Schelling's favourable book had appeared in 1802, and in a footnote to the fifth number of *The Friend*, Coleridge writes of his intention to give: "hereafter an account of the life of Giordano Bruno, . . . a vigorous mind struggling after truth, amid many prejudices, which from the state of the Roman Church, in which he was born, have a claim to much Indulgence."[36] Henry Hallam's remark of 1839 that it is "not uncommon in modern books to find an eulogy on the philosopher of Nola"[37] suggests that other writers before 1850 shared Coleridge's admiration for Bruno. Hallam's tone is far less adulatory. In the second volume of his *Introduction to the Literature of Europe* he finds that Bruno's doctrines are unoriginal and dogmatic in their reduction of the "most subtle and incomprehensible mysteries into positive aphorisms of science."[38] Pater borrowed a copy of this volume from Queen's College library in December 1863 and may have absorbed something of Hallam's view of Bruno's philosophy as fundamentally amoral.[39]

Various images of Bruno emerged during the 1870s and the 1880s, different commentators championing him as a symbol of the "valiant soldier of the right, a fearless defender of his belief, a magnanimous advocate of truth."[40] This picture of his life as a "struggle against authority in favour of reason,"[41] was enhanced by John Tyndall's Belfast lecture of 1874, in which he claimed that Bruno was an important forerunner of modern science and especially of the new physics.[42] The other image was of Bruno as an intensely religious man. This was the kind of view taken by Ian Frith in his biography of 1887 in which Bruno is presented as an untainted hero.[43]

However, it was the rationalists who became the greatest champions of Bruno, regarding him as an example of their own struggle against superstition. The tone had already been set by G. H. Lewes in his influential *Biographical History of Philosophy*.[44] Writing in the same tradition, Annie Besant extravagantly describes Bruno as "this grandest hero of Freethought, this man who lived and died so nobly that he carved his name forever on the marble temple of Fame."[45] Isa Blagden, writing in *Fraser's Magazine* in 1871, also celebrates Bruno as a "martyr for freedom of thought and liberty of opinion"; similarly, Arthur Moss declares that "Freethought has had no more ardent lovers, philosophy no more diligent students, persecution no more fearless victims, than Bruno and Spinoza."[46]

This veneration of Bruno reached its peak in the mid-1880s and led to some opposition—shown in the earnest debate about the historical certainty of Bruno's having been burnt at the stake.[47] The English National Committee was set up in 1885 in connection with an international group formed to ensure the erection of a monument to the memory of Bruno. New heights of praise were reached in the *Agnostic Annual* for the same year, 1885:

> Hero of heroes, hail! No nobler name
> Gleams 'mid the galaxy of human pride;
> Nor brighter story lights the scroll of Fame
> Than that which tells the world how BRUNO died![48]

Swinburne had been a founder member of the English committee and in 1889 wrote a commemorative poem on the occasion of the unveiling of the statue:

> Cover thine eyes and weep, O Child of hell,
> Grey spouse of Satan, Church of name abhorred.
> . . . Rome, redeemed at last
> From all the red pollution of thy past,
> Acclaims the grave bright face that smiled of yore
> Even on the fire that caught it round and clomb
> To cast its ashes on the face of Rome.[49]

Similarly, though less emotionally, J. A. Symonds was to write of Bruno in 1886 as that "most illustrious example of the school exterminated by reactionary Rome."[50]

It was amidst this atmosphere of anti-Catholic feeling that Pater's article appeared in the same month as C. E. Plumptre's article on Bruno in the *Westminster Review*. Plumptre finds it appropriate to compare Bruno and Shelley but points out that, whereas Shelley warred against all religion, Bruno only rebelled against sham faith.[51] Karl Blind's "Giordano Bruno and the New Italy" had already been printed in the *Nineteenth Century* in July of the same year. Both Blind's and Plumptre's accounts lay stress on the notion of Bruno as a martyr for science. Blind, for example, identifies the neo-platonist elements of Bruno's thought which caused him to strive "for greater beauteousness" and also sees him as a precursor of Darwin and evolutionary thought, for although "unaided by exact science, he anticipated in a general way the scientific results of ages to come."[52] This is also a theme in Pater's article which points out how "already Bruno had measured the space which Bacon would fill, with room, perhaps, for Darwin also."[53] However, like Blind, Pater's emphasis is equally upon Bruno as a religious individual. His study of him is primarily the study of a religious temperament, but without the sentimentality of the religious image of Bruno that had characterized Frith's biography two years before Pater's article appeared. Pater's portrait may therefore be seen as combining the religious and rationalist elements of other commentators. He anticipates the dual response adumbrated by Brinton and Davidson in their addresses on Bruno, published in Philadelphia in 1890. Brinton sees Bruno primarily as a physicist and sceptic; Davidson suggests that Bruno's search was essentially a religious one.

For Pater, just as Montaigne practises Platonic dialogue, so Bruno, as an interpreter of Plato formulates a dialectic between sensual and spiritual desires.[54] He remains "a lover and a monk."[55] Within the context of *Gaston* it would seem then that the protagonist discovers in Bruno's system not only a theoretical justification for the integration of mind and matter, soul and body, but also an example of the fulfilment to be found in attaining such harmony. However, Pater's response remains ambivalent, the text casting doubts on the morality of Bruno's doctrines. The manuscripts also reveal a curious further echo of the initial attraction to Bruno, signalling Pater's fascination with the cruel shadow of Bruno's doctrine, whatever the ethical objections which continue to be signalled. In the dark world of Valois Paris, as portrayed in the manuscripts, the voices of the sceptic Montaigne and the idealist Bruno become conflated through the indifference with which they are both associated.

Gaston is initially attracted to Montaigne's "jealously guarded indifference of soul."[56] After the massacre of St. Bartholomew's Day however, Gaston considers the weakness of his uncommitted position and "his own helplessness amid the obscure forces around him, which would fain compromise the indifferent."[57] Bruno's doctrine of indifference, as expounded in chapter six, conflicts with the ideal of aesthetic discrimination, presaging the collapse of "the distinction . . . between what was right and wrong in the matter of art."[58] This failure of artistic taste is linked to a breakdown of moral order in which the distinctions between art and life, good and evil are eroded and pain and pleasure are no longer separable. Yet within such a breakdown, Gaston is irresistibly pulled towards Montaigne and Bruno: "[B]oth alike recommending though from opposite points in the speculative circle their doctrine of 'indifference': yes of moral indifference. It presented itself in fact as neither more nor less than the weighted theoretic equivalent to the actual situation."[59] In confirmation of that attraction, Gaston is "magnetically" drawn to the tower of Marguerite de Valois. Gaston's ascent is likened to the moment when Ulysses "approaches the palace of Circe."[60] Marguerite welcomes Gaston and Jasmin to her "charmed circle/area" by "flinging wide the doors upon them suddenly like Homer's sorceress."[61] Once within the court, Gaston adopts the position of distanced observer: "For, as with physical delicacies, if you wished to sip, as you might wine, . . . the singularly attempered character of the so gifted Margaret a calm though kindly indifference was in fact the proper condition for doing so."[62] However, as he edits Marguerite's text with its "entanglement of beauty with evil,"[63] events suggest that Gaston's indifference, like that of Montaigne and Bruno, is also an evasion of moral responsibility. Gaston is linked to the "indifferent" Parisian public who gather to watch the execution of Jasmin's devoted young servant Raoul in chapter ten of the *Gaston* manuscripts.[64] The description of Raoul's death may be read as a fantasy of homosexual submission to suffering. The boy emerges into the "heat" of the square, into the "long shadow" of a Paris under the influence of Bruno.[65] Neither Gaston, nor Jasmin the implied watcher, are directly represented, but are displaced amongst the "aristocratic sightseers" looking on.[66] As in the arena passage of *Marius*, details of horrific death are supplied, while the apparent concentration of the passage is on the crowd's response: a mixture of morbid fascination and sentimentality.

At the end of the chapter Gaston is led to reflect on the evil effects which flow from accidental or deliberate callousness. While Marguerite's cruelty to La Mole may be deliberate, Jasmin's is unintentional. The outcome in both cases is, however, the same. Gaston is therefore linked through his accidental cruelty towards Colombe to Jasmin, and through him to that of Marguerite and the whole age. The policy of experiencing all things "indifferently" is, he realizes, a limiting one,[67] yet it remains the appropriate philosophy of his day:

Observe, touch, taste of all things, indifferently!—So his philosophic guides had steadily recommended—guides he might *seem* indeed to have encountered quite casually on the/his way, whose judgements/theories nevertheless as he then actually was seemed to come to him with nothing less than axiomatic force.[68]

Within this charmed circle, traditional distinctions are blurred and Gaston's voice lost amidst those of Montaigne and Bruno. The philosophers, in turn, are missing. Their views are echoed both through the, again absent, figure of Brantôme, who "would have concurred alike with the 'new gospel' of the philosophic monk and/as with the Gascon worldling's . . . doctrine of 'indifference'," and through the portrayal of Henri III as a figure capable of the unexpected in keeping with Montaigne's "doctrine of 'ondoyancy' of life/man/the world."[69] The indifferent Gaston becomes merely a watcher of events, "thoughtfully looking on with us all along."[70] Gaston does not emerge again as a distinct persona until chapter thirteen, when he rediscovers the true Renaissance spirit and its "preoccupation with the perennial . . . interests of life."[71] Presumably such moral seriousness would have been necessary to free Gaston from the decadence revealed in the earlier parts of the text. However, whatever change of heart may have been envisaged for his protagonist, Pater's acknowledgement of the decadent implications of Montaigne's and Bruno's indifferent philosophies remains a challenge to the comfortable assumptions of his contemporaries.

Pater thus resists the tendency of the 1880s simply to incorporate Montaigne and Bruno into its liberal tradition and identifies the irony of his society's appropriation of them as symbols of its supposed moral and intellectual tolerance. The ambivalence of Pater's response may perhaps best be understood both as a reflection of his own acknowledged conflicting impulses, and as his reflection upon the unacknowledged strains inherent within the contemporary British admiration for Bruno and Montaigne. As with the mirrors frequently mentioned in the *Gaston* manuscripts, it seems then that we look into the text only in order to recover shifting images; "double and treble reflections of the mind upon itself."

Notes

———— 1

LAUREL BRAKE & IAN SMALL
Pater in the 1990s

1.   Rene Wellek, *A History of Modern Criticism*, vol. 4 *The Later Nineteenth Century* (New Haven: Yale University Press, 1965), 381.

———— 2

BILLIE ANDREW INMAN
Estrangement and Connection:
Walter Pater, Benjamin Jowett, and William M. Hardinge

1.   Thomas Wright, *The Life of Walter Pater*. 2 vols. (London: Everett, 1907), I, 255-56.
2.   Laurel Brake, "Judas and the Widow: Thomas Wright and A. C. Benson as Biographers of Walter Pater: The Widow," *Prose Studies*, 4 (1981), 48. The essay is reprinted in Philip Dodd, ed., *Walter Pater: An Imaginative Sense of Fact* (London: Frank Cass, 1981), 39-54. The passages from Benson's *Diary* discussed by Brake have been printed by R. M. Seiler in *Walter Pater: A Life Remembered* (Calgary, Alberta: University of Calgary, 1987), 253-61.
3.   Richard Ellmann, "Oscar at Oxford," *New York Review*, 29 March 1984, 26.
4.   Ibid.
5.   Richard Ellmann, *Oscar Wilde* (New York: Knopf, 1988), 60-61.
6.   Ibid., 60.
7.   In a telephone conversation in November 1985, Richard Ellmann directed me to Dr. Kadish, who directed me to the Gell family and to Hardinge's article on Jowett cited herein. I express gratituted to Dr. Kadish and to Major Gell, who provided the letters for me to read and gave me permission to quote from them and photocopy them. The series of letters from the Gell Correspondence that I cite are the *B* series (Arnold Toynbee), and the MIL series (Alfred Milner). The letters have been laminated, arranged by dates, numbered, and placed in manila envelopes. I read Toynbee's letters to Philip Lyttleton Gell, 1873-1881; Jowett's letters to Gell 1873-1892 [Series A; none cited]; and Milner's to Gell, 1873-1879. MIL 6, 7, and 8, the most pertinent to the

paper, are in an envelope labelled *1874*. The numbers and dates correspond to those given in the *National Register of Archives*, listed by T. W. M. Jaine for the Royal Commission on Historical Manuscripts in 1975, of which the Derbyshire County Record Office in Matlock has a copy. Much of the correspondence is of a business type, related mainly to the British South Africa Company. The personal correspondence is in Section VI: Correspondence Mostly Between P. L. Gell and Alfred Milner (cr. Viscount Milner, 1902). Most of the pertinent letters are in subdivision HMC/64. Milner also saved an extensive body of correspondence which is now held by the Bodleian Library and indexed in a separate *Catalogue*. However, no letters pertaining to Hardinge are indexed.

8.   Hardinge states that he "had the misfortune to lose both . . . [his] parents in ten months" (William Money Hardinge, "Some Personal Recollections of the Master of Balliol," *Temple Bar* 103 [October 1894]; repr. in *Littel's Living Age* 203 [1 December 1894], 557), and that after his father's death he "paid the master a visit of many days at his own house, dating from Monday, February 28th, 1876 . . . a visit during which his house was literally mine, whether he was there or away." The death date of Hardinge's father, Henry Hardinge, M.D., is given in the *Calendar of the Grants of Probate and Letters of Administration Made in the Probate Registries* (London, 1876) at Somerset House, London, as 28 January 1876. Milner tells Gell on 6 February 1876: "Hardinge has lost his father—great loss I should think" (MIL 1/20). Hardinge's mother, Jane Hardinge, had died on 26 March 1875 of cerebral hemorrhage, with her son present (death certificate from St. Catherine's House, London).

9.   Ellmann, *Oscar Wilde*, 60.

10.   John Dixon Hunt places the beginning of the road project at Hinksey in the spring of 1874 (*The Wider Sea: A Life of John Ruskin* [London: Dent, 1982], 350), and Alon Kadish dates the first planning meeting on 16 March 1874 (Alon Kadish, *The Life and Death of Arnold Toynbee, 1852-1883* [Durham: Duke University Press, 1986], 34.)

11.   Ellmann, *Oscar Wilde*, 61.

12.   William Money Hardinge, "Some Personal Recollections of the Master of Balliol," *Littel's Living Age*, 557.

13.   Gell Correspondence, B1/1.

14.   Ibid., MIL 1/6.

15.   B 1/2. This paragraph continues as follows: "Milner will tell you more: now [next word smudged] but his real friends know the circumstances & of course you will say nothing about them: Hardinge was really very grateful to you for all your kindness & seemed to feel your not being up during the matter very much: he had a sort of wish to go down by the same sea-side place as you: but I fancy there are very strong objections which you will understand: though I think in some respects the plan is a good one. Especially I don't think for your sake, in your present state of health it would be at all good, though you know best about that, of course." Toynbee's letter, with full date, 11 March 1874, contains this line: "Hardinge seemed very sensible to your kind offer to go with him to the sea." But apparently they did not go. Toynbee wrote Gell on 9 April 1874: "Will you write to Hardinge? He is lonely Im afraid, though his never-ending doubleness of which he seems hardly conscious is reason enough for men ceasing to have to do with him—but nothing but infinite patience from the few of us who have tried to help him can save him—for his father plainly says he will turn him from the house if anything of the kind happens again—and if that does happen God knows what will become of him." B 1/3.

16.   MIL 1/6.

17. MIL 1/7.

18. MIL 1/8.

19. Hardinge, "Some Personal Recollections of the Master of Balliol," 557.

20. Ibid., 554.

21. Ibid., 561.

22. Bodleian MS. Eng. misc. e 459, from 17 January 1874.

23. It has been suggested "Miss Pater" might refer to Pater himself. I do not think so. Such a usage would have been out of keeping with the style of Milner's letters. Although Milner was capable of levity, irony, and sarcasm, he treats Hardinge's crisis consistently with straightforward seriousness. Also, I think that if Pater had been trying to send Hardinge home, Milner would have felt prompted to comment either on Pater's duplicity or Hardinge's misinterpretation of the relationship. In the nineteenth century "Miss" was the title of the eldest unmarried sister; I therefore thought at first that Hester, not Clara, would have been "Miss Pater." However, Sir Michael Levey has convinced me that the sister who took action is more likely to have been Clara than Hester: "Although of course Miss Pater was, as you say, the proper form for referring to the elder sister, anyone not aware of her or of the sisters' ages *might* have referred in that way to Clara. . . . To illustrate . . . I cite Wilde's letter to Wemyss Reid (Hart-Davis, 1962, 195), where he writes of hoping to get among contributors to the *Lady's World*, in 1887, 'Miss Pater,' where surely he meant Clara? Clara's gravitating all the time towards university circles is possibly another pointer to considering if it was she who became involved" (Letter dated 21 August 1988).

24. Leonard Montefiore was destined to have an even shorter life than Arnold Toynbee. After studying law, he returned to Balliol and took his B.A. in 1878. Then he went out to Newport, Rhode Island, where in 1879 he died.

25. Mallock had taken the B.A. in 1874, but apparently had remained at Oxford. He had never lodged in college. Book I, Chapter I-III, of *The New Republic* would appear in *Belgravia* four months later, or June 1876, and the serial publication would extend to December. Mallock, who had won the Newdigate Prize for Poetry in 1871, had published *Every Man His Own Poet, The Inspired Singer's Recipe Book* in 1872, in which he had given the recipe for writing a poem like Tennyson, Browning, Arnold, and others. He had by this time written most of the poems that were to appear in *Poems by William Hurrell Mallock* (New York: George W. Fitch, 1880). While *The New Republic* was appearing in *Belgravia*, he published an article entitled "*The Golden Ass* of Apuleius" in *Fraser's Magazine* (n.s. 14 [1876], 363-74). He published his central philosophical book, *Is Life Worth Living?* (New York: John Wurtels Lovell), dedicated to Ruskin, in 1880. Mallock believed that unless modern man could find a new basis for religious faith, he would sink deeper and deeper into misery. The position that he advocates in this book is exactly that described by Pater in "The Will as Vision" in *Marius the Epicurean*, the only difference being that Marius was able to effect the will to believe only once or twice and Mallock thought it to be the only acceptable state of mind.

26. MIL 1/20.

27. Wright, *The Life of Walter Pater*, I, 256.

28. William Hurrell Mallock, *Memoirs of Life and Literature* (New York and London: Harper, 1920), 67.

29. Ibid., 79.

30. Ibid., 80-82.

31. Ibid., 87.

32. *The New Republic, or, Culture, Faith and Philosophy in an English Country House*, 2 vols. (London: Chatto and Windus, 1877); see especially I, 22, 134, 163; II, 136, 144, 158, 179.

33. Ibid., II, 130.

34. *Monumens du culte secret des dames romaines, pour servir de suite aux Monumens de la vie privée des XII Césars* [by Pierre François Hugues, called d'Hancarville], who states that it was published by Sabellus in Caprée, in 1784. For a discussion of this book, see my "Laurence's Uncle's Book, or Shades of Baron d'Hancarville in Mallock's *New Republic*," *ELT Special Series No. 4* (1990), 67-76.

35. Geoffrey Faber, *Jowett: A Portrait with a Background* (Cambridge: Harvard University Press, 1957), 378.

36. Ibid.

37. Ibid., and Mallock, *The New Republic*, I, 14.

38. [Charles Edward Hutchinson], *Boy-Worship* (Oxford, 1880), 12-13.

39. The remainder of the sonnet is as follows:

> One was Narcissus by a wood-side well,
> And on the moss his limbs and feet were white;
> And one, Queen Venus, blown in for my delight
> Across the blue sea in a rosy shell;
> And one, a lean Aquinas in his cell,
> Kneeling, his pen in hand, with aching sight
> Strained towards a carven Christ; and of these three
> I knew not which was fairest. First I turned
> Towards the soft boy, who laughed and fled from me;
> Towards Venus then; and she smiled once, and she
> Fled also. Then with teeming heart I yearned,
> O Angel of the Schools, towards Christ with thee! (II, 130-31)

Either Hardinge or Mallock was capable of writing this sonnet, but presumably Mallock wrote it, since it is a part of his book and since it expresses a type of eclecticism that was anathema to him.

40. Faber, *Jowett: A Portrait with a Background*, 92-93.

41. "Some Personal Recollections of the Master of Balliol," 557-60.

42. Watts-Dunton, quoted by Oswald Doughty in *Dante Gabriel Rossetti: A Victorian Romantic*, 2nd ed. (London: Oxford University Press, 1960), 616.

43. Evelyn Abbott and Lewis Campbell, *The Life and Letters of Benjamin Jowett*, 3 vols. (New York: E. P. Dutton, 1897), II, 111.

44. "Some Personal Recollections of the Master of Balliol," 557.

45. Ibid., 562.

46. William Money Hardinge, *Clifford Gray: A Romance of Modern Life* (London: Smith, Elder, 1881), 80-81.

47. If Raffalovich's use of *saw* in this passage is literal, the reference cannot be to Hardinge's first encounter with Pater, since Raffalovich was only ten years old in 1874.

48. Alexander Michaelson [Marc André Raffalovich], "Walter Pater. In Memoriam," *Blackfriars*, 9 (1928), 469-70.

49. "The Myth of Demeter and Persephone," *Greek Studies* (London: Macmillan, 1895), 108.

50. *Pater and His Reading, 1874-1877, with a Bibliography of His Library Borrowings, 1878-1894* (New York: Garland, 1990), especially pp. xxiv-xxxiii, 140, 204.

51. Walter Pater, *The Renaissance: Studies in Art and Poetry*, 2nd ed. (London: Macmillan, 1877), 7-8.

3

GERALD MONSMAN

Editing Pater's *Gaston de Latour*:
The Unfinished Work as "A Fragment of Perfect Expression"

1. Walter Pater, *Gaston De Latour* (London: Macmillan, 1896), "Preface."
2. Elizabeth Falsey, "Special Collections Report: The Pater Manuscripts at Houghton, Harvard University," *English Literature in Transition*, 27:2 (1984), 155.
3. Walter Pater, *Marius the Epicurean* (London, Macmillan, 1910), I, 9.
4. Charles Lamb, "Oxford in the Vacation," *The Essays of Elia* in *The Works of Charles Lamb* (Edition de Luxe), Alfred Ainger, ed. (London: Chesterfield Society, 1883), 18, 300.
5. William Sharp, "Some Personal Reminiscences of Walter Pater," *Atlantic Monthly*, 74 (December 1894), 805.
6. Hans Walter Gabler, ed. James Joyce, *Ulysses: The Corrected Text* (New York: Vintage Books, 1984), 649-50.
7. Hans Walter Gabler, ed. James Joyce, *Ulysses: A Critical and Synoptic Edition* (New York: Garland, 1984), III, 1892–95.
8. Letter of April or May 1894, *Letters of Walter Pater*, Lawrence Evans, ed. (Oxford: Clarendon, 1970), 153, n.2.
9. Gosse, "Walter Pater," *Critical Kit-Kats* (London: Heinemann, 1896), 262-64.
10. Unpublished correspondence, Bodelian Library, University of Oxford. See also Shadwell's letter to Clara of 7 September 1894 and his preface to *Greek Studies* (1896).

4

IAN SMALL

Editing and Annotating Pater

1. See G. Thomas Tanselle, "Textual Criticism and Deconstruction," *Studies in Bibliography*, 43, (1990), 1-33.
2. The Pater correspondence in Macmillan archive in the British Library contains no reference to any edition after the 1892.
3. For example, the editions by Parker, Tuell, and Levey follow the Library edition, but for different and quite implausible reasons. See Walter Pater, *Marius the Epicurean*, E. Adams Parker, ed. (London: Macmillan, 1931); Walter Pater, *Marius the Epicurean*, Anne Kimball Tuell, ed. (New

York: Macmillan, 1926); and Walter Pater, *Marius the Epicurean*, Michael Levey, ed. (Harmondsworth: Penguin, 1985).

4.   G. Thomas Tanselle, "The Editorial Problem of Final Authorial Intention," *Studies in Bibliography*, 29 (1976), 169.

5.   Jerome McGann, "Shall These Bones Live?" in *The Beauty of Inflections* (Oxford: Clarendon Press, 1985), 91. McGann does offer a systematic programme for taking full account of the history of a text.

6.   See Michael Black, "Editing a Constantly-Revising Author: The Cambridge Edition of Lawrence in Historical Context," in *D.H. Lawrence Centenary Essays*, Mara Kalnins, ed. (Bristol: Bristol Classical Press, 1986).

7.   Hans Walter Gabler, "The Synchrony and Diachrony of Texts: Practice and Theory of the Critical Edition of James Joyce's *Ulysses*," *TEXT*, 1 (1981), 305-26.

8.   See, in particular, Claire Badaracco, "The Editor and the Question of Value: Proposal," *TEXT*, 1 (1981), 41-43; and Fredson Bowers, "The Editor and the Question of Value: Another View," *TEXT*, 1 (1981), 45-73.

9.   See Ian Small, "Critical Opinion: Annotating 'Hard' Nineteenth-Century Novels," *Essays in Criticism*, 36 (1986), 281-93.

10.   Walter Pater, *Miscellaneous Studies* (London: Macmillan, 1895), 184.

11.   Martin C. Battestin, "A Rationale of Literary Annotation: The Example of Fielding's Novels," *Studies in Bibliography*, 34 (1981), 1-22.

12.   Ibid., 19-20.

13.   See Ian Jack, "Novels and Those 'Necessary Evils': Annotating the Brontës," *Essays in Criticism*, 32 (1982), 320-30; and Stephen Wall, "Annotated English Novels?," *Essays in Criticism*, 32 (1982), 1-14.

14.   See, for example, Hans-Robert Jauss, *Towards an Aesthetic of Reception* (Manchester: Manchester University Press, 1985).

5

LAUREL BRAKE

The Discourses of Journalism:
"Arnold and Pater" Again—and Wilde

1.   T. S. Eliot, "Arnold and Pater," *Bookman*, 72 (1930), 1-7.

2.   See Walter Pater, "Style," *Fortnightly Review*, 50 o.s. (1888), 730.

3.   Frank Harris, "Walter Pater," *Contemporary Portraits*, 2nd series (New York: Frank Harris, 1919), 212.

4.   See Linda Dowling, "Pater, Moore and the Fatal Book," *Prose Studies*, 7 (1984), 168-78. Dowling suggests additional antecedents for "Style," namely Newman's "Literature" in *The Idea of a University*, George Moore's *Confessions of a Young Man*, and Flaubert: it has long been noted that sections of Pater's review of Flaubert's correspondence (*Pall Mall Gazette*, 25 Aug. 1888) are embedded in "Style." Eliot's exclusion of Wilde has been challenged by Richard Ellmann in *The*

Artist as Critic (London: W. H. Allen, 1969), and Regenia Gagnier in *Idylls of the Market-Place* (London: Scolar, 1987).

5.   Oscar Wilde, "The Decay of Lying: A Dialogue," *Nineteenth Century*, 25 (1889), 35-56; "The True Function and Value of Criticism," *Nineteenth Century*, 28 (1890), 123-47, 435-59.

6.   W. S. Landor, *Imaginary Conversations of Literary Men and Statesmen* (2nd ed; London: Henry Colburn, 1826).

7.   Frederic Harrison, "Culture: a Dialogue," *Fortnightly Review*, 8 o.s. (1867), 603-14.

8.   R. H. Super, "Vivacity and the Philistines," *Studies in English Literature* 6 (1966), 629-37.

9.   Oscar Wilde, "Shakespeare and Stage Costume," *Nineteenth Century*, 17 (1885), 800-18.

10.   Oscar Wilde, "Pen, Pencil, and Poison: A Study in Green," *Fortnightly Review*, 45 n.s. (1889), 41-54.

11.   See Ann Parry, "The Intellectuals and the Middle Class Periodical Press: Theory, Method and Case Study," *Journal of Newspaper and Periodical History*, 4:3 (1989), 19, for a different estimate of *Macmillan's Magazine*.

12.   [Anon. review], "Macmillan and Co.," *Bookman*, 1 (1891), 34.

13.   "Prefatory Note," in Matthew Arnold, *Essays in Criticism. Second Series* (London: Macmillan, 1888).

14.   Matthew Arnold, "Shelley," *Nineteenth Century*, 23, (1888), 23-39.

15.   Matthew Arnold, "Count Leo Tolstoi," *Fortnightly Review*, 48 o.s. (1887), 783-99.

16.   [Samuel H. Jeyes], "*The Picture of Dorian Gray*," *St James Gazette* (24 June 1890), 3-4.

17.   Darrel Mansell, "Matthew Arnold's 'Study of Poetry' in its Original Context," *Modern Philology*, 83 (1986), 279-85.

18.   *The Complete Prose Works of Matthew Arnold*, R. H. Super, ed. 11 vols. (Ann Arbor: University of Michigan Press, 1960-77), III, 258.

19.   Unpublished letter, T. H. Ward to Macmillan (24 Feb. 1879). Macmillan Archive, British Library.

20.   Walter Pater, *Greek Studies* (London: Macmillan, 1895). See William Shuter, "Pater's Reshuffled Text," *Nineteenth Century Literature*, 43 (1989), 500-25, where it is shown (p. 504) that Pater used passages from "The Marbles of Aegina" in *Plato and Platonism* (1893).

21.   [Anon. review], "M. Feuillet's *La Morte*," *Macmillan's Magazine*, 55 (1886), 97-105. On this review, see Gerald Monsman, *Walter Pater's Art of Autobiography* (New Haven: Yale University Press, 1980), 27.

22.   George Moore, *Literature at Nurse*, Pierre Coustillas, ed. (Hassocks, Sussex: Harvester, 1976); and "A New Censorship of Literature," *Pall Mall Gazette* (10 Dec. 1884), 1-2.

23.   Moore, *Literature at Nurse*, 18.

24.   Oscar Wilde, "The Soul of Man Under Socialism," *Fortnightly Review*, 55 o.s. (1891), 306.

25.   Richard Burton, ed., *The Book of the Thousand Nights and a Night* (Benares: Kamashastra Society, 1885).

26.   Ibid., xvii.

27.   [Walter Pater], "Ferdinand Fabre: An Idyll of the Cevennes," *Guardian* (12 June 1889), 911-12.

28.   Walter Pater, "A Chapter on Plato," *Macmillan's Magazine*, 66 (1892), 31-38.

29.   [Walter Pater], "Four Books for Students of English Literature," *Guardian* (17 Feb. 1886), 246-47; and Walter Pater "English at the Universities," *Pall Mall Gazette* (27 Nov. 1886), 1-2.

30.   See *Letters of Walter Pater*, Lawrence Evans, ed. (Oxford: Clarendon Press, 1970), 106.

31.   "Mr. Pater's Last Volume," *Speaker*, 1 (22 March 1890), 320.

32.   Frank Harris, "Walter Pater," 215.

33.   Frank Harris, *Oscar Wilde, His Life and Confessions*, 2 vols. (New York, Frank Harris, 1918). Harris claims that Pater refused his request out of awareness of personal danger, and finally wrote a review out of a sense of duty. While the *Fortnightly* continued to publish Wilde's most controversial work after *The Picture of Dorian Gray* appeared, it never published a review of the novel.

34.   Walter Pater, "A Novel by Mr. Oscar Wilde," *Bookman*, 1 (1891), 59-60.

35.   Matthew Arnold, "The Study of Poetry," *Essays in Criticism. Second Series*, 1.

36.   Pater, "Style," 730.

6

J. P. WARD

An Anxiety of No Influence:
Walter Pater on William Wordsworth

1.   See Linda Dowling, *Language and Decadence in the Victorian Fin de Siècle* (Princeton: Princeton University Press, 1986).

2.   Michael Millgate, *Thomas Hardy* (Oxford: Oxford University Press, 1982), 273.

3.   Walter Pater, *Appreciations* (London: Macmillan, 1889), 57.

4.   Harriet Martineau, *Autobiography* (London: Virago, 1980), II, 239.

5.   *Appreciations*, 85-87.

6.   Ibid., 221-22.

7.   Walter Pater, *The Renaissance* (Oxford: Oxford University Press, 1986), xxxi.

8.   *Appreciations*, 40.

9.   Ibid., 49-50.

10.   See F. W. Bateson, *Wordsworth: A Re-interpretation* (London: Longman, 1954), 38; Geoffrey Hartmann, *Wordsworth's Poetry* (New Haven: Yale University Press, 1964), Part II; "An Interview with Louis Simpson," *The Wordsworth Circle*, 13, (1982).

11.   *Appreciations*, 48.

12.   Michael Levey, *The Case of Walter Pater* (London: Thames and Hudson, 1978), 153.

13.   *Prelude*, 1805. XI, 328-29.

14.   *Appreciations*, 51-52.

15.   Ibid., 52-58.

16.   Ibid., 52.

17.   Walter Pater, *Marius the Epicurean*, Michael Levey, ed. (Harmondsworth: Penguin, 1985), 122.

18.   Ibid., 38.

19. *Appreciations*, 3.
20. Ibid., 7-12.
21. *Prelude* 1805. XI, 307-15.

—————— ▬▬▬ —————— 7

LESLEY HIGGINS

Essaying "W. H. Pater Esq.":
New Perspectives on the Tutor/Student Relationship
Between Pater and Hopkins

1.   Gerard Manley Hopkins, "To R. B.," in W. H. Gardner and N. H. MacKenzie, eds., *The Poems of Gerard Manley Hopkins*, 4th ed. (Oxford: Oxford University Press, 1967), 108. Hereafter *Poems*.

2.   Claude Colleer Abbott, ed., *Further Letters of Gerard Manley Hopkins*, 2nd ed. (London: Oxford University Press, 1955), 255. Hereafter, *Further Letter*.

3.   See especially David Downes, *Victorian Portraits: Hopkins and Pater* (New York: Bookman Associates, 1965); Gerald Monsman, *Walter Pater* (Boston: Twayne, 1977); and Alison Sulloway, *Gerard Manley Hopkins and the Victorian Temper* (New York: Columbia University Press, 1972).

4.   Hopkins's well-known journal entry early in May 1866 begins "Coaching with W. H. Pater this term." See Humphry House and Graham Storey, eds., *The Journals and Papers of Gerard Manley Hopkins* (London: Oxford University Press, 1959), 133. Hereafter, *Journals and Papers*.

5.   As Monsman and others have pointed out, it was Liddon who helped J. R. McQueen block Pater's plans for ordination in 1862. See Monsman, *Walter Pater*, 23-24; and Robert Seiler, ed., *Walter Pater: A Life Remembered* (Calgary: University of Calgary Press, 1987), 228-29, 233-35.

6.   Liddon MS. Diary, 1864, entries for 8 and 10 February. The diaries are the property of Liddon House, St. Margaret's Church (Mayfair), London.

7.   According to Edmund Gosse, Jowett was "so struck with [Pater's] power that he very generously offered to coach him for nothing" in 1860. (See *Critical Kit-Kats* [New York: Dodd, Mead and Co., 1896], 248). Monsman states that "during the 1861 Lent term" Pater "prepared a weekly essay" for Jowett (Monsman, *Walter Pater*, 24). Both sources repeat the story that Jowett once confided to Pater, "I think you have a mind that will come to great eminence." Pater's tribute to Jowett can be found in Lawrence Evans, ed., *Letters of Walter Pater* (Oxford: Oxford University Press, 1970), 267.

8.   Samuel Brooke (1844-1898) was at Corpus Christi College from 1862 to 1866. Cleverness got Brooke elected to the Old Mortality Society in February 1863, approximately the same time as Pater joined; narrow-mindedness impelled him to quit the Society a year later and establish his own rival organization, the Hexameron Society. Brooke's diaries are housed in Corpus Christi, MS. CCC 498 (1-6). The quotations are cited from the entries for 20 and 29 Feb. 1864. See also Monsman, "Old Mortality at Oxford," *Studies in Philology*, 67 (1970), 359-89; and *Walter Pater*, 30-31. Pertinent excerpts from Brooke's diary are published in Seiler, *Walter Pater: A Life Remembered*, 11-13.

9.   [Edmund Geldart] Nitram Tradleg, *A Son of Belial: Autobiographical Sketches* (London: Trubner and Co., 1882; reissued by University Microfilms International, 1976), 167-70.

10.   *Journals and Papers*, 133.

11.   *Journals and Papers*, 138.

12.   Walter Pater, *Gaston de Latour* (London: Macmillan, 1910), 89. Unless otherwise indicated, all references to Pater's published work will be cited from the ten-volume Library Edition.

13.   Brasenose brewed its own beer until 1886. Its lone literary distinction was that every Shrove Tuesday a new set of "Ale verses" was recited at the college's pancake supper party. In 1885, E. F. MacPherson penned an affectionate lampoon of Pater. See *Brasenose College Quatercentenary Monographs* (Oxford, 1909), II, 297.

14.   John Buchan, "Nine Brasenose Worthies," ibid. II, 3-4.

15.   Humphry Ward, "Brasenose, 1864-1872," ibid. II, 73. Charles Mallet lists Brasenose's distinctions as "pre-eminence in rowing, games, and sport." See Mallett, *A History of the University of Oxford*, vol. III, *Modern Oxford* (London: Methuen, 1927), 407.

16.   *Further Letters*, 20.

17.   A notebook now catalogued as MS. D.XII in the Campion Hall, Oxford Collection.

18.   D.XII, f.1.

19.   Walter Pater, *Plato and Platonism*, 175, 184.

20.   A. C. Benson, *Walter Pater* (London: Macmillan, 1906), 25.

21.   Ibid.

22.   Ibid.

23.   Jowett's lists of prospective essay topics are found among his papers in the Jowett Collection of Balliol College, Oxford.

24.   Ward, "Brasenose, 1864-1872," 74.

25.   D.III.6, f.18.

26.   *Plato and Platonism*, 177.

27.   D.III.1, f.1.

28.   Ibid., ff.1 and 4.

29.   Pater, "Coleridge's Writings," *Westminster Review*, 85 (1866), 49.

30.   "Coleridge's Writings," 53.

31.   Ibid., 57.

32.   D.III.1, f.3 and f.4.

33.   "Coleridge's Writings," 57.

34.   Walter Pater, *Miscellaneous Studies*, 51.

35.   D.III.1, f.5.

36.   D.III.4, f.14.

37.   See especially Hopkins's essay "The Life of Socrates" (D.II.6), a paper of 1865 written for Jowett.

38.   D.III.3, ff.12-13.

39.   "Coleridge's Writings," 52.

40   D.III.3, f.10.

41.   Ibid.

42.   D.III.3, f.9

43.   In several outlines for lectures written in the 1857-1865 period Jowett analyzes "Whether virtue or knowledge can be taught?" and whether "knowledge is virtue" (Jowett Collection, Box B). See also Hopkins's essay "The Life of Socrates" (D.II.6).

44. D.III.6, f.21.

45. *Plato and Platonism*, 187.

46. Ibid., 193-94.

47. D.III.6, ff.21-22.

48. *Gaston de Latour*, 160.

49. D.VI.7.

50. For Pater's translation of *Symposium*, Steph. 210, see *Plato and Platonism*, 121-23.

51. D.III.4, f.15.

52. Ibid.

53. *Plato and Platonism*, 97.

54. D.XII.1, f.1.

55. Ibid., f.2.

56. Billie A. Inman, *Walter Pater's Reading: A Bibliography of his Library Borrowings and Literary References, 1857-1873* (New York: Garland, 1981), 187.

57. Walter Pater, "Poems by William Morris," *Westminster Review*, n.s. 34 (1868), 149.

58. D.IX.3.

59. Ibid., f.1.

60. Although "Winckelmann" appears in *The Renaissance*, I shall be quoting from the serial version of the essay that Hopkins would have read at that time. "Winckelmann," *Westminster Review*, 87 (1867), 36-50.

61. *Miscellaneous Studies*, 16.

62. "Winckelmann," 50. In his "Preface" to *The Renaissance*, Pater is much more blunt, calling all metaphysical questions "unprofitable" p. x.

63. According to Lionel Tollemache, Jowett's response to a student "who had been reading him an essay with a strong metaphysical flavour" was: "It is remarkable what a fascination metaphysics seems to possess for the human mind. It is like falling in love. But you get over it after a time." See Lionel Tollemache, *Benjamin Jowett, Master of Balliol* (London: Edward Arnold, 1895), 72-73.

64. "Coleridge's Writings," 49.

65. Ibid., 48.

66. D.IX.3, f.8.

67. Ibid., ff.7-8.

68. Ibid., ff.8-9.

69. Ibid., f.9.

70. "Winckelmann," 45.

71. D.I.5.

72. D.I.6.

73. D.V.1.

74. Notes from an undated (1850s-1860s) black leather-covered notebook, inscribed inside the front cover, "1. True art colourless like water." (Jowett Collection, Balliol College, Box B). Another thick notebook containing "Lectures on Greek Literature—Nov.1871" reveals that Jowett punctuated his discourse with references to classical inscriptions, monuments and statues, especially the "monuments to be found in the British Museum" (Jowett Collection, Balliol College, Box A, f.20).

75. Jowett Collection, Box B, ff.1-2.

76. D.III.1, f.1.

77.   D.III.2, f.7.

78.   George Grote, *Plato, and the Other Companions of Sokrates* (London: John Murray, 1865), III, 50.

79.   *Marius the Epicurean*, II, 23.

80.   *The Renaissance*, 141.

81.   *Plato and Platonism*, 268.

82.   D.III.5, f.17.

83.   Ibid., f.15v.

84.   Ibid., f.18.

85.   "Coleridge's Writings," 54.

86.   Ibid., 55.

87.   *Miscellaneous Studies*, 50-51.

88.   *Renaissance*, 242-43.

89.   Pater employs this unusual term to great advantage in his essay on "Coleridge's Writings." The "unity of aim" in Greek philosophy is the function of an "unfixed poetical prepossession" (54); morality is described as "a groundless prepossession until transformed into a religious recognition of a spiritual world" (56).

90.   D.XII, ff.7-8.

91.   *Marius the Epicurean*, II, 20.

8

F. C. McGrath

Pater Speaking Bloom Speaking Joyce

1.   See my chapter on Pater's "Theory of Expression" in *The Sensible Spirit: Walter Pater and the Modernist Paradigm* (Tampa: University of South Florida Press, 1986), 184-214. For some other views of Pater's style, see Paul Barolsky, "From Mannerism to Modernism: The Playful Artifice of Walter Pater," *University of Hartford Studies in Literature*, 16: 2/3 (1984), 47-57; William E. Buckler, "The Poetics of Pater's Prose: 'The Child in the House'," *Victorian Poetry*, 23:3 (1985), 281-88; Edmund Chandler, "Pater on Style," *Anglistica*, 11 (1958), 1-100 (Copenhagen: Rosenkilde and Bagger, 1958); Zilpha E. Chandler, "An Analysis of the Stylistic Techniques of Addison, Johnson, Hazlitt, and Pater," *University of Iowa Humanistic Studies*, 4 (1928), 75-89; David J. DeLaura, "Some Victorian Experiments in Closure," *Studies in the Literary Imagination*, 8 (1975), 19-35, and "Newman and the Cult of Style," *The Victorian Newsletter*, 51 (1977), 6-10; Linda Dowling, "Pater, Moore and the Fatal Book," *Prose Studies*, 7:2 (1984), 168-78, and *Language and Decadence in the Victorian Fin de Siècle* (Princeton: Princeton University Press, 1987); John J. Duffy, "Walter Pater's Prose Style: An Essay in Theory and Analysis," *Style*, 1 (1967), 45-63; Stanley Fish, *Is There a Text in This Class?* (Cambridge, MA: Harvard University Press, 1980), 30-35; G. S. Fraser, "Walter Pater: His Theory of Style, His Style in Practice, His Influence," *The Art of Victorian Prose*, George Levine and William Madden, eds. (New York: Oxford University Press, 1968); Billie A. Inman "Pater's Appeal to His Readers: A Study of Two of Pater's Prose Styles," *Texas Studies in Literature and Language*, 14 (1973), 643-66; Wolfgang Iser, *Walter*

Pater: The Aesthetic Moment, David Henry Wilson, trans. (Cambridge: Cambridge University Press, 1987); Lionel Johnson, "The Work of Mr. Pater," *Fortnightly Review*, ns. 56 (1894), 352-67; John R. Reed, "Decadent Style," *North American Review*, 266:4 (1981), 59-61; Ian Small, "Computational Stylistics and the Construction of Literary Readings: Work in Progress," *Prose Studies*, 7:3 (1984), 250-60; Julia Whitsitt, "The Vision Within: Pater's Style and Radical Individualism," *New Orleans Review*, 8:2 (1981), 173-76.

2.   Walter Pater, *Appreciations* (London: Macmillan, 1910), 8.

3.   For Pater's anticipation of contemporary thought on language, see Harold Bloom, "Introduction" to *Selected Writings of Walter Pater* (New York: New American Library, 1974), viixxxi; Dowling, *Language and Decadence*; J. Hillis Miller, "Walter Pater: A Partial Portrait," *Daedalus*, 105:1 (1976), 97-113; Gerald Monsman, "Pater Redivivus," *The Victorian Experience: The Prose Writers*, Richard A. Levine, ed. (Athens: Ohio University Press, 1982), 203-39, and *Walter Pater's Art of Autobiography* (New Haven: Yale University Press, 1980); and Nathan A. Scott, Jr., "Pater's Imperative—To Dwell Poetically," *New Literary History: A Journal of Theory and Interpretation*, 15:1 (1983), 93-118.

4.   Ian Fletcher, "Walter Pater," in *Walter Pater: Modern Critical Views*, Harold Bloom, ed. (New York: Chelsea House, 1985), 68.

5.   Walter Pater, *Plato and Platonism* (London: Macmillan, 1910), 190.

6.   A. Walton Litz, *The Art of James Joyce* (London: Oxford University Press, 1964), 34; and J. S. Atherton, "The Oxen of the Sun," *James Joyce's Ulysses: Critical Essays*, Clive Hart and David Hayman, eds. (Berkeley: University of California Press, 1974), 315.

7.   Anthony Burgess, *Here Comes Everybody: An Introduction to Joyce for the Ordinary Reader* (London: Faber and Faber, 1965), 156.

8.   Atherton, "The Oxen of the Sun," 313-16.

9.   Karen Lawrence, *The Odyssey of Style in Ulysses* (Princeton: Princeton University Press, 1981), 144.

10.   Ibid. 145; and Michael Groden, *Ulysses in Progress* (Princeton: Princeton University Press, 1977), 50.

11.   Wolfgang Iser, *The Implied Reader: Patterns of Communication in Prose Fiction from Bunyan to Beckett* (Baltimore: The Johns Hopkins University Press, 1974), 192, 202.

12.   Harry Blamires, *The Bloomsday Book: A Guide through Joyce's Ulysses* (London: Methuen, 1966), 162.

13.   Colin MacCabe, *James Joyce and the Revolution of the Word* (New York: Barnes and Noble, 1979), 126.

14.   Fredric Jameson, *Nationalism, Colonialism and Literature: Modernism and Imperialism*. Field Day Pamphlet 14 (Derry: Field Day Theatre Company, 1988), 21.

15.   The most thorough exploration of the Modernist, multiple perspectives approach to "Oxen of the Sun" and to *Ulysses* in general is Iser, *The Implied Reader*, 179-233.

16.   These drawings are reproduced in Richard Ellmann, *James Joyce* (rev. ed.; New York: Oxford University Press, 1982), plates XXXIX and LI, following 482.

17.   James Joyce, *Ulysses* (New York: Random House, 1986), 344.

18.   Since most of the Pater passages Joyce copied into his notebook are not memorable, I have listed them below for anyone who desires to pursue Joyce's use of Pater further. Joyce's transcriptions contain inaccuracies and he did not identify the passages except to list some under the heading of "Marius the Epicurean" and some under the heading of "Imaginary Portraits." All those

he listed as being from *Marius* are from volume one. Of those he listed under "Imaginary Portraits," eleven are from *Imaginary Portraits* and the last four are from volume two of *Marius*. The order below is the order in which they appear in Joyce's notebook (*James Joyce: Notes, Criticism, Translations, & Miscellaneous Writings*, Hans Walter Gabler, ed., 2 vols. [New York: Garland, 1979], II, 384-89). Long passages are listed by their opening and closing phrases.

They comprehended a multitude . . . in which were those well-remembered roses. (*Marius the Epicurean* [London: Macmillan, 1910], I, 106-07).

Down the dewy paths the people were descending . . . like a wild picture drawn from Virgil. (*Marius*, I, 161-62).

The temple of Antoninus and Faustina was still fresh . . . though the birds had built freely among them. (*Marius*, I, 173).

Marius could distinguish, could distinguish clearly, the well known profile, between the floating purple curtains. (*Marius*, I, 177).

The nostrils and mouth seemed capable almost of peevishness . . . the flesh had scarcely been an equal gainer with the spirit. (*Marius*, I, 191).

The discourse ended almost in darkness . . . and at no time had the winter roses from Carthage seemed more lustrously yellow and red. (*Marius*, I, 211).

It might be almost edifying . . . as neatly as if it were a stocking . . . (*Marius*, I, 239). [At the beginning of this quotation Joyce wrote in parentheses "Marsyas."]

And meantime those dreams of remote and probably adventurous travel . . . in the foldings of the hillside. ("Duke Carl of Rosenmold," *Imaginary Portraits*, 134).

. . . a marvellous tact of omission . . . ("A Prince of Court Painters," *Imaginary Portraits*, 6). [After this quotation Joyce wrote in parentheses "Watteau."]

Methinks I see him there . . . over which the sun is sinking. ("A Prince of Court Painters," *Imaginary Portraits*, 10).

. . . "The evening will be a wet one." . . . and the secular trees themselves will hardly outlast another generation. ("A Prince of Court Painters," *Imaginary Portraits*, 32).

He was always a seeker after something in the world that is there in no satisfying measure, or not at all. ("A Prince of Court Painters," *Imaginary Portraits*, 44).

The pavement of the choir . . . in a sudden oblique ray of ghastly dawn. ("Denys L'Auxerrois," *Imaginary Portraits*, 69).

. . . a flask of lively green glass . . . ("Denys L'Auxerrois," *Imaginary Portraits*, 56).

. . . the riotous and earthy heat of [old] paganism [itself] . . . ("Denys L'Auxerrois," *Imaginary Portraits*, 56). [Joyce omitted the words in brackets.]

Tears rose in the eyes of needy children . . . after scattered hedge-nuts or dried vine-tendrils. ("Denys L'Auxerrois," *Imaginary Portraits*, 67).

From a comfortless portico . . . the like of which one was used to hear. ("Duke Carl of Rosenmold," *Imaginary Portraits*, 127).

. . . the young Duke had often peered at the faded glories of the immense coroneted coffins, the oldest shedding their velvet tatters around them. ("Duke Carl of Rosenmold," *Imaginary Portraits*, 138).

. . . his goodwill sunned her wild-grown beauty into majesty . . . in the wood-sides and on the hilltops. ("Duke Carl of Rosenmold," *Imaginary Portraits*, 148-49).

The air there . . . in its slow, wise, maturing work. (*Marius*, II, 65-66). [This passage was cited by George Saintsbury, *A History of English Prose Rhythm* (1912; Bloomington: Indiana University Press, 1965), 425-26.]

Lastly, herb and tree had taken possession . . . against the wide realms of sunset. (*Marius*, II, 96).

Men and women came to the altar successively . . . with an increasing mysticity and effusion the rite proceeded. (*Marius*, II, 137).

Among the captives . . . in his misshapen features, and the pale, servile, yet angry eyes. (*Marius*, II, 197).

19. Walter Pater, *Marius*, I, 191; *James Joyce: Notes, Criticism, Translations*, II, 385.
20. Pater, *Imaginary Portraits*, 127; *James Joyce: Notes, Criticism, Translations*, II, 387-88.
21. Pater, *Imaginary Portraits*, 32; *James Joyce: Notes, Criticism, Translations*, II, 387.
22. Lionel Johnson, "The Work of Mr. Pater," 356-57; and George Saintsbury, *A History of English Prose Rhythm*, 420-21.
23. Roland Barthes, *Mythologies* (London: Granada, 1972), 127.
24. Walter Pater, *The Renaissance: Studies in Art and Poetry* (London: Macmillan, 1910), 136.
25. Walter Pater, "Poems by William Morris," *Westminster Review*, 90 (1868), 300.
26. Ibid., 305.
27. Ibid., 301.
28. Ibid., 302.
29. Joyce, *Ulysses*, 344.

30. Ibid., 320.

31. Robert Janusko, *The Sources and Structures of James Joyce's "Oxen"* (Ann Arbor: UMI Research Press, 1983), 64, 95, 103.

32. Joyce, *Ulysses*, 94-95.

33. Ibid., 344.

34. A. Walton Litz, *The Art of James Joyce*, 36.

35. Richard Ellmann, Introduction to *My Brother's Keeper* by Stanislaus Joyce (New York: Viking, 1958), xix.

36. Oscar Wilde, *The Artist As Critic: Critical Writings of Oscar Wilde*, Richard Ellmann, ed. (New York: Random House, 1968), 305, 316.

9

PAUL TUCKER

Pater as a "Moralist"

1. See David DeLaura, *Hebrew and Hellene in Victorian England: Newman, Arnold, and Pater* (Austin: University of Texas Press, 1969), 179. Cf. T. S. Eliot, "Arnold and Pater" in *Selected Essays*. (3rd ed. London: Faber, 1951), 439; Frank Kermode, *The Romantic Image* (1957; Glasgow: Collins, 1976), 33; and Ian Fletcher, *Walter Pater* (1959; Harlow: Longmans, 1971), 15.

2. "He began as an aesthete, and ended as a moralist. By faithful and self-restraining cultivation of the sense of harmony, he appears to have risen from the perception of visible beauty to the knowledge of beauty of the spiritual kind, both being expressions of the same perfect fittingness to an ever more intense and various and congruous life"; repr. in Robert Seiler, ed. *Walter Pater: The Critical Heritage* (London: Routledge & Kegan Paul, 1980), 294. Cf. Ruth Child's comment: "He began his work with an emphasis on art for art's sake, but progressed gradually to a greater and greater emphasis on the ethical function of art." (*The Aesthetic of Walter Pater* [1940; New York: Octagon, 1969], 10.)

3. See, for example, Kermode, *The Romantic Image*, 33; Richard L. Stein, *The Ritual of Interpretation* (Cambridge: Harvard University Press, 1975), 261; and Hilary Fraser, *Beauty and Belief: Aesthetics and Religion in Victorian Literature* (Cambridge: Cambridge University Press, 1986), 198.

4. See Seiler, *The Critical Heritage*, 297.

5. An exception appears to be Wohlee Choe. See "Walter Pater's 'Romantic Morality'," *Victorian Newsletter*, 72 (1987), 12-17.

6. Stein, *The Ritual of Interpretation*, 261-62.

7. Fraser, *Beauty and Belief*, 198.

8. Ibid.

9. Ibid., 199-200.

10. Ibid.

11. Ibid., 201.

12. Walter Pater, "Coleridge's Writings" (1866); repr. in *English Critical Essays: Nineteenth Century*, Edmund D. Jones, ed. (Oxford: Oxford University Press, 1971), 22.

13. Pater, *Studies in the History of the Renaissance*, (1873; London: Macmillan, 1910), 55-56.

14. Pater, "Coleridge's Writings," 456.

15. Ibid.

16. Walter Pater, *Appreciations* (1889; London: Macmillan, 1910), 183.

17. Auguste Comte, *Système de politique positive ou Traité de sociologie instituant la Religion de l'Humanité*, 4 vols. (Paris, 1851-1854), IV, 282.

18. Antimo Negri, *Augusto Comte* (Rome: Armando, 1971), 301.

19. David Hume, *A Treatise of Human Nature* (1739-1740; Harmondsworth: Penguin, 1987), 632.

20. Ibid., 630.

21. "Sympathy, appreciation, a sense of latent claims in things which even ordinary good men pass rudely by—these on the whole are the characteristic traits of its artists [the artists of the Renaissance], though it may still be true that 'aesthetic propriety, rather than strict conceptions of duty, ruled the conduct even of the best'; and at least they never 'destroyed pity in their souls' " (Pater, review [1875] of *The Renaissance in Italy: The Age of the Despots*, by J. A. Symonds; repr. in *The Renaissance: Studies in Art and Poetry: The 1893 Text*, Donald Hill, ed. [Berkeley: University of California Press, 1980], 199).

22. "And, working ever close to the concrete, to the details, great or small, of actual things, books, persons, and with no part of them blurred to his vision by the intervention of mere abstract theories, he has reached an enduring moral effect also, in a sort of boundless sympathy" (Pater, *Appreciations*, 109).

23. Pater, *Appreciations*, 184.

24. T. R. Wright, *The Religion of Humanity: The Impact of Comtean Positivism on Victorian Britain* (Cambridge: Cambridge University Press, 1986), 199.

25. M. H. Abrams, *The Mirror and the Lamp: Romantic Theory and the Romantic Tradition* (1953; London: Oxford University Press, 1977), 332.

26. Pater, *Appreciations*, 184.

27. Walter Pater, "Poems by William Morris," *Westminster Review*, n.s. 34 (October, 1868), 312.

28. Alasdair MacIntyre, *A Short History of Ethics* (New York: Macmillan, 1966), 84.

29. Pater, "Poems by William Morris," 312.

30. Ibid., 311.

31. See Billie Andrew Inman, *Walter Pater's Reading: A Bibliography of His Library Borrowings and Literary References, 1858-1873* (New York: Garland, 1981), 14-19, 58-60, 68-72. For the "higher morality," see particularly 59.

32. Remo Bodei, *Scomposizioni: forme dell'individuo moderno* (Turin: Einaudi, 1987), 127.

33. Radoslav A. Tsanoff, "Fichte, Johann Gottlieb," *The Encyclopedia of Philosophy* (1967), 195.

34. *Einige Vorlesungen über die Bestimmung des Gelehrten* [*On the Mission of the Scholar*] (1794); *Über das Wesen des Gelehrten* [*On the Essence of the Scholar*] (1805); *Fünfe Vorlesungen über die Bestimmung des Gelehrten* (1811).

35. J. G. Fichte. *Werke*, I. H. Fichte, ed. (1845-46; Berlin: de Gruyter, 1971), VI, 331.

36. See Gerald Monsman, "Old Mortality at Oxford," *Studies in Philology*, 67 (July 1970), 359-89; "Pater, Hopkins and Fichte's Ideal Student," *South Atlantic Quarterly*, 70 (1971), 367-70; and *Walter Pater* (London: Twayne, 1977), especially 31.

37. "The true and immediate mode of being in the divine idea requires of us that we become, and therefore that we deplore our being's standing still at any given moment" (Fichte, *Werke*, VI, 387); "The following rule is good for all men, and even more for the scholar. Let him forget what he has done as soon as he has done it, and let him think only of what he still has to do" (Fichte, *Werke*, VI, 329). (All translations from Fichte are my own.)

38. Pater, "Coleridge's Writings," 448.

39. Ibid.

40. Fichte, *Werke*, V, 469.

41. "To suppose that what is called 'ontology' is what the speculative spirit seeks, is the misconception of a backward school of logicians. Who would change the colour or curve of a roseleaf for that *ousia achromatos, asahematistos, anaphes* ("colourless, formless, intangible essence" [transcribed from Greek in original]). A transcendentalism that makes what is abstract more excellent than what is concrete has nothing akin to the leading philosophies of the world. The true illustration of the speculative temper is not the Hindoo, lost to sense, understanding, individuality; but such an one as Goethe, to whom every moment of life brought its share of experimental, individual knowledge, by whom no touch of the world of form, colour, and passion was disregarded" ("Coleridge's Writings," 423). As a measure of the distance between Pater and Fichte with regard to the ontological status of the self, it is to be noted that in *Die Anweisung zum seligen Leben* Fichte adopts precisely the Platonic terminology (*Phaedrus*, 247 C) that Pater rejects above to express the self's divine parentage, notwithstanding its otherwise finite condition: "What you see is eternally you yourself; but you are not it as you see it, nor do you see it as you are it. You are it in so far as you are unchanging, pure, without form or colour. Only this reflection, which is you yourself, and from which you therefore can never separate yourself;—only the reflection breaks it up into infinite rays and forms" (Fichte, *Werke*, V, 458).

42. Pater, "Poems by William Morris," 312.

43. Ibid., 311.

44. But through its association with art the morality of "sympathy" itself acquires a broader, theoretical significance. For art may be seen as a model not only of judgment but also of representation.

45. Pater, "Coleridge's Writings," 423.

46. Pater, "Poems by William Morris," 311.

47. The confluence of ethical and theoretical motives in Pater's ethic of "passion" may be illustrated by a further comparison with classical ethics, especially with the ethical systems of the Hellenistic philosophies, with their private outlook and defensive, consolatory stance. If "[p]hilosophy, as many have said, responded to the unsettled age of the Hellenistic monarchs by turning away from disinterested speculation to the provision of security for the individual" (A. A. Long, *Hellenistic Philosophy: Stoics, Epicureans, Sceptics* [2nd ed. London: Duckworth, 1986], 3), Pater's ethic of "passion" answers a similar need, although the state of insecurity it moves from is not of a political but of a theoretical order: modern philosophy and natural science had seemingly undermined the very fabric of experience. The theoretical concerns of the "Conclusion" explain why one might, practically speaking, think it "almost anticlimactic" (Stein, *The Ritual of Interpretation*, 256).

48. DeLaura says that Pater "uses a swarm of words suggesting refined, passive, sensuous, largely visual experience—observation, mood, insight, variegated, dramatic, see, senses, eye, lifted horizon, strange dyes and flowers, curious odors, art works, the face of one's friend, discriminate, splendor of experience, see and touch, curiously test new opinions, new impressions, regard—which beget a second swarm of terms suggesting intense momentary thrills, frissons: delicious recoil, race,

drift, flight, tremulous, dissolution, pulsations, rouse, startle, ecstasy, exquisite passion, excitement, irresistibly real and attractive, the focus of 'vital forces', melts, grasp, stirring, desperate effort, 'courting' impressions" (DeLaura, *Hebrew and Hellene*, 226). It seems to me that DeLaura's characterization of the kind of experience named by his first group as "passive" has to some extent confused the two sets of terms, and that as a result certain words have been misplaced. Moreover, although his aim is to give a picture of the "Paterian ideal" through Pater's key-words, he has indiscriminately included terms from the earlier, expository paragraphs of the "Conclusion," whose referent is not the subject addressed or described in the final paragraphs.

49. Unlike German, English does not have two words to express these two different conceptions of experience. For an account of the separation of the concept of "Erlebnis"—(an) immediately lived experience—from that of "Erfahrung"—the having experience of something—in the second half of the nineteenth century, see Hans-Georg Gadamer, *Truth and Method* (2nd ed. London: Sheed and Ward, 1979), 55-63; and Leonardo Amoroso, *L'estetica come problema* (Pisa: ETS, 1988).

50. Pater, "Coleridge's Writings," 423.

51. From the Greek for "things perceptible by the senses."

52. Pater, "Coleridge's Writings," 422-23.

53. Ibid., 423.

54. As perhaps all scepticism does. Cf. Merleau-Ponty: "Le scepticisme a deux faces. Il signifie que rien n'est vrai, mais aussi que rien n'est faux." *Eloge de la philosophie* (1953; rpt. Paris: Gallimard, 1963, 321.)

55. See David DeLaura, *Hebrew and Hellene*, 224; and Gerald Monsman, *Walter Pater*, 57.

56. Pater, "Poems by William Morris," 309.

57. Ibid., 305.

58. Ibid.

59. Ibid., 303.

60. Ibid., 312.

61. Adrian Stokes, *The Critical Writings*, 3 vols. (London: Thames & Hudson, 1978), III, 339.

62. G. W. F. Hegel, *Introduction to Aesthetics: Being the Introduction to the Berlin Aesthetics Lectures of the 1820s*, T. M. Knox, trans. (Oxford: Clarendon Press, 1979), 7.

63. Ibid., 7-8.

64. Cf. Richard Wollheim, who unjustifiably limits Pater's interest in Hegel's schematic distinction between Form and Content to one "registered predominantly on a more psychological level." (Wollheim, "Walter Pater as a Critic of the Arts," in *On Art and the Mind* [London: Allen Lane, 1973], 171-72.)

65. Pater, *The Renaissance*, 206.

66. Ibid., 230.

67. Cf. Wolfgang Iser, who makes a similar point about Pater's criticism of Renaissance painting, but robs it of positive theoretic point by subordinating it to the pure indeterminacy of what he calls "mood": "Art, then, is an in-between region of undecidedness, separating itself from a single metaphysical interpretation of the world without being committed to rejecting such an interpretation. . . . Mood has replaced metaphysical hierarchies, and for Pater it is mood that determines art. . . . Art removes the intentionality of a challenging reality, and replaces it with a transitional reality that neither rejects the old nor the new, but remains a mood in which contrasts

lose their firm outlines and begin to merge" (Wolfgang Iser, *Walter Pater: The Aesthetic Moment*, D. H. Wilson, trans. [Cambridge: Cambridge University Press, 1987], 40).

68. Pater, *The Renaissance*, 125.

69. Ibid., 231.

70. Pater, "Poems by William Morris," 311.

71. Pater, *The Renaissance*, 48.

72. Ibid., 56.

73. Cf. Iser: "The inherent contradictions impair the symbolic qualities of the paintings [of the Madonna and of Venus]. Yet this seems to have been done deliberately; the gradual effacing of the symbolic significance gives expression to an emerging mood" (*Walter Pater: The Aesthetic Moment*, 41).

10

RICHARD DELLAMORA

Critical Impressionism as Anti–Phallogocentric Strategy

1. See Ian Small, "Introduction," in Walter Pater, *Marius the Epicurean: His Sensations and Ideas* (Oxford: Oxford University Press, 1986), vii-xxii.

2. W. David Shaw, *The Lucid Veil: Poetic Truth in the Victorian Age* (Madison: University of Wisconsin Press, 1987), 168.

3. Cited by Shaw, 168.

4. See Linda Dowling, *Language and Decadence in the Victorian Fin de Siècle* (Princeton: Princeton University Press, 1986); Robert Crawford, "Pater's *Renaissance*, Andrew Lang, and Anthropological Romanticism," *ELH*, 53 (1986), 849-79; and Morse Peckham, *Victorian Revolutionaries: Speculations on Some Heroes of a Culture Crisis* (New York: Braziller, 1970), ch. 5.

5. Walter Pater, *Appreciations with an Essay on Style* (London: Macmillan, 1910), 68-69, 66.

6. Ibid., 104. [Love is the] father of delicacy, of splendour, of luxury, of the Graces, of desire, and of longing.

7. Ibid., 103-104.

8. Walter Pater, *Studies in the History of the Renaissance* (London: Macmillan, 1873), viii.

9. Pater, *Letters*, Lawrence Evans, ed. (Oxford: Clarendon Press, 1970), 13.

10. Quoted in Jeffrey Wallen, "On Pater's Use and Abuse of Quotation," *Arnoldian*, 14 (Winter 1986), 1.

11. See Wayne Koestenbaum's discussion of *The Waste Land* in *Double Talk: The Erotics of Male Literary Collaboration* (New York: Routledge, 1989), ch. 4.

12. J. Hillis Miller, "Walter Pater: A Partial Portrait," *Daedalus*, 105 (1976), 98.

13. Ibid., 106.

14. Ibid., 108.

15. See my discussion of the passage in *Masculine Desire: The Sexual Politics of Victorian Aestheticism* (Chapel Hill: University of North Carolina Press, 1990), 139-40.

16. Miller, 99.

17. Quoted by Miller, 102.

18. Ibid., 106.

19. Ibid., 112.

20. See Monique Wittig, "The Straight Mind," *Feminist Issues*, 1 (1980), 103-11.

21. Walter Pater, *Miscellaneous Studies* (London: Macmillan, 1910), 143, 144, 143-44, 164. In Miller's/Freud's terms, the murder of Hyacinth might be seen as the psychological destruction of desire, fixed at an "adolescent homosexual stage," in the Prior.

22. Crawford, 867.

23. See Richard M. Dorson, "The Eclipse of Solar Mythology," *Myth: A Symposium*, Thomas A. Sebeok, ed. (Philadelphia: American Folklore Society, 1955).

24. Quoted in Crawford, "Pater's *Renaissance*, Andrew Lang, and Anthropological Romanticism," 865.

25. Ibid., 859.

26. See Robert Peters, "The Cult of the Returned Apollo: Walter Pater's *Renaissance* and *Imaginary Portraits*," *PRR*, 2 (1981), 53-69.

27. Pater, *Miscellaneous Studies*, 188.

28. Miller, 108.

29. Ibid., 109.

30. Ibid.

31. Walter Pater, *The Renaissance: Studies in Art and Poetry: The 1893 Text*, Donald L. Hill, ed. (Berkeley: University of California Press, 1980), 165.

32. Wallen, "On Pater's Use and Abuse of Quotation," 15.

33. See Ibid., 17.

34. See Peter Clarke, *Liberals and Social Democrats* (Cambridge: Cambridge University Press, 1978).

35. See Patrick Brantlinger, *Rule of Darkness: British Literature and Imperialism, 1830-1914* (Ithaca: Cornell University Press, 1988), 202.

36. Matthew Arnold, *Complete Prose Works*, R. H. Super, ed., 11 vols. (Ann Arbor: University of Michigan Press, 1960), III, 145-46.

37. John Lee, Tim Garrigan, and Bob Connell, "Toward a New Sociology of Masculinity," *Theory and Society*, 14 (1985), 587.

38. I adapt the phrase, "homosexual existence," from Adrienne Rich, "Compulsory Heterosexuality and Lesbian Existence," *Signs*, 5 (1980), 631-60.

39. Sharon Bassett, "*Marius* and the Varieties of Stoic Will: 'Can the Will Itself Be an Organ of Knowledge, of Vision?' " *ELT*, 7 (1984), 57.

40. Arnold, *Complete Prose Works*, III, 149.

41. Daniel T. O'Hara, *The Romance of Interpretation: Visionary Criticism from Pater to de Man* (New York: Columbia University Press, 1985), 16.

42. Walter Pater, *Marius the Epicurean: His Sensations and Ideas*, 2 vols. (London: Macmillan, 1910), II, 66.

43. Ibid., II, 68.

44. Ibid., II, 72.

45. Ibid., II, 70.

46. O'Hara, *The Romance of Interpretation*, 41; emphasis added.

47. Pater, *Marius*, II, 115.

48. The final phrase is from the second edition of 1885, II, 110.

49. Walter Pater, *Studies in the History of the Renaissance*, 92; and *Imaginary Portraits* (London: Macmillan, 1910), 52-53.

50. Pater, *The Renaissance*, Hill, ed., 106.

51. Ibid., 105.

52. Miller, 101.

53. In the present context, by revisionary masculine discourses I mean discourses which attempt to enlarge masculine capacities for relationship while remaining principally concerned with male-female relations. See Percy Bysshe Shelley, *Complete Works*, 10 vols; Roger Ingpen and Walter E. Peck, eds. (London: Benn, 1965), VI, 325; and, as I indicate below, Pater's "Denys l'Auxerrois."

54. See Robert K. Martin, *Hero, Captain, and Stranger: Male Friendship, Social Critique, and Literary Form in the Sea Novels of Herman Melville* (Chapel Hill: University of North Carolina Press, 1986), ch. 2.

55. Ibid., 54.

56. Pater, *Imaginary Portraits*, 54.

57. Pater, *Miscellaneous Studies*, 156, 164.

58. Miller, 112.

59. Nancy K. Miller, *Subject to Change: Reading Feminist Writing* (New York: Columbia University Press, 1988), 91.

60. Ibid., 100 fn. 21.

61. Miller, "Ariadne's Thread: Repetition and the Narrative Line," in *Interpretation of Narrative*, Mario J. Valdes and Owen J. Miller, eds. (Toronton: University of Toronto Press, 1978), 159.

62. Ibid., 164.

63. See Joseph Allen Boone, "Mappings of Male Desire in Durrell's *Alexandria Quartet*," *South Atlantic Quarterly*, 88 (1989), 73-106; and Lee Edelman, "Homographesis," *Yale Journal of Criticism*, 3 (1989), 189-207.

----- **11**

HAYDEN WARD

"The Last Thing Water Wrote": Pater's "Pascal"

1. Michael Levey, *The Case of Walter Pater* (London: Thames and Hudson, 1978), 230.

2. Walter Pater, *Letters of Walter Pater*, Lawrence Evans, ed. (Oxford: Clarendon Press, 1970), 156-57.

3. Clara Pater's letter of transmittal to Gosse, dated 13 November 1895, prefaces the bound manuscript, in the Bodleian Library (Ms. Don d. 84).

4. Among the writers who discuss "Pascal" in relation to Pater's own religious position are Germain D'Hangest, *Walter Pater: l'homme et l'oeuvre*, 2 vols. (Paris: Didier, 1961), 2: 251-52; David J. DeLaura, *Hebrew and Hellene in Victorian England* (Austin: University of Texas Press, 1969), 338ff.; and John J. Conlon, *Walter Pater and the French Tradition* (Lewisberg, PA: Bucknell University Press, 1982), 160-63.

5. Conlon, 155-56.

6.   Walter Pater, *Appreciations* (London: Macmillan, 1910), 137-38.

7.   Walter Pater, *Marius the Epicurean*, 2 vols. (London: Macmillan, 1910), 1, 150. In the notes to his edition of *Marius* (Harmondsworth: Penguin, 1985), 306, Michael Levey identifies the quotation as from the ante-penultimate paragraph of Pascal's *Entretiens avec M. de Saci sur Epictete et Montaigne* (1655) and notes that Pater repeats the point in the Pascal essay (*Miscellaneous Studies* [London: Macmillan, 1910], 85).

8.   Pater, *Miscellaneous Studies*, 69.

9.   Ibid., 80.

10.   Ibid., 63.

11.   Ibid., 67.

12.   Blaise Pascal, *The Provincial Letters*, Alban Krailsheimer, trans. (Harmondsworth: Penguin, 1967), 167. Pater quotes part of this passage in Pascal's French original: "C'est proprement à la vérité qu'il appartient de rire parce qu'elle est gaie, et de se jouer de ses ennemis parce qu'elle est assurée de sa victorie" (*Miscellaneous Studies*, 72). Krailsheimer has also translated the *Pensées* (Harmondsworth: Penguin, 1966).

13.   *Miscellaneous Studies*, 68.

14.   Although Pater does not say so explicitly, the process he describes Pascal as undergoing, as his commitment to Jansenism deepens, is analogous to the process of Newman's gradual turning away from the ahistorical Anglican Church to the truly "developed" Roman Church. The apparently casual reference to Newman's *Apologia* that Pater makes in defining the tone of *The Provincial Letters* has implications throughout the entire essay on Pascal.

15.   Ibid., 70.

16.   Ibid., 77. Somewhat overstating the case, Germain D'Hangest concludes his analysis of the Pascal essay by applying the term *agonia* to the tension, in Pater himself, of residual skepticism and the will to believe (D'Hangest, 2: 252).

17.   Hugh Davidson writes of *Port-Royal* (1840) that Sainte-Beuve "evokes [an] image of Pascal, that of the reader of Montaigne and the man of the world who brought into a theological debate new notes of humor, playfulness, and a certain fashionable indifference," in *Blaise Pascal* (Boston: Twayne, 1983), 114-15. These are the qualities that Pater, too, emphasizes in discussing *The Provincial Letters*.

18.   Richard M. Chadbourne, *Charles Augustin Sainte-Beuve* (Boston: Twayne, 1977), 114-15.

19.   Alban Krailsheimer, *Pascal* (Oxford: Oxford University Press, 1980), 51. I am much indebted to Krailsheimer's analysis of Pascal's argument vis-à-vis Montaigne, especially pages 50-59.

20.   Ibid., 53.

21.   Walter Pater, *Gaston de Latour* (London: Macmillan, 1910), 93.

22.   Walter Pater, *Plato and Platonism* (London: Macmillan, 1910). See especially the chapter called "The Genius of Plato"—for instance, 125-26.

23.   Walter Pater, *Essays from "The Guardian"* (London: Macmillan, 1910), 67-68.

24.   For a useful, brief discussion of Pascal's "Augustinian" views in relation both to Pater and to Leslie Stephen, see Noel Annan, *Leslie Stephen: The Godless Victorian*, rev. ed. (New York: Random House, 1984), 263-64.

25.   Leslie Stephen, *Studies of a Biographer*, 4 vols. (London: Duckworth, 1898-1902), 2, 241-84.

26.   In the introduction to his translation of the *Pensées* (21), Krailsheimer disputes the accuracy of calling the Jansenists "Calvinists" of the Roman Catholic Church; moreover, he says that Pascal cannot be called a "Jansenist" except by way of loose affiliation. However, that Pater believed him a kind of Calvinist is explicit in his essay.

27.   See Davidson, 85: "One may safely say, I think, that every important term in the *Pensées* is involved in some kind of semantic paradox." Davidson's comments on Pascal's "nongeometrical way of defining words" help to explain what Pater regards as a puzzling, and disabling, contradiction.

28.   Matthew Arnold, *Lectures and Essays in Criticism*, vol. 3 of *Complete Prose Works of Matthew Arnold*, R. H. Super, ed. (Ann Arbor: University of Michigan Press, 1962), 230.

29.   "The Writings of Cardinal Newman," Houghton Ms. bMsEng1150 (12). Although it is undated, the essay may be from the early 1880s, when Pater was planning *Marius the Epicurean*, a work much indebted to Newman's *Grammar of Assent* (as DeLaura explains in *Hebrew and Hellene*, 314-26), which was originally published in 1870 and appeared in a new edition in 1881. *The Grammar* is a recurring focal point in Pater's discontinuous manuscript pages. As its title indicates, Pater's manuscript cannot date from before 1879.

30.   As DeLaura notes (308), Pater's passing allusion to Newman in the essay on Winckelmann (*The Renaissance: Studies in Art and Poetry: The 1893 Text*, Donald L. Hill, ed. [Berkeley: University of California Press, 1980], 159) defines Newman as a champion of the idea of "culture." The view is much the same in the incomplete, unpublished essay of several years later. Needless to say, DeLaura, a distinguished Catholic scholar, finds Pater's understanding of Newman inadequate, because it is much too selective.

12

J. B. BULLEN

The Historiography of *Studies in the History of the Renaissance*

1.   Claude Lévi-Strauss, *The Raw and the Cooked*, John and Doreen Weightman, trans. (Harmondsworth: Penguin, 1986), 13.

2.   Walter Pater, *Appreciations* (1889; London: Macmillan, 1900), 5-6.

3.   Roland Barthes, *The Rustle of Language*, Richard Howard, trans. (Oxford: Blackwell, 1986), 138.

4.   Ibid., 137-38.

5.   Ibid., 137.

6.   Gerald Monsman, *Walter Pater's Art of Autobiography* (New Haven: Yale University Press, 1980), 13.

7.   Walter Pater, *Marius the Epicurean* (1885; London: Macmillan, 1914), I, 117.

8.   In the second edition of 1877 it became *The Renaissance: Studies in Art and Poetry*.

9.   Stephen Bann, *The Clothing of Clio* (Cambridge: Cambridge University Press, 1984), 36.

10.   Walter Pater, *The Renaissance: Studies in Art and Poetry*, Donald Hill, ed. (Berkeley: University of California Press, 1980), 44.

11.   Ibid., 45.

12. Ibid., 44.

13. Walter Pater, *Miscellaneous Studies* (London: Macmillan, 1895), 257.

14. Walter Pater, "Coleridge's Writings," *Westminster Review*, 29 n.s. (1866), 114.

15. Walter Pater, "Winckelmann," *Westminster Review*, n.s. 31 (1867), 83. My emphasis.

16. Walter Pater, "Poems by William Morris," *Westminster Review*, n.s. 34 (1868), 307. My emphasis.

17. "Poems by William Morris," 302-303.

18. Ibid., 308.

19. Ibid., 305.

20. Pater, "Winckelmann," 94-95.

21. J. B. Bullen, "Walter Pater's Interpretation of the Mona Lisa as a Symbol of Romanticism," *The Romantic Heritage*, ed. Karsten Engelberg (Copenhagen: Publications of the Department of English, University of Copenhagen, 1983), 139-52.

22. Pater, *The Renaissance*, 97.

23. A. C. Swinburne, "Notes on Designs of the Old Masters at Florence," *Fortnightly Review*, n.s. 4 (1868), 17.

24. Ibid., 16.

25. Pater, *The Renaissance*, 45.

26. Monsman, *Walter Pater's Art of Autobiography*, 24.

27. Pater, *The Renaissance*, 98.

28. Monsman, *Walter Pater's Art of Autobiography*, 24.

29. Pater, *The Renaissance*, 184.

30. Théophile Gautier, "Leonardo Da Vinci," in *Les Dieux et les demidieux de la peinture*, par Théophile Gautier, A. Houssaye et P. de Saint-Victor (Paris: Morizot, 1864), 8.

31. Quoted by Richard Dellamora, "Pater's Modernism: The Leonardo Essay," *University of Toronto Quarterly*, 47 (1977), 135.

32. Pater, *The Renaissance*, 188.

13

M. F. MORAN

Pater's Mythic Fiction: Gods in a Gilded Age

1. See, for example, Robert Peters, "The Cult of the Returned Apollo: Walter Pater's *Renaissance* and *Imaginary Portraits*," *Journal of Pre-Raphaelite Studies*, 2 (1981), 53-69; and Gerald Monsman, *Walter Pater's Art of Autobiography* (New Haven: Yale University Press, 1980), 5.

2. R. T. Lenaghan, "Pattern in Walter Pater's Fiction," *Studies in Philology*, 58 (1961), 69-91.

3. Ibid., 74, 76.

4. Sloane Frazier, "Two Pagan Studies: Pater's 'Denys L'Auxerrois' and 'Apollo in Picardy'," *Folklore*, 81 (1970), 280-81.

5.   Wolfgang Iser, *Walter Pater: The Aesthetic Moment*, David Henry Wilson, trans. (Cambridge: Cambridge University Press, 1987), 126; Steven Connor, "Myth as Multiplicity in Walter Pater's *Greek Studies* and 'Denys L'Auxerrois'," *Review of English Studies*, n.s. 34 (1983), 28-42.

6.   Lenaghan, "Pattern in Walter Pater's Fiction," 74.

7.   Ibid., 75.

8.   Quoted in James Kissane, "Victorian Mythology," *Victorian Studies*, 6 (1962), 9.

9.   Ibid., 14.

10.   Janet Burstein, "Victorian Mythography and the Progress of the Intellect," *Victorian Studies*, 18 (1975), 314.

11.   F. C. McGrath, *The Sensible Spirit: Walter Pater and the Modernist Paradigm* (Tampa: University of South Florida Press, 1986), 65.

12.   Walter Pater, *Greek Studies: A Series of Essays* (London: Macmillan, 1895), 100.

13.   Ibid., 2.

14.   Ibid., 45.

15.   Ibid., 22-23.

16.   Ibid., 3.

17.   Christopher Nash, "Myth and Modern Literature," in *The Context of English Literature 1900-1930*, Michael Bell, ed. (London: Methuen, 1980), 166, 167.

18.   McGrath, 149-50.

19.   Pater, *Greek Studies*, 13.

20.   Ibid., 95.

21.   Ibid., 22.

22.   Ibid., 23.

23.   R. D. Stock, *The Holy and the Daemonic from Sir Thomas Browne to William Blake* (Princeton: Princeton University Press, 1982), 17.

24.   Pater, *Greek Studies*, 16.

25.   Ibid., 13-14.

26.   Ibid., 111.

27.   Ibid., 23.

28.   Ibid., 111.

29.   Ibid., 37.

30.   Ibid., 28-29. Gerald Monsman identifies the centrifugal tendency with Dionysus, the centripetal with Apollo. He suggests that Pater's own aesthetic propensity for order, rationality, and the ultimate expression of the Absolute can be seen in his typical (Apollonian) heroes who nonetheless share with Dionysus an incarnation "in time and space . . . enduring the pangs of death" (*Pater's Portraits: Mythic Patterns in the Fiction of Walter Pater* [Baltimore: Johns Hopkins Press, 1967], 18, 22). It is worth noting, however, that in "Denys L'Auxerrois" and "Apollo in Picardy" the displaced god figures seem to share many common features, and these similarities tend to overshadow Nietzschean readings like those of Monsman and Lenaghan. The association of both Denys and Apollyon with such characteristics as natural vitality, creative individuality, and strangeness is highlighted at the expense of the traditional distinctions made between Dionysus and Apollo in classical mythology. Indeed, some scholars suggest that the cults of the two gods were eventually assimilated one by the other in the classical world (see, for instance Walter F. Otto, *Dionysus: Myth and Cult*, Robert B. Palmer, trans. [Bloomington: Indiana University Press, 1965], 207).

31.   Pater, *Greek Studies*, 31.

32. Ibid., 140; emphasis added.

33. Connor, "Myth as Multiplicity," 30-31. Connor goes on to point out (32-33) that "Pater apprehended myth as always in a state of Becoming" and "was little interested in patterns of historical reconciliation and progression." But Connor also admits that Pater's "relativistic viewpoint" necessarily implicates the "contemporary world" in moments of historical conflict between "earlier" and "later ways of thinking": a position that supports Pater's concern with *both* "the irresolvable ambiguity of myth" *and*, in my view, its cultural expressiveness.

34. McGrath makes a similar point in considering Pater's expressive and functionalist view of myth: "so with Pater both myth and philosophy express in their respective forms an indwelling spirit that is analogous to the cohesive and informing vision an artist renders in the concrete matter of his art" (201).

35. Cf. Burstein, 319. Burstein usefully charts the growing Victorian concern with the particular mode of thought informing mythic discourse: "Like the mythic mind, the language of myth seemed to have fused subjective and objective impressions; thus, in myth single words gathered many aspects of experiential phenomena into dense but coherent symbols."

36. Cf. Connor, 42, who makes a similar point but to support a more traditional reading of "Denys L'Auxerrois" as a tale which momentarily resolves contradictions rather than emphasizing their inevitability in the modern age.

37. Walter Pater, "Apollo in Picardy," in *Miscellaneous Studies: A Series of Essays* (London: Macmillan, 1899), 122.

38. Walter Pater, "Denys L'Auxerrois," in *Imaginary Portraits* (London: Macmillan, 1896), 64.

39. See, for example, Robert and Janice A. Keefe, *Walter Pater and the Gods of Disorder* (Athens: Ohio University Press, 1988), 136. They connect these mythic stories to the Victorian debate between Hebraism and Hellenism.

40. Pater, *Miscellaneous Studies*, 124, 122.

41. Pater, *Imaginary Portraits*, 78.

42. Pater, *Miscellaneous Studies*, 136. Sloane Frazier in "Two Pagan Studies" links monastery and pigeon-house in terms of their "artificiality and complacency" which Apollyon destroys in order to re-assert his "pagan harmony" (283-84).

43. Pater, *Miscellaneous Studies*, 133.

44. Ibid., 131.

45. Pater, *Imaginary Portraits*, 80-81.

46. Ibid.

47. See Christine van Boheemen-Saaf, *Between Sacred and Profane: Narrative Design and the Logic of Myth from Chaucer to Coover* (Amsterdam: Rodopi, 1987). Mythic decomposition involves the distribution of a "complex of attributes" between different but related individuals. Pater does not literally split his mythological counterparts, but metaphorically suggests they are uneasily divided between opposing characteristics by signalling certain inexplicable but sudden reversals in their behaviour and demeanour. For example, Hermes finds Denys "like a double creature, of two natures, difficult or impossible to harmonise" (*Imaginary Portraits*, 75).

48. Pater, *Imaginary Portraits*, 73.

49. Ibid., 87.

50. Claude Lévi-Strauss, "The Structural Study of Myth," in *Structural Anthropology*, Claire Jacobson and Brooke Grundfest Schoepf, trans. (Harmondsworth: Penguin, 1972), 226.

51. F. C. McGrath's treatment of Denys and Apollyon offers a similar perspective—not so much through the expression of difference but by focussing on the artistic potential of the characters. For McGrath they represent a concept of "the artist as an alien figure cleansing his age" (98). However, such a reading does not take full account of the ways in which cleansing and creativity are simultaneously activated and thwarted in the narrative.

52. Pater, *Imaginary Portraits*, 67, 68.

53. Ibid., 68-69.

54. Pater, *Miscellaneous Studies*, 122.

55. Pater, *Imaginary Portraits*, 87.

56. Pater, *Miscellaneous Studies*, 144.

57. Ibid., 123, 122.

58. Nash, "Myth and Modern Literature," 166.

59. Roland Barthes, *Mythologies*, Annette Lavers, trans. (London: Granada, 1973), 109.

60. Pater, *Imaginary Portraits*, 70-71.

61. Pater, *Miscellaneous Studies*, 132.

62. Ibid., 146.

63. Pater, *Imaginary Portraits*, 57, 88.

64. Ibid., 60, 59, 75.

65. Pater, *Miscellaneous Studies*, 135.

66. Pater, *Imaginary Portraits*, 63-64; emphasis added.

67. Ibid., 76.

68. Pater, *Miscellaneous Studies*, 131, 138.

14

BERNARD RICHARDS

Pater and Architecture

1. *The Works of Walter Pater*, 8 vols. (London: Macmillan, 1910), I, 210.

2. Ibid., I, 210-11. In his edition of *The Renaissance* (Berkeley and Los Angeles: University of California Press, 1980), Donald Hill identifies the source of the comparison as Hegel's *Aesthetik*, I, 449-50 (trans. Knox, I, 358).

3. For a survey, see James S. Curl, *The Egyptian Revival* (London: Allen & Unwin, 1982).

4. The "Postscript" was originally published as "Romanticism" in *Macmillan's Magazine* (November 1876). It was revised for *Miscellaneous Studies* (1895), and the final paragraph was added.

5. *Works of Pater*, I, x.

6. Ibid., V, 245.

7. Ibid., V, 249.

8. Ibid., VIII, 132-33.

9. In *The Dilemma of Style: Architectural Ideas from the Picturesque to the Post-Modern* (London: John Murray, 1987).

10. *Works of Pater*, III, 123.

11. Ibid., III, 118.

12. Ibid., IV, 50.
13. Ibid., IV, 49.
14. Ibid., VI, 279.
15. Ibid., VIII, 127.
16. Ibid., VIII, 138-39.
17. Ibid., VIII, 140.
18. Ibid., VIII, 141.
19. Ibid., VIII, 139.
20. Ibid., IX, 5.
21. Ibid., IX, 6.
22. Ibid., VIII, 109.
23. Ibid., VIII, 110.
24. Ibid., VIII, 115.
25. Ibid., VIII, 113-14.
26. Ibid., VIII, 119.
27. Ibid., VIII, 119.
28. Ibid., VIII, 135.
29. Ibid., IX, 77-78.
30. Ibid., I, 134.
31. Ibid., VIII, 178.
32. Ibid., VIII, 148.
33. Ibid., VIII, 152.
34. Ibid., VIII, 154.
35. Ibid., VI, 279.
36. Ibid., VIII, 155.
37. Ibid., I, 176.
38. Ibid., V, 23.
39. Ibid., V, 261.
40. In quoting this passage from the "Postcript" to *Miscellaneous Studies* (127) J. M. Crook mistakenly dates it 1874. In fact it is an addition of 1889. This means that it was written *after* work on T. G. Jackson's extraordinarily eclectic New Quad had begun at Pater's college, Brasenose.
41. All of these buildings are illustrated in Mark Girouard's *The Victorian Country House* (New Haven: Yale University Press, 1979) and his *Sweetness and Light: the 'Queen Anne' Movement 1860-1910* (Oxford: Clarendon Press, 1977).

15

ANNE VARTY

The Crystal Man: A Study of "Diaphaneitè"

1. See Gerald Monsman, "Pater, Hopkins, and Fichte's Ideal Student," *SAQ* 70 (1971), 365-76; and "Pater's Aesthetic Hero," *UTQ* 40 (1971), 136-51. See also B. A. Inman, *Walter*

Pater's Reading: A Bibliography of His Library Borrowings and Literary References 1858-1873 (New York: Garland, 1981), 74-75.

2.   Walter Pater, "Diaphaneitè," *Miscellaneous Studies*, C. L. Shadwell, ed. (London: Macmillan, 1895), 259. The very title of the essay is mysterious. *Diaphaneitè* is not an English word, nor, as the accentuation suggests, is it a French word. If we transliterate *Diaphaneitè* into ancient Greek, it assumes the form of a second person plural imperative verb: "[You shall] become transparent!" or "shine through!" This reinforces the sense of the essay as a manifesto or imperative command for the future.

3.   Inman, 74-75.

4.   Monsman, "Pater's Aesthetic Hero," 137-40.

5.   Donald L. Hill, ed., *The Renaissance: Studies in Art and Poetry* (Berkeley and Los Angeles: University of California Press, 1980), 410-43.

6.   Walter Pater, "Winckelmann," *Westminster Review* ns. 31 (1867), 94.

7.   "Diaphaneitè," 258.

8.   *The Renaissance*, 189.

9.   Walter Pater, *Plato and Platonism* (London: Macmillan, 1910), 135.

10.   For Pater's early interest in Carlyle, see Inman, 7.

11.   See Monsman, "Pater, Hopkins, and Fichte's Ideal Student."

12.   Thomas Carlyle, "The Hero as Poet," *On Heroes and Hero-Worship and the Heroic in History*, H. D. Traill, ed.; *The Works of Thomas Carlyle*, (London: Chapman and Hall, 1897-99), V, 105.

13.   Thomas Carlyle, *The French Revolution: A History* (1837), *Works*, III, 46.

14.   "Diaphaneitè," 256.

15.   G. H. Lewes, *The Life of Goethe* (1855; London: Smith, Elder and Co. [1863], 1864). A letter from Anthony Trollope to Lewes, dated 13 December 1863, thanking him for a copy of the *Life*, confirms its publication date. See *The George Eliot Letters*, Gordon S. Haight, ed. (New Haven: Yale University Press, 1978), VIII, 315. While there is no bibliographical evidence that Pater ever borrowed this book from a library, and he did not own a copy of it, Pater's interest in Goethe was so lively and the book so influential, that it is most improbable that he was not familiar with it.

16.   Lewes, 259, 277, 299.

17.   Ibid., 20.

18.   "Diaphaneitè," 257.

19.   Inman, 49.

20.   G. W. F. Hegel, *Aesthetics: Lectures on Fine Art*, T. M. Knox, trans. (Oxford: Oxford University Press, 1975), I, 20.

21.   "Winckelmann," 112.

22.   Hegel, II, 712-13.

23.   Ibid., 713.

24.   "Diaphaneitè," 255; and "Winckelmann," 103.

25.   "Winckelmann," 99.

26.   Lewes, 222.

27.   "Diaphaneitè," 258.

28.   "Winckelmann," 84.

29.   "Diaphaneitè," 254-55; and "Winckelmann," 88-89.

30.   "Diaphaneitè," 254; and "Winckelmann," 102.

31.   "Diaphaneitè," 255.

32. "Winckelmann," 103.

33. Ibid., 80.

34. Ibid., 88.

35. Carlyle, *Works*, V, 81.

36. Pater, "Duke Carl of Rosenmold," *Imaginary Portraits* (London: Macmillan, 1910), 152. This choice of diction may have been influenced by Kant's essay "Beantwortung der Frage: Was ist Aufklärung?" which ends by distinguishing between finished and unfinished process: "Leben wir jetzt in einem *aufgeklärten* Zeitalter? . . . Nein, aber whol in einem Zeitalter der *Aufklärung*." *Kants Gesammelte Schriften*, hersg. Könichlich Preussischen Akademie der Wissenschaften, (Berlin: Georg Reimer, 1912), VIII, 40.

37. "Duke Carl of Rosenmold," 153.

38. Ibid., 122-23.

39. "Diaphaneitè," 255.

40. "Winckelmann," 86.

41. "Duke Carl of Rosenmold," 126-27.

42. J. D. Passavant, *Rafael von Urbino und sein Vater Giovanni Santi* (Leipzig: F. A. Brockhaus, 1839), I, 302.

43. Johannes Winckelmann, Brief "An Berendis," Nothenitz, 17 Sept. 1754, *Briefe*. hersg. Walter Rehm (Berlin: de Gruyter, 1952-1957), I, 153.

44. Ibid., Brief "112 An Berendis," Dresden, 4 June 1755, *Briefe*, I, 176.

45. Ibid., my translation.

46. "Duke Carl of Rosenmold," 129.

47. "Winckelmann," 107.

48. "Duke Carl of Rosenmold," 133.

49. Ibid., 145.

50. Ibid., 143; and Goethe, *Wilhelm Meisters Lehrjahre*, Erich Trunz, hersg. *Goethes Werke. Hamburger Ausgabe.* (Hamburg: Erich Trunz, 1967), VII, 431.

51. Lewes, *Life of Goethe*, 170.

52. "Duke Carl of Rosenmold," 153.

53. *Female Characters of Goethe. From the Original Drawings of William Kaulbach. With Explanatory Text by G. H. Lewes* (London: Cassell, Petter, and Galpin, 1867), 23ff. Goethe's own account of the skating episode is in *Dichtung und Wahrheit, Werke*, X, 84-85.

—————— **16** ——————

JANE SPIRIT

Nineteenth–Century Responses to Montaigne and Bruno:
A Context for Pater

1. Work by DeLaura, Knoepflmacher, and Young exemplify this approach. See David DeLaura, *Hebrew and Hellene in Victorian England: Newman, Arnold and Pater* (Austin: University of Texas Press, 1969); Ulrich Knoepflmacher, *Religious Humanism and the Victorian Novel* (Princeton: Princeton University Press, 1965); and Helen Young, *The Writings of Walter Pater*

(Lancaster: Bryn Mawr College, 1933). More recently Linda Dowling places Pater's choice of a second-century Roman setting against the background of the "significant revaluation" of "the idea of Roman decadence" that occurred during the nineteenth century. James Lubbock also alters the perspective from which *Marius* has been regarded, arguing that Pater's main concern is not with Marius as a figure of concealed autobiography, but with the historical period represented. See Linda Dowling, "Roman Decadence and Victorian Historiography," *Victorian Studies*, 28 (1985), 579-605; and James Lubbock, "Walter Pater's *Marius the Epicurean*: The Imaginary Portrait," *Journal of the Philologial Quarterly*, 41 (1962), 475-91.

2.   Patricia Clements demonstrates Pater's immense but concealed debt to Baudelaire, revealed particularly in the portrait of Ronsard in *Gaston*. John Coates traces the submerged intention of *Imaginary Portraits*. Ian Small points out how Pater's work creates a "web of intertextual relationships" and how, as in the case of religious citation, this is used to "controvert" any "simple notion of authority." See Patricia Clements, *Baudelaire and the English Tradition* (Princeton: Princeton University Press, 1985); John Coates, "Aspects of the Intellectual Context of Pater's Imaginary Portraits," *Yearbook of English Studies*, 15 (1985), 93-108; and the Introduction by Ian Small to Walter Pater, *Marius the Epicurean*, Ian Small, ed. (Oxford: Oxford University Press, 1986).

3.   Richard Wollheim, "The Artistic Temperament," *TLS* (22 September 1978), 1045.

4.   I am most grateful to Mr. John Sparrow for permission to quote from the manuscripts in his possession. References to these unpublished chapters are denoted MS, followed by chapter and folio numbers.

5.   Donald Frame, *Montaigne in France, 1812-1852* (New York: Columbia University Press, 1940), vii.

6.   *The New Monthly Magazine and Literary Journal*, 19 January 1827, 28.

7.   Walter Landor, *Imaginary Conversations*, T. Earle Welby, ed. (London: Chapman and Hall, 1928), VII, 148.

8.   Thomas Carlyle, *Montaigne and other Essays, Chiefly Biographical* (London: James Gowan, 1897), 3.

9.   Ibid., 4-6.

10.   Cooper-Willis comments that the "the fact that Montaigne has been described by many writers as 'licentious,' in view of certain admissions of laxness in sex matters which he makes, has for many people disposed of the whole question of his 'morality,' as if morality and continence were one and the selfsame thing." See Irene Cooper-Willis, *Montaigne* (London: Alfred A. Knopf, 1927), 13.

11.   Alexander Vinet, *Montaigne; The Endless Study, and other Miscellanies*, Robert Turnbull, trans. (New York: M.W. Dodd, 1850), 58.

12.   R. W. Church, "The Essays of Montaigne," in *Oxford Essays* (London: John Parker, 1857), 239-283.

13.   John Owen, *Skeptics of the French Renaissance* (London: Macmillan, 1893), 423.

14.   F. D. Maurice, *Moral and Metaphysical Philosophy* (London: Griffin, Bohn, and Co., 1872), 151.

15.   See Arthur Tilley, *The Literature of the French Renaissance* (Cambridge: Cambridge University Press, 1904), II, 165.

16.   Bayle St. John, *Montaigne the Essayist: A Biography* (London: Chapman and Hall, 1858), I, 336.

17.   In Lecky's view Montaigne deserved admiration for believing that "it was the part of a wise man to remain poised with an indifferent mind between opposing sects. As a consequence of this he taught . . . the innocence of error and the evil of persecution." W. E. H. Lecky, *The History of the Rise and Influence of the Spirit of Rationalism in Europe* (London: Green, Longmans, Roberts and Green, 1865), II, 63.

18.   Matthew Arnold, "On Translating Homer," in *The Complete Prose Works of Matthew Arnold*, R. H. Super, ed. (Michigan: University of Michigan Press, 1960), I, 174.

19.   "Emerson," *Complete Prose Works of Matthew Arnold*, X, 175.

20.   "George Sand," Ibid., 188.

21.   Lynn Linton, "A Practical Philosopher," *Chambers Journal of Popular Literature, Science and Art*, 11 (12 May 1894), 291.

22.   Walter Pater, *Gaston de Latour* (London: Macmillan, 1896), 138.

23.   Ibid., 136.

24.   Ibid., 140.

25.   Ibid., 141.

26.   Pater's influence here may be detected in the enlarged version of "The Portrait of Mr. W. H.," in which Wilde discusses the Renaissance revival of the spirit of Hellenism and of Platonic theory. He mentions, for example, the love of "Michael Angelo" and "Tomanasio Cavalieri," saying that: "[t]he same idea is put forward in Montaigne's noble essay on Friendship, a passion which he ranks higher than the love of brother for brother, or the love of man for woman. See Oscar Wilde, *The Portrait of Mr. W. H.*, Vivyan Holland, ed. (London: Methuen and Co., 1921), 45.

27.   *Gaston*, 130.

28.   Ibid., 131.

29.   Ibid., 117.

30.   Ibid., 130-31.

31.   Ibid., 112, 144.

32.   Ibid., MS, ch. 8, f.21.

33.   James Joyce, "The Day of the Rabblement," in *The Critical Writings of James Joyce*, Ellsworth Mason and Richard Ellmann, eds. (London: Faber, 1959), 69.

34.   See Giordano Bruno, *The Ash Wednesday Supper*, E. Gosselin and L. Lerner, trans. (Hamden, Connecticut: Archon, 1977), 22f.

35.   Frances Yates, *Giordano Bruno and The Hermetic Tradition* (1964; London: Routledge and Kegan Paul, 1978), 450.

36.   S. T. Coleridge, *The Friend* (1809: London: Gale and Curtis, 1812), 89.

37.   Henry Hallam, *Introduction to the Literature of Europe in the Fifteenth, Sixteenth and Seventeenth Centuries* (Paris: Bawdry's European Library, 1839), II, 92.

38.   Ibid., II, 96.

39.   Billie Andrew Inman, *Walter Pater's Reading 1858-1873*, (New York: Garland, 1981), 66.

40.   J. H. Browne, "Giordano Bruno," *Atlantic Monthly*, 38 (Nov. 1876), 557.

41.   Ibid., 550.

42.   In his address given on 9 August 1874, Tyndall suggested that by his insistence that "[m]atter is not the mere naked, empty *capacity* which philosophers have pictured her to be, but the universal mother" Bruno had come close to modern scientific thought. See John Tyndall, *Fragments of Science* (London: Longmans, Green and Co., 1879), 156.

43.   Ian Frith comments that "by the way of poetry Bruno became a philosopher; Love of art made him a lover of men; love of the true and beautiful made him the worshipper of God." See Ian Frith, *The Life of Giordano Bruno* (London: Trubner, 1887), 307.

44.   Lewes portrays Bruno as "a preacher, young, handsome, gay, and worldly—as a poet, not as a fanatic." See G. H. Lewes, *Biographical History of Philosophy* (1845-1846; London: Parker and Son, 1857), 316.

45.   Annie Besant, *Giordano Bruno* (London: Watts and Co., 1887), 1.

46.   Isa Blagden, "Giordano Bruno," *Fraser's Magazine*, 3 (Mar. 1871), 364; Arthur Moss, *Bruno and Spinoza* (London: Watts and Co., 1885), 3.

47.   R. C. Christie examined the evidence for Bruno having died at the stake and found it to be incontrovertible. His findings were disputed by J. P. B. Stuart, who scorned those wanting to erect a monument to Bruno's memory, a view which was in its turn dismissed by C. E. Plumptre. See: R. C. Christie, "Was Giordano Bruno Really Burned?" *Macmillan's Magazine*, 52 (May-Oct. 1885), 435-40; J. P. B. Stuart, *Essays on Foreign Subjects* (London: Alexander Gardner, 1901); and C. E. Plumptre, "Giordano Bruno and the Scottish Reviewer," *Antiquary* 19 (March and April 1889), 110-14 and 146-51.

48.   *Agnostic Annual* (1885), 23.

49.   A. C. Swinburne, "The Monument of Giordano Bruno," in *Swinburne's Collected Poetical Works* (London: Heinemann, 1924), 1081-82.

50.   J. A. Symonds, *The Renaissance in Italy* (London: Smith, Elder and Co., 1886), VII, 139.

51.   C. E. Plumptre, "Giordano Bruno: His Life and Philosophy," *Westminster Review*, 132 (August 1889), 117-37.

52.   Karl Blind, "Giordano Bruno and the New Italy," *Nineteenth Century* 26 (July 1889), 115 and 119.

53.   Walter Pater, "Giordano Bruno, Paris: 1586," *Fortnightly Review*, 46 (August 1889), 234. Apart from the additional introduction establishing the figure of Gaston listening to Bruno there are no great differences between the article and chapter versions. However, the chapter does insert a new paragraph emphasizing the significance of Bruno's doctrine of indifference to Gaston (*Gaston*, 196-97). Other changes slightly alter the emphasis of the later version. In the article version, for example, Pater writes of how Bruno "the escaped monk, is still a monk: his philosophy, impious as it might seem to some, a new religion" ("Giordano Bruno," 241). In the chapter version this is made more emphatic by the alteration of the last clause to "a religion; very new indeed, yet a religion" (*Gaston*, 191). The "earlier physical impulses" which make Bruno always a "lover and a monk" despite the superseding of "religion and love" by intellectual ardour ("Giordano Bruno," 238) are, in the book version, made more specifically "physically erotic" impulses (*Gaston*, 181), associated with Bruno's early enthusiasm for "religion and physical love" (*Gaston*, 183).

54.   *Gaston*, 175.

55.   Ibid., 183.

56.   Ibid., 123.

57.   Ibid., 161.

58.   Ibid., 200.

59.   Ibid., MS, ch. 9, f. 16.

60.   Ibid., ch. 9, f. 17.

61.   Ibid., ch. 9, f. 21.

62.   Ibid., ch. 10, f. 13.

63. Ibid., ch. 10, f. 14.
64. Ibid., ch. 10, f. 32.
65. Ibid., ch. 10, f. 33.
66. Ibid., ch. 10, f. 33.
67. Ibid., ch. 10, f. 37.
68. Ibid., ch. 10, f. 37.
69. Ibid., ch. 9, f. 6 and ch. 11, f. 37.
70. Ibid., ch. 11, f. 35.
71. Ibid., ch. 13, f. 21.

Contributors

LAUREL BRAKE (Ph.D. London) is Lecturer in Literature at Birkbeck College, University of London. Her principal research interests are Victorian—non-fictional prose and the press, and she admits to a taste for theory, bibliography and editing. Co-founder and co-editor of the *Pater Newsletter* and, with Aled Jones and Lionel Madden, of *Investigating Victorian Journalism* (1990), she has co-edited a theory number of *Victorian Periodical Review* (1989) and edited *The Year's Work in English Studies* since 1981. She has published articles on Pater, and on Victorian biography, criticism, and the press. Currently she is working on a biography of Pater and a book on Victorian prose. She is also an editor of a volume of the forthcoming edition of Pater's *Collected Works*.

J. B. BULLEN is a graduate of Cambridge University; he was Junior Research Fellow at Balliol College, Oxford, and is now Reader in English Literature at Reading University. He has a long-standing interest in the relationship between literature and the visual arts, and he has published on the writings of George Eliot, Dickens, Browning, Ruskin, Pater and many others in the field. In 1986 Oxford University Press published his full-length study of Hardy's novels, *The Expressive Eye: Fiction and Perception in the Work of Thomas Hardy*. He also published *Post-Impressionism in England: The Critical Reception* (1988) and he edited Roger Fry's *Vision and Design* (1981) and Clive Bell's *Art* (1987). Dr. Bullen is at present working on a book entitled *The*

Myth of the Italian Renaissance in the Nineteenth Century which will be published by Oxford University Press.

RICHARD DELLAMORA (Ph.D., Yale University) teaches in the Department of English, in Women's Studies, and in the Cultural Studies Program at Trent University in Peterborough, Ontario. He is the author of *Masculine Desire: The Sexual Politics of Victorian Aestheticism* (1990), and his "Traversing the Feminine in Oscar Wilde's *Salomé*" appears in *Victorian Sages and Cultural Discourse: Renegotiating Gender and Power* (1990), edited by Thaïs Morgan. Dellamora is currently continuing his studies in the construction and contestation of masculine gender-norms in late nineteenth and twentieth-century literary and critical texts.

LINDA DOWLING is currently a fellow of the Rutgers Center for Historical Analysis and Visiting Fellow in the English Department at Princeton University. She is author, most recently, of *Language and Decadence in the Victorian fin de Siècle.*

LESLEY HIGGINS (Ph.D., Queen's) is an Assistant Professor in the English Department of York University (Toronto, Canada). Her work on Pater and Hopkins is complemented by studies in gender, identity politics, and textual transmission. Her articles on Walter Pater and Gerard Manley Hopkins have appeared in *Texas Studies in Literature and Language, Hopkins Quarterly, The Month, The New Welsh Review* and *Dalhousie Review*. She has also published on Thomas Hardy and T.S. Eliot. In addition to editing Hopkins's Oxford essays and notebooks, she is currently completing a book-length study of Pater and Hopkins.

BILLIE ANDREW INMAN (Ph.D., Texas), Professor of English at University of Arizona, is General Editor of the nine-volume *Collected Works of Pater*, in progress. She is author of *Walter Pater's Reading: A Bibliography of His Library Borrowings and Literary References, 1858-1873* (1981), and *Pater and His Reading, 1874-1877, with a Bibliogra-*

phy of His Library Borrowings, 1878-1894 (1990), as well as various essays on Pater, including " 'Sebastian van Storck': Pater's Exploration into Nihilism," in *Nineteenth-Century Fiction* (March 1976) and "The Intellectual Context of Walter Pater's 'Conclusion'," in *Prose Studies, 1800-1900* (May 1981).

F. C. MCGRATH (Ph.D., Texas), Associate Professor of English at University of Southern Maine, is author of *The Sensible Spirit: Walter Pater and the Modernist Paradigm* (1986). He has published articles on Pater, W. B. Yeats, T. S. Eliot, James Joyce, and the contemporary Irish playwright Brian Friel. He is currently working on a book on Friel and Irish cultural politics, *Language, Illusion, and Politics.*

GERALD MONSMAN (Ph.D., Johns Hopkins) is Professor of English and former Head of the Department of English at the University of Arizona. His publications include *Confessions of a Prosaic Dreamer: Charles Lamb's Art of Autobiography* (1984), *Walter Pater's Art of Autobiography* (1980), *Walter Pater* (1977), *Pater's Portraits: Mythic Pattern in the Fiction of Walter Pater* (1967), and essays on Olive Schreiner, Gerard Manley Hopkins, Victorian selfhood, Romantic heroism, and literary interpretation. He is currently completing a book-length study of Schreiner's fiction.

MAUREEN F. MORAN (Ph.D., London) was Principal Lecturer and Head of the English Section at the West London Institute of Higher Education and now directs the Institute's undergraduate degree programme. She completed her Ph.D. dissertation on Pater's place in the Victorian critical tradition and has written variously on John Galt, Pater, and twentieth-century British and Canadian fiction. For some years she served as an Associate Editor of *The Year's Work in English Studies.* Her current research interest is in elements of comic disorder and subversion in contemporary writing.

BERNARD RICHARDS is a Fellow and Tutor at Brasenose College, Oxford, and a Lecturer in English at Oxford University. He has published an anthology of Victorian poetry (1980) and a critical study of Victorian poetry (1988) in the Longmans Literature in English series. In addition he has published a wide range of articles from Shakespeare to present-day literature in many scholarly journals. He is also a regular contributor to *The Times*, *The Sunday Telegraph* and *The Independent* on literary and cultural subjects. He is co-editor of a literary magazine (principally for VIth Formers) launched in 1990, *The English Review*.

IAN SMALL is senior lecturer in English at the University of Birmingham. He read English at the University of Reading and took a Ph.D. in 1972. He has written widely on late nineteenth-century English literature, and he is co-general editor of the forthcoming multi-volume Oxford English Texts edition of the *Complete Works* of Oscar Wilde. His publications include *The Aesthetes* (1979), editions of Oscar Wilde's society dramas (1980-1983), and an edition of Walter Pater's *Marius the Epicurean* (1986). His most recent book is *Conditions for Criticism: Authority, Knowledge and Literature in the Late Nineteenth Century* (1991). He has also co-edited two collections of essays by various hands on the impact of France upon British intellectual life: *Studies in Anglo-French Cultural Relations* (1988) and *The French Revolution and British Culture* (1989).

JANE SPIRIT received both her B.A. in English literature and M.A. in Literature and the Visual Arts from Reading University. Her Ph.D. thesis on the use of pain in Pater's fiction was completed in 1988 at Queen Mary College, London. She is currently teaching the Open University's arts foundation and modern literature courses and is preparing articles on *Marius* and on the image of Byzantium in modernist texts.

PAUL TUCKER read English Literature at Cambridge University, after which he received an M.Litt. from Oxford, with a thesis on the fiction of Walter Pater. Since 1983 he has been teaching English language at the University of Pisa. He has published articles on Pater and is currently editing and translating *Marius the Epicurean* for the Italian publisher Studio Tesi. He is also working on a linguistic study of Pater's narrative technique. Another research interest is John Ruskin, especially his late Tuscany and early Tuscan art. The latter will be the subject of an exhibition, organised in collaboration with the Ruskin Gallery of Sheffield, to be held in England and Italy in late 1992.

ANNE VARTY (D.Phil., Oxford), Lecturer in the Departments of English and Drama and Theatre Studies at Royal Holloway and Bedford New College, University of London, is currently working on a series of articles on Pater and the visual arts, and Pater and Platonism. She is British editor and co-author of a forthcoming history of European literature, commissioned by Hachette for publication in 1991. A book on modern Dream Theatre is also in progress.

HAYDEN WARD (Ph.D., Columbia), Associate Professor of English at West Virginia University, was from 1970 to 1990 the assistant editor of *Victorian Poetry*. He is now editor. He has published articles on Browning, Tennyson, Stevenson, and Pater and at present he is the American editor of *The Pater Newsletter*. He is also currently working on the edition of Pater's writings.

J. P. WARD holds degrees from the universities of Toronto, Cambridge and Wales. He was formerly Senior Lecturer in English at University of Wales, Swansea and is now a tutor in extramural studies at Birkbeck College, University of London. His books include *Poetry and the Sociological Idea* (1981), *Wordsworth's Language of Men* (1984), and *The English Line: Poetry of the Unpoetic from Wordsworth to Larkin* (1991). He has published articles on Wordsworth, nineteenth-century thought and a number of twentieth-century poets. He was editor of *Poetry Wales* from 1975 to 1980. He is currently writing studies of *As You Like It* for the Harvester Shakespeare New Readings series, and of Hardy's poetry for the Open University Press.

Index

Pater in the 1990s

Dust Jacket, Title-page
Contents page & Text

Designed by

Robert Langenfeld
&
Kathleen Mason Driskell

Using WordPerfect 5.1
Typeface ITC Galliard

ELT Press Production Assistants
Julia Belcher, Rebecca Lasley
& Kathleen Mason Driskell

Printer: Thomson-Shore, Inc.
Production Coordinator, Diane Nourse
Dexter, Michigan U. S. A.
1991